CITIZENSHIP, NATIONALITY AND MIGRATION IN EUROPE

Throughout Europe longstanding ideas of what it means to be a citizen are being challenged. The sense of belonging to a nation has never been more in flux. Simultaneously, nationalistic and racist movements are gaining ground and barriers are being erected against immigration.

Citizenship, Nationality and Migration in Europe examines how concepts of citizenship have evolved in different countries and varying contexts. It explores the interconnection between ideas of the nation, modes of citizenship and the treatment of migrants.

Adopting a distinctive multi-disciplinary and international approach, this collection brings together leading experts from several fields including political studies, history, law and sociology. By juxtaposing four European countries – Britain, France, Germany and Italy – and setting current trends against a historical background, it highlights important differences and exposes similarities in the urgent questions surrounding citizenship and the treatment of minorities in Europe today.

David Cesarani is Professor of Modern Jewish Studies and Co-Director of the Centre for Jewish Studies at Manchester University. **Mary Fulbrook** is Professor of German History at University College London and Director of the UCL Centre for European Studies.

CITIZENSHIP, NATIONALITY AND MIGRATION IN EUROPE

Edited by David Cesarani and Mary Fulbrook

London and New York

First published 1996
by Routledge
11 New Fetter Lane, London EC4P 4EE

Simultaneously published in the USA and Canada
by Routledge
29 West 35th Street, New York, NY 10001
Routledge is an International Thomson Publishing company

Phototypeset in Garamond by
Intype London Ltd

Printed and bound in Great Britain by
TJ Press (Padstow) Ltd, Padstow Cornwall

British Library Cataloguing in Publication Data
A catalogue record for this book is available from the British Library

Library of Congress Cataloging in Publication Data
Citizenship, nationality, and migration in Europe / edited by
David Cesarani and Mary Fulbrook.
p.   cm.
Includes bibliographical references and index.
1. Citizenship—Europe, Western.   2. Nationalism—
Europe, Western.   3. Europe, Western—Emigration
and immigration—Government policy.
I. Cesarani, David.   II. Fulbrook, Mary, 1951–
JN94.A92C57   1996
323.6'094—dc20   95–38744
                                                                CIP

ISBN 0–415–13100–6 (hbk)
0–415–13101–4 (pbk)

CONTENTS

CONTENTS

NOTES ON CONTRIBUTORS

David Cesarani is Professor of Modern Jewish Studies and Co-Director of the Centre for Jewish Studies at Manchester University.

Mary Fulbrook is Professor of German History at University College London and Director of the UCL Centre for European Studies. Her most recent books include *Anatomy of a Dictatorship: Inside the GDR, 1949–1989, The Divided Nation: Germany 1918–1990* and *National Histories and European History* (editor).

Elspeth Guild, Baileys Shaw and Gillett.

Tony Kushner is Marcus Sieff Lecturer and Director of the Centre for Jewish/non-Jewish Relations at the University of Southampton.

Enrico Pugliese, Department of Sociology, University of Naples.

Carlo Ruzza, Department of Sociology, University of Essex.

Karen Schönwälder is Lecturer in German History at the School of Slavonic and East European Studies, University of London.

Oliver Schmidtke, Department of Social Sciences, Humboldt Universitaet, Berlin.

Max Silverman is Senior Lecturer in French at the University of Leeds.

Yasemin Nuhoğlu Soysal is Associate Professor of Sociology at Harvard University and an affiliate of Harvard's Center for European Studies.

Patrick Weil, Institut d'Etudes Politiques, Paris.

LIST OF TABLES

ACKNOWLEDGEMENTS

This collection of essays grew out of a conference organised jointly by the Centre for European Studies, University College London, and the Wiener Library and Institute of Contemporary History, London on 21–22 September 1994 at University College London. It was supported by grants from the Centre for European Studies, the Institute of Contemporary History and the Friedrich Ebert Foundation. Klaus Funken, of the Ebert Foundation, assisted in the planning of the conference and arranged with the Foundation a generous grant without which the event and this publication would not have been possible.

1

INTRODUCTION

David Cesarani and Mary Fulbrook

Who is a citizen? Who is entitled to be part of a 'national' community, and who is to be excluded? Who may cross what boundaries and borders, reside and work within particular states, and who may not? What perceptions do insiders have of outsiders? How do different communities within states behave towards each other, define, manipulate and act upon their mutual perceptions?

In every community, there are common-sense understandings of who belongs, and who does not. Societies the world over have developed conceptions of 'self' and 'other', the 'civilized' and the 'barbarians', those who belong and those who are 'beyond the pale'. Identities have been forged on the basis of many possible imagined attributes: the myth of common ancestry, the inheritance of blood, the binding force of tribal tradition, custom and belief are historically among the most widespread. With the rise of nation states in the late eighteenth to late twentieth centuries, new elements of definition began to emerge; notions of citizenship defined by common ideals and the right to reside in the country of birth rather than of ancestry began to overlay or displace the primacy of kinship. Perceiving something of a sea-change in bases of identity in the modern era, historians and social scientists have for some time been grappling with an attempt to define the concept of national identity.[1]

However one seeks to define concepts of citizenship and national identity, 'imagined communities' attain an extraordinary impact as real social phenomena in which people believe and on which they act. The French sociologist Émile Durkheim's injunction to 'treat social facts as things' becomes brutally relevant when people are attacked or murdered because of (imagined) 'racial inferiority', or when families are torn apart and relatives sent 'home' by officials paid to guard borders and prevent the entry of 'illegal immigrants'.

1

Self-definitions of communities and the movement of peoples are phenomena stretching back through thousands of years of human history. In each age, however, there are new features and new issues. The current situation in Europe has a number of distinctive features. Global processes of the internationalization of the economy, enhanced communications networks, and transnational institutions and cultural currents have over a considerable period of time been changing the character and functions of nation states. Processes of European integration over the post-war decades have led to fundamental changes within the European Union, many of which have not yet been comprehended – or even registered – by citizens of European states. Since the fall of the Iron Curtain in 1989, there have been major upheavals in the broader European context, with increased levels of migration from eastern to western Europe for both political and economic reasons. The massive geopolitical earthquakes in south-eastern Europe, the Middle East and elsewhere in the last few years have been accompanied by heightened political tensions within the western European states. Right-wing movements, present already in the 1980s, have capitalized on the changes of the 1990s to seek to expand their electoral support. Less organized, apparently spontaneous racism has become more visible and frightening, as in the case of reunified Germany – of particular resonance, half a century after the demise of the Hitler regime. For many people in the 1990s, the current situation appears disturbingly turbulent and uncertain.

The recent rise of racism and xenophobia in Europe has focused public attention on issues concerning asylum-seekers and economic migrants. Yet migration is not a new phenomenon in Europe, and has not always been associated with inter-group violence. Immigrant communities have often been successfully integrated and new social and national identities have developed over time.

Bringing together international experts from a range of disciplines, this volume explores key questions concerning patterns of migration and different national policies, and their relation to political, social and cultural processes. Part One begins by examining the broader global and European context. Parts Two and Three then focus on four selected countries – Britain, France, Germany and Italy – within the broader European context. Controlled comparisons among these four countries allow for careful exploration of some of the major arguments in what is often a rather confused and emotive set of debates on an issue of great current interest and public concern.

The book examines a series of interrelated questions across the four cases. First, how do ideas and definitions of citizenship and nationality change over time? Under what conditions do they change very quickly? What changes cause a problematization of previously unexamined assumptions? How are these changes and associated tensions resolved (or not)?

Second, how far are ideas of the national community inclusive or exclusive? To what extent does the state generate and how does it sustain definitions of national identity? What other factors (media, social policies, etc.) are important in constructing a sense of identity?

Finally, the book confronts the following questions: Under what conditions are perceived differences politicized, to form the basis of serious cleavage and conflict? What factors mitigate against conflict and foster harmony or the celebration of difference?

THE CURRENT SITUATION IN EUROPE

On 26 March 1995 'Schengenland' came into existence. This is the informal term that denotes the area comprising seven European Union (EU) states between which internal border controls have been abolished under the terms of the Maastricht Treaty. Despite the fact that internal passport controls have been waived by the participant countries only at the price of massively strengthened external border controls, right-wing politicians throughout the EU have adopted an anti-Schengen stance and raised the spectre of a 'flood' of immigrants entering the union from north Africa and eastern Europe. As a result, it is increasingly likely that the prospect of 'Fortress Europe' will be realized as governments act to stop volatile electorates falling prey to the alarums of right-wingers.[2]

Changes in citizenship and nationality within the EU have thus had, and continue to have, a concordant effect on immigration controls as well as the rights of resident immigrants and asylum-seekers trying to join them. So one paradoxical effect of European unity and the greater internationalism of the Europeans (within Europe) has been a strengthening of Eurocentrism, a sort of higher xenophobia directed against Muslims and the modern version of the Mongol hordes – east Europeans attempting to escape the economic rubble of communism.[3]

The seven Schengen states are France, Germany, the Benelux countries, Spain and Portugal. Greece, Italy and Austria will soon join, while the Scandinavian countries are still debating the matter. The British Conservative Government in 1995 was resolutely opposed to any relaxation of frontier controls. Several leading British politicians expressed misgivings about the trend of EU policy on citizenship, immigration and nationality. One minister, Charles Wardle, even resigned from the government in protest against what he alleged was the loss of sovereign rights to regulate immigration. Thanks to these politicians and to newspapers such as the *Daily Mail,* which ran immigration scare stories on its front page throughout February and March 1995, these issues were set to figure prominently in the next British General Election. The British Home Secretary, Michael Howard, soon signalled that even tougher measures against illegal immigrants were in the pipeline. New anti-immigration laws featured in the proposed legislation revealed by the Conservative Government for the 1995/6 session of Parliament, a legislative package which was designed with one eye on a General Election.[4]

The revived salience of immigration as a party-political issue in Britain is mirrored throughout Europe. Several of the chapters in this book examine these trends in detail. Here it will suffice to mention that French presidential contenders Jean-Marie Le Pen and Philippe de Villiers both inscribed anti-immigrant and anti-Maastricht slogans on their election banners. Like the British right, they see European integration eroding each country's power to control the influx of aliens. In October 1994, Jörg Haider's Freiheitliche Partei Österreichs (Austrian Freedom Party) won over 22 per cent of the votes in the Austrian General Election after a campaign in which anti-immigration rhetoric played a large part.[5]

How is it possible to explain the paradox of insurgent nationalism at a time of European integration? What role do the very mechanisms of integration play in the exclusion of non-Europeans? To what extent are we witnessing a continuity of European racisms, or are there new forces at work as we near the end of the twentieth century? These are some of the questions which this volume sets out to answer. It approaches the interlocked phenomena of citizenship, nationality and migration from an interdisciplinary standpoint. There are chapters by historians, political scientists, sociologists and lawyers. This combination has been chosen to illustrate the deep, historical context for current political debates around migration. Too often the challenge which migration sets for concepts of citizenship and nationality is treated as contemporary. Consequently, important lessons go unlearned and analytical tools are blunted. This volume tries to understand the synchronic relationships between migration, citizenship, national identity and nationality alongside their dynamic relationship over time.

THE CASES FOR COMPARISON: BRITAIN, FRANCE, GERMANY AND ITALY

Four countries have been selected for examination. Each one represents different attributes of the debate.

Britain is an 'old country' with a reputedly stable constitutional system, but a weak notion of citizenship and a confused definition of nationality. The mixture of *jus soli* (nationality derived from place of birth) and *jus sanguinis* (nationality acquired by descent or blood) reflects the long evolution of England towards becoming the dominant party in a domestic and then a global empire. Throughout British history immigration has been a catalyst for defining and amending nationality and citizenship.

France in the modern era pioneered the definition of an active citizenship that was inclusive of all who accepted the principles of the Revolution and French culture. The availability of French citizenship to the children of immigrants on condition of their education in, and identification with, French culture expresses the idea of the French nation as a 'daily plebiscite'. Yet the very presence of immigrants who utilize the right to be different against the universalism of the rights of the citizen has caused French people to reassess the nexus between citizenship and ethnic nationality.

Citizenship in Germany has, until recently, been shackled to an exclusive, ethnic sense of nationality and was passed on according to the principle of *jus sanguinis*. The predominance of ethnic nationality stemmed from the singular history of the German nation. However, it is now being challenged. Developments in Germany over the last forty years, connected in part with immigration, have forced a reconsideration of the ethnic basis of citizenship.

Italy, like Germany, is an old nation but a relatively new state. Unlike the previous examples, until quite recently it was not a country of immigration. The Italian response to immigration has exposed latent assumptions about national identity, while attempts to accommodate citizenship to the new realities of mass immigration have foundered on the curious, postmodern character of the global movement of people. Immigration to Italy poses problems quite unlike those faced in Britain, France or Germany in earlier periods.

All four countries are members of the EU as well as signatories to international conventions governing human rights, refugee issues and asylum. Since immigration, citizenship and nationality issues are quite dramatically affected by transnational agreements and political associations, this volume begins with chapters relating the theory and practice of citizenship law and rights at international level to more limited national loci.

In chapter 2, Yasemin Soysal challenges the established dichotomy between forms of belonging to nations on the basis of either civic or ethnic components. She argues that since 1945 a person's identity as a member of a nation has been uncoupled from their rights. International migration, supra-national associations and the discourse of human rights have created an alternative need and source for the legitimation of individual and collective rights other than membership of a nation. For example, the International Labour Organisation defines and monitors the observance of the rights of migrant workers, demanding and obtaining for them entitlements which at one time only citizens of a country might customarily have expected to receive. 'What we have is a trend towards a new model of membership anchored in deterritorialized notions of persons rights' (see p. 21).

Elspeth Guild explains the rapidly changing nature of European citizenship and nationality (chapter 3). Under the Maastricht Treaty citizens of individual EU member states acquired a second citizenship: that of the EU. Guild shows that according to most agreed legal criteria this citizenship is also a form of nationality: it confers rights on EU citizens in third-party states. However, the internal operation of this citizenship is unusually messy and confusing. The contradictions illustrate Yasemin Soysal's assertion that 'classical conceptions of citizenship are no longer adequate in understanding the dynamics of membership and belonging in contemporary Europe' (p. 21).

The difference between old and new forms of membership and their derived rights has generated tension. The assertion of non-territorial rights grinds against common notions of sovereignty. The population of a particular state ends up as a tiered social formation, with different groups having different bundles of rights. Ironically, the universal language of human rights that is legitimated by reference to international conventions and guarded by international judicial instruments actually incites particularism and intolerance. Ethnic groups, national groups and almost any collectivity of people who define themselves as a 'nation' demand the universal right to self-determination: the right to be different. The result, as seen in the former Yugoslavia, can be chaotic and bloody. Many of these ethnic and national conflicts are historically rooted, which underlines the need for a historical perspective to the current fluid, and bewildering, state of citizenship and nationality.

The British case (chapter 4) exemplifies the fluid nature of national identity, its interaction with nationality and citizenship. The concept of citizenship was always weak in England. Subjecthood was the preferred mode of belonging to the nation and persisted into the modern era by virtue of Parliament's assumption of the sovereign's mantle. Access to political rights was, at various times, restricted due to the confessional nature of the state. Despite the pre-eminence of *jus soli*, full belonging was predicated upon belonging to the national church: Anglicanism and Englishness were fused together. The creation of the United Kingdom and the British Empire necessitated a flexible category of belonging, which was supplied by the perpetuation of allegiance to the crown by British subjects throughout the empire. However, the emergence of the dominions and the entrenchment of racial thinking led to a bifurcation of white and non-white British subjects.

The racialization of belonging was not unprecedented: Jewish immigrants to Britain at the turn of the century had been the object of hostile attention on racist grounds. But mass immigration from the colonies and the New Commonwealth after 1945 strongly accentuated the desire to draw the criteria for national belonging more tightly and to exclude non-white peoples. By the late-1970s, immigration controls and citizenship were overdetermined by considerations of 'race', even if disguised as cultural concerns. The struggle over the definition of an exclusive or an inclusive national identity is still not resolved, but the treatment of immigrants and non-white citizens bears the marks of a dominant exclusivist ethos.

Since the late nineteenth century, French citizenship has been inclusive and non-ethnic. But Patrick Weil (chapter 5) fears that this tradition is under threat paradoxically because of European integration and the extension of voting rights to non-nationals in EU member states. The Maastricht Treaty allows each EU member state to determine who 'belongs' according to their own nationality laws. This latitude was permitted out of recognition for the sovereignty of member states and rested on the essentialism of nationality: it was assumed that each nation state had criteria for belonging that were unique and which could not be standardized. As a result, a sharp distinction was drawn between French nationality and German nationality, which Weil regards as a false polarity with unfortunate consequences. It confirmed the Germans in their chosen mode of 'ethnic nationality' at just the time when it was most appropriate to modify it. By perpetuating the French notion of an elective citizenship, symbolized by voting, it created the grounds for an ethnic backlash. Weil worries that focusing citizenship around voting rights may actually perpetuate the otherness and inequality of immigrants.

In France since 1889, duration of residence and socialization into French culture have been critical to gaining citizenship. Contrary to Renan's rhetorical flourish that the nation was a daily plebiscite, most Frenchmen only exercised this choice symbolically on certain occasions, such as voting in national elections (see note 38).

> There is no differentiation in the French social imagination between identity, citizenship and nationality, between local and national citizenship. It is for this reason that the creation of a citizenship that is enlarged to include all foreigners or only Europeans (as envisioned by the Treaty of Maastricht) which would break the bonds between the vote, citizenship, nationality and identity is still very hotly contested.
>
> (Weil, this volume, p. 81)

A profligate dissemination of voting rights might provoke an assertion of ethnic identity in order to answer the question 'who is a French person?'. Weil concludes that it would have been far better to sweep away separate nationalities and create a genuine European nationality with a common citizenship carrying common rights, and one that was accessible to non-Europeans. At present, Weil regards EU law as deepening the cleavage between European voters and non-European non-voters without any guarantee that the latter will ever gain full political rights.

German national identity has been resolutely ethnic and exclusive in character (chapter 6). At the time of German unification in 1871 many ethnic Germans lived outside the boundaries of the German state, while many non-Germans lived within it. After 1913, citizenship was linked to the notion of a nationality inherited by *jus sanguinis*. This sense of the nation was maintained after the demise of the Third Reich, notwithstanding the perversion of ideas about the *Volk*, or people, committed by the Nazis. In 1945 Germany was a divided nation; large numbers of ethnic Germans were being uprooted and driven towards Germany. In order not to foreclose the possibility of reunion and to enable the absorption of the ethnic German refugees, West Germany adopted the *völkish* definition of citizenship. The East

Germans, like the West Germans, initially hoped that the division of Germany was temporary and avoided setting up a separate nationality. When the division petrified, the East Germans formulated a socialist concept of nationality that was supposed to differentiate them from that of the West. Ironically, while East Germans seem never to have lost their sense of ethnic nationhood, young West Germans developed a more cosmopolitan and inclusive idea of Germanness.

The pre-eminence of an ethnic identity helped to undermine the East German state and facilitate reunification in 1989. The down-side of this was the exclusion of guestworkers and long-term settlers from the nation and citizenship. This regime of closure became increasingly untenable when nationalism led to attacks on foreigners in Germany, many of whom had been there longer than ethnic Germans pouring in from the former Soviet Bloc. It was further undermined since the new ethnic German arrivals, who often knew little of German or Germany, found themselves in a superior position to 'immigrants' who had been born and raised in the country.

The situation was exacerbated in the early 1990s by the influx of asylum-seekers, whose entry was facilitated by the post-war sense of the nation as a riposte to Hitlerism. This was the 'double legacy' of the Third Reich. As Fulbrook remarks, 'while it was extremely hard to acquire rights of citizenship and political representation, it was conversely relatively easy to enter Germany as a refugee seeking political asylum' (p. 101). In 1993–4, in an attempt to resolve this paradox, the German Government scaled down its constitutional obligation to accept refugees, while at the same time relaxing the rules under which long-term settlers could obtain German nationality and citizenship. The country now stands at a crossroads where questions of identity, nationality and rights intersect. Fulbrook concludes:

> The united Germany of the 1990s, having achieved arguably the closest it has ever come to being a 'nation state' . . . must now seriously ask whether the concept of a putative German 'national identity' cannot usefully be divorced from that of citizenship entitlement.
>
> (p. 103)

The pattern of immigration to Germany since the 1950s, detailed by Karen Schönwälder in chapter 10, follows the classic model. As German industry soaked up the pool of cheap labour created by ethnic Germans who had fled from or been driven out of territories in eastern Europe, it turned to migrant labour from southern Europe.

From 1954 it was policy to recruit industrial workers from Italy and Turkey. The influx of foreign workers could be managed relatively easily because, for one reason, they were concentrated in heavy industry and manufacturing in a few urban centres. When the presence of a large foreign population attracted adverse comment in the early 1970s, it was possible for the government to respond with integrative policies aimed at improving the living conditions of 'guestworkers' and assimilating their families into German society so as to reduce antagonism towards them. But what can be done with an immigrant labour force that is heterogeneous, mobile, dispersed, outside the social institutions and fraternities associated with industrial societies, and for the most part clandestine? This is the dilemma facing Italians, who grapple with the wave of immigration that has, within the last decade, reversed Italy's traditional position as a net exporter of population.

Despite its history as a country of emigration with a long-established interest in Italian communities in other countries, Enrico Pugliese (chapter 7) shows that Italy has had little experience of handling the challenges posed by mass immigration. The agencies delegated to collect information on population inflows found themselves ill-equipped to provide even basic raw data. Although public debate focuses on immigrants from the Third World, the numbers provided by these agencies refer to the unassorted total that includes the large number of resident foreigners from other EU countries and the USA. As a result, the number of non-white, Muslim immigrants, to whom alone the term is confined in popular discourse, is grossly inflated. But the means to correct it and present a more accurate appraisal hardly exist. Third World immigration followed the decline of manufacturing in Italy, the expansion of service industries and the burgeoning of the 'informal' economy. Immigrants are sucked into precarious service jobs or employed illegally under exploitative conditions. The immigrant population is highly diverse, emanating from a dozen countries, and spread over a wide range of occupations, most of which are non-unionized. Pugliese remarks that 'We are at the forefront of a post-industrial migration . . . the great integrative institutions typical of industrial societies, in particular the trade unions, have by necessity a much reduced role.' (See p. 114.)

The liberal policy of extending rights to migrant workers has been frustrated by their clandestine *modus operandi*, itself a function of the new global economy of migration. Amnesties were offered to illegal immigrants to tempt them to regularize their position and extend to them a form of social and economic citizenship. However, their attraction to employers lies in the fact that they carry no costs in terms of employers' welfare contributions. So employers and the immigrants' sense of their own marketability dictate that they remain a semi-covert presence. Many register with the authorities to regularize their status, but claim to be unemployed in order to avoid jeopardizing their jobs. Ironically, this inflates the statistics of 'unemployed, sponging foreigners' so beloved of right-wing agitators and only worsens their overall position! Since the early 1990s, internal pressure to restrict immigration have conjoined with the imperatives of Schengen. Italy toughened its immigration controls and resolved to cease being the soft underbelly of 'Fortress Europe'. A relatively liberal policy of civic inclusion, which was facilitated by a relaxed sense of national identity, was turned into a policy of rigid exclusion that mirrored a sharper sense of Italianness.

In Italy the question of political rights for foreigners or access to full citizenship is still a nascent issue. In Britain non-white immigrants were, from the outset, citizens with full legal and political rights. The challenge to this inclusivity followed only many years after the creation of large immigrant communities. However, its dominant expression does not lie in political movements seeking to disenfranchise or repatriate immigrants and settlers. Tony Kushner (chapter 8) maintains that the politicization of difference should not be seen as confined to far-right parties such as the National Front (NF) or British National Party (BNP). To take this view is to erect an alibi for deep currents of racism in British society which can be plumbed using the research material of Mass Observation. This reveals that liberalism places strict limits on the forms of difference that are tolerable to people who regard themselves as anti-racist. 'Cultural diversity is quite all right unless it produces culture clashes ... in essence problems of ethnic diversity are blamed on the immigrants' (see pp. 133–4). In other words, the prejudices of the majority are universalized as cultural norms to which members of ethnic minorities are expected to conform, or else. The forms of difference that are acceptable are 'theme park differences'.

Kushner concludes that 'Ultimately, pluralism has to be subsumed under the hegemony of what is seen as true English national identity' (p. 136). Yet this identity is increasingly racialized and access to it is getting more exclusive. Contrary to analyses of racism that focus on far-right parties and accept that difference is problematic, a fact of life to be exploited by the unscrupulous, Kushner retorts that 'the

11

basis of conflict is not difference itself, but Englishness as a racialized and in recent years, a politicized, exclusive project' (p. 140).

Despite France's divergent political tradition, developments there follow a pattern similar to Britain's, according to Max Silverman (chapter 9). Citizenship was supposed to be a universal category, articulating the citizen into a neutral state. In fact, 'Citizenship was merged with cultural conformity, the second seen as the condition of and the means to attain the first'. Hence the assertion of the cultural rights and identity of immigrants is seen as an 'invasion' of the state and a challenge to the French political ethos. Ironically, the aggressive deployment of particularity has been facilitated by the rampant individualization of society due to consumerism, *laissez-faire* market theories and the 'privatization' of the state. Identity in postmodern France has been de-institutionalized; the latent tension between the particular man and the universal citizen has become apparent. Silverman thus shows how the combined effects of free market capitalism and migration have disarticulated citizenship, nationality and culture. There is a desperate need to reunite the individual with a citizenship that is not culture-bound and exclusive, and to create a politics that accepts and functions with diversity.

As Karen Schönwälder shows in the case of West Germany (chapter 10), there are greater political dividends to be gained from pursuing the politics of exclusivity than the politics of cultural and ethnic pluralism. Yet the racialization of difference and the current spate of attacks on immigrants and asylum-seekers was not foredoomed; it was a consequence of conscious political manipulation and incitement by the media. From 1954 to 1964 West Germany welcomed migrant labour, even if the warm reception for Italians was patronizing and, in part, based on guilty feelings about Germany's conduct towards its ally during the war. When migrant labourers formed settled communities which attracted hostile attention in the late 1960s and during the 1970s, the state stepped in with integrationist policies. Rhetoric about an 'invasion' of foreigners remained marginal to political discourse. Xenophobia only emerged into the open on a large scale in the late 1970s and was connected with the search for a West German national identity. It attained prominence with the electoral politics of Helmut Kohl in 1982 and his subsequent conduct of government.

Chancellor Kohl encouraged debate about patriotism and national identity; he deliberately sought to rehabilitate the German past, to give Germans a history they could be proud of. Politicians began to describe hostility to foreigners as a 'healthy' expression of national identity and defence of national culture. As economic difficulties worsened in the wake of reunification there was pressure from below against 'foreigners'. Instead of countering this popular prejudice, politicians and the media colluded with it. This process culminated in the revocation of Germany's liberal asylum laws, symbolizing a politicization of difference that was all the sadder for being neither natural nor inevitable.

There can be few more blatant, or successful, efforts at constructing difference than the Northern Leagues in Italy. Carlo Ruzza and Oliver Schmidtke (chapter 11) show how Umberto Bossi and his followers artfully manufactured a Northern Italian identity which had no ethnic, linguistic or cultural basis. Yet the sense of belonging, rooted in the notion of residence in a certain area and an elective affinity with a group of people defined against outsiders, facilitated political mobilization and proved immensely flexible. The Lega (Leagues) took a region and defined its ethos against Southerners and immigrants. The construction of a *Feindbild* or 'enemy picture' was crucial to imagining this fictitious community: 'The definition of an enemy is crucial, as it supports social identities' (see p. 194).

Yet the Northern Leagues found that a strictly regional identity constricted their political ambitions. Ruzza and Schmidtke explain that in order to expand their electoral base, socially and territorially, the Leagues defined new enemies. Foreigners replaced Southerners, many of whom were settled in the North and, unlike aliens, had the vote. Corrupt central government now served to highlight the assiduous, frugal and upright habits of folk living in Northern Italy (as against Northern Italians). From 1992, the Leagues occupied seats in the Italian Parliament and set their sights on national power. They now adopted a federalist agenda that would justify the conquest of central state institutions. In order to appear respectable, anti-immigrant rhetoric was toned down, but the assault on corrupt central government continued.

'In the case of the Lega. . . . the image of communal belonging is strategically used in a form of political mobilization that exceeds what is traditionally known as regionalism' (see p. 201). How was this feat possible? Ruzza and Schmidtke argue that the collapse of Marxism and traditional integrative ideologies left a vacuum which could be filled with neighbourhood, village, town, district and so forth. The regional policy of the EC encouraged the development of regional identities and lent them a certain economic viability. The growth of immigration offered an outsider group against which to define native virtues, while the globalization of culture encouraged a defiant localism. Ethnic belonging would not do, but the individualism of the 1980s and notions of choice made it legitimate for people to opt into an identity.

With Ruzza and Schmidtke we return to our point of departure: transnational communities, theories of group rights, the globalization of culture, migration and economic change. The Italian example demonstrates vividly the possibilities and dangers of constructing and exploiting difference in a political context.

NOTES

1 See for example: E. J. Hobsbawm, *Nations and Nationalism since 1780* (Cambridge: Cambridge University Press, 1990); Benedict Anderson, *Imagined Communities* (London: Verso, rev. edn., 1991); E. Gellner, *Nations and Nationalism* (Oxford: Blackwell, 1983); John Hutchinson and Anthony Smith (eds), *Nationalism* (Oxford: Oxford University Press, 1994); M. Fulbrook (ed.), *National Histories and European History* (London: UCL Press, 1993).
2 Tony Bunyon, 'Borders go down, walls go up', *Guardian*, 15 February 1995.
3 See Liz Fetke and Frances Webber, *Inside Racist Europe* (London: Institute of Race Relations, 1994).
4 *Guardian*, 14 March 1995; 24 March 1995.
5 *Guardian*, 27 March 1995; *Observer*, 8 May 1994. For the background see: Richard Mitten, 'Jörg Haider, the Anti-immigrant Petition and Immigration Policy in Austria', *Patterns of Prejudice* 28(2), 1994, pp. 27–47; Cas Mudde, 'One against all, All against one! A portrait of the Vlaams Blok', *Patterns of Prejudice* 29 (1), 1995, pp. 5–28. See also note 2 above, and Institute of Jewish Affairs/European Centre for Research and Action on Racism and Antisemitism, *Political Extremism and the Threat to Democracy in Europe* (London: IJA/CERA, 1994).

Part I

THE INTERNATIONAL CONTEXT

2

CHANGING CITIZENSHIP IN EUROPE

Remarks on postnational membership and the national state[1]

Yasemin Nuhoğlu Soysal

Recently, it has been very fashionable to define German citizenship as ethnic citizenship and French citizenship as a civic one (Dumont 1994, Brubaker 1992). Civic citizenship defines belonging on the basis of participation through rights and obligations. Ethnic citizenship on the other hand denotes community-based notions of belonging through particularistic identities. Even though this categorization may have analytical appeal in understanding the ways that self-definitions of nations differ, I do not see these two components (rights on the one hand, and identities on the other) as profound differentiating factors across national citizenships.

I would rather argue that national citizenship – as an ideology and as an institutional practice – have always embodied both of these components. Throughout European nation-buildings, and at various stages of it, the European states have made claims on various peoples on the basis of both of these components. The historical formation of the modern polity describes a process that encloses citizenship within territorially based national units (Bendix 1964). This national closure of citizenship was achieved, on the one hand, by the extension of rights and benefits to different strata of the civil society; on the other, by attributing some distinctiveness – 'shared' values, language, blood, history or culture – to the collective citizenry. The first of these acts transformed previously excluded populations into citizens, whereas the second ensured the exclusivity in membership. Hence, the process of nation-building brought together the principle of nationality and the principle of rights in the very body of citizenship.

My goal in this chapter, however, is not to inquire into the historical development of national citizenship in Europe. Rather, I will focus on the changes in the institution of citizenship in the post-war era. The underlying argument of my presentation is that in the post-war era citizenship has undergone a profound change, through which the two major components of citizenship – identity and rights – are increasingly decoupled. Rights that were once associated with belonging in a national community have become increasingly abstract, and defined and legitimated at the transnational level. Identities, in contrast, are still perceived as particularized and territorially bounded. Thus, what was brought together by the French Revolution and the following two centuries of nation-building efforts no longer 'naturally' belong together. In the post-war era, profound changes in the organization and ideologies of the global system have complicated the national order of citizenship and introduced new dynamics for membership in national polities. In the following, I will discuss these post-war changes and their implications for the meaning and organization of citizenship in Europe.

The predominant conceptions of modern citizenship, as expressed in both scholarly and popular discourses, posit that populations are organized within nation-state boundaries by citizenship rules that acclaim 'national belonging' as the legitimate basis of membership in modern states. As such, national citizenship is defined by two foundational principles: a congruence between territorial state and the national community; national belonging as the source of rights and duties of individuals as well as their collective identity. Hence, what national citizenship denotes is a territorially bounded population with a specific set of rights and duties, excluding others on the ground of nationality.

Several post-war global developments have undercut these foundational principles of citizenship, and have contributed to the expansion of membership beyond the boundaries of national collectivities. Let me briefly cite four of these developments:

1 Post-war internationalization of labour markets. As a consequence of this there have been massive migratory flows to Europe, not only from the immediate European periphery but from 'distant lands', and this has complicated the existing national and ethnic composition of European countries. The list of sending and receiving countries has grown impressively with time, with new combinations that are undermining political and geographical distances

18

and rationalities (for example, Vietnamese in Romania, Chinese in Moscow, Nigerians in Turkey, Turks in Israel, etc.).

2 Massive decolonizations after 1945, which led to the mobilization of newly independent states at the international level, and ushered in an awareness and assertion of their 'rights' within universalistic parameters. This, in turn, contributed to the broadening and recasting of the global discourse of rights. Parallel to the celebration and codification of 'different but equal cultures' and 'otherhood' through transnational agencies such as the UN and UNESCO, new social movements have emerged around individual and collective rights, contesting the accepted notions of citizenship in European polities. Consequently, a variety of cultures and identities have been incorporated into the social domain and institutions of citizenship: women, gays and lesbians, environmentalists, increasingly regional identities and youth subcultures, as well as immigrants.

3 The emergence of multi-level polities, as we observe with the gradual unfolding of the European Union (Marks and McAdam 1993; Schmitter 1992). As much as the development of the EU implies the diffusion and sharing of sovereignty among local, national and transnational political institutions, the nature of making claims, acquiring rights and mobilizing identities also change. The existence of multi-level polities creates new opportunities for social mobilizing and advancing demands within and beyond national boundaries. And the EU citizenship itself breaches the link between the status attached to citizenship and national territory, by conferring rights which are not necessarily located in a bounded nation state.

4 A fourth development is the increasing intensification of the global discourse and instruments on individual rights. This emphasis on rights is expressed through a codification of 'human rights' as a world-level organizing principle in legal, scientific and popular conventions. As legitimized and celebrated by various international codes and laws, the discourse of human rights ascribes universal rights to the person, independent of membership status in a particular nation state. Even though they are frequently violated as a political practice, human rights increasingly constitute a world-level index of legitimate action and provide a hegemonic language for formulating claims to rights above and beyond national belonging.

19

In the post-war era, this elaboration of individual rights as an abstract universal category has created an inventive ground upon which more expensive claims for rights can be advanced by various groups in society, and has led to the introduction and amplification of new forms of rights – for women, children, minorities, and even for animals and plants (Turner 1986).

The increasing codification and elaboration of human rights as a global principle is especially pertinent to the membership and rights of post-war immigrants in Europe. In their case, ideologies and instruments of human rights, which privilege individuals independent of a necessary belonging into a national collectivity, have been very influential in the expansion of many citizenship rights to these populations. In particular, the national court systems, which increasingly activate transnational human rights conventions as the basis of their decisions, have contributed substantially to the expansion of foreigners' rights. In many cases, their decisions, typically presented as inalienable rights of personhood, have undermined the national order of distributing rights. Also, many transnational organizations such as the International Labour Organisation and the Council of Europe have taken an active interest in immigrant populations by situating them within the bounds of human rights discourse, thus contributing to the redefinition of their status and expansion of their rights in the host countries.

Today, even though a large proportion of immigrants in Europe have not been incorporated into a formal scheme of citizenship, they are nevertheless incorporated into many rights and privileges of citizenship. Actually, one of the most striking characteristics of the post-war immigrants is their predominantly non-citizen status. An estimated 15 million immigrants in Europe are foreigners in their countries of residence; they do not hold a formal citizenship status. (And restrictive procedures for citizenship are only a partial explanation for their foreignness. Surveys have repeatedly shown that there has not been an urgent demand among immigrants themselves to take on the citizenship of their country of residence, either. When there is a demand, it is usually accompanied by demands for dual citizenship.) The majority of the immigrant populations have a permanent resident status, however, which is a status not very easily distinguishable from a formal citizenship status in terms of the rights and privileges it confers. Permanent residents of European host polities are entitled to full civil rights and have access to a set of social services and economic rights almost identical to those available to national citizens, including public education, health benefits, various welfare schemes and free access to labour markets. The right that differentiates national citizens from resident foreigners is the national voting right. Local voting rights, on the other hand, are extended to non-citizen populations in a number of European countries.

Thus, post-war immigrants who are not directly part or full members of the national community are still entitled to rights and protection by a state which is not 'their own', and are being incorporated into a wide range of rights and privileges that were originally reserved only for nationals. This status constitutes an anomaly for the predominant conceptions of citizenship, which assume a 'natural' dichotomy between citizens and aliens; and it is highly correlated with the increasing dominance of global ideologies and institutions of individual rights in the post-war era.

What are the implications of all these global changes for the meaning and organization of citizenship in Europe? First, all these trends imply that the nation state as a territorial entity is no longer the source of legitimacy for individual rights (though, as I argue later, the materialization of rights are still organizationally vested in the state). The post-war changes in the organization and ideologies of the global system have increasingly shifted the institutional and normative basis of citizenship to a transnational level and have extended rights and privileges associated with it beyond national boundaries.

Second, classical conceptions of national citizenship are no longer adequate in understanding the dynamics of membership and belonging in contemporary Europe. The trends I discussed suggest a profound rewriting of the rules that define the membership of individuals in European polities. National citizenship or a formal nationality is no longer a significant construction in terms of how it translates into certain rights and privileges, as attested by the status of post-war immigrants. Rights, participation and representation in a polity are increasingly matters beyond the vocabulary of national citizenship. What we have is a trend towards a new model of membership anchored in deterritorialized notions of personal rights. This new model that I call postnational differs in various dimensions from the classical model of national citizenship, which came into place or rather crystallized only in the first part of this century and which still continues to inform much of our understanding of membership in national polities. I have elaborated this postnational model (and its varying dimensions from the national model) elsewhere (Soysal

1994). Here I would like to mention the three most important differences.

The first difference regards *the territorial dimension of citizenship*. As I already indicated, the classical model is nation-state bounded. Citizenship entails a territorial relationship between the individual and the state (Weber 1968; Bendix 1964). It postulates well-defined, exclusionary boundaries and state jurisdiction over the national population within those boundaries. The model thus implies a congruence between membership and territory; only German nationals are entitled to the rights and privileges the German state affords – nobody else.

The boundaries of postnational citizenship are fluid; a Turkish guestworker need not have a primordial attachment to Berlin (or to Germany for that matter) to participate in Berlin's public institutions and make claims on its authority structures. By holding citizenship in one state (Turkey) while living and enjoying rights and privileges in a different state (Germany), Turkish guestworkers violate the presumed congruence between membership and territory. Another indicator of the fluidity of postnational membership is the increasing acquisitions of dual nationality across Europe. Switzerland, Belgium and the Netherlands recently passed legislation allowing dual citizenship. In Germany, it is a hotly debated issue but the Berlin city administration has been allowing dual citizenship since the 1990s.

The fluid boundaries of membership do not necessarily mean fluid boundaries of the nation state. On the contrary, as we know, all European states are trying to reinforce their national boundaries through restrictive immigration policies. What makes postnational membership fluid is the fact that individuals can forward claims or demands independent of national boundaries, and that rights are granted even when individuals do not belong to formal national collectivity. Thus, while states reinforce more and more strict boundaries, at the same time, transnational pressures toward a more expansive membership and individual rights penetrate the same national boundaries and profoundly transform the nature of citizenship.

A second difference between postnational and national citizenship concerns *rights and privileges*. The classic order of the western nation state is centred around formal equality in the sense of uniform citizenship rights. Citizenship assumes a single status; all citizens are entitled to the same rights and privileges. The postnational model, on the other hand, implies multiplicity of membership – a principal organizational form for empires and city states. As it is the case with post-war immigrants, the distribution of rights among various immigrant groups and citizens is not even. In the emerging European system, certain groups of migrants are more privileged than others; legal permanent residents, political refugees, dual citizens and the nationals of common-market countries have more rights than temporary residents or those residents who do not hold a legal status. Thus, what is increasingly in place is a plurality of membership forms.

The third difference between postnational and national models regards *the basis and legitimation of membership*. In the classical model, shared nationhood constitutes the basis of membership. This nationhood may be constituted differently in different countries – it might assume a subscription to a political ideal, a culture or ethnicity – but it is still the shared nationhood that justifies equal rights and obligations. In that sense, the basis of legitimacy for individual rights is located within the nation state.

In the new model, the membership of individuals is not solely based on the criteria of nationality; their membership and rights are legitimated by the global ideologies of human rights. Thus, universal personhood replaces nationhood; and universal human rights replace national rights. The justification for the state's obligations to foreign populations goes beyond the nation state itself. The rights and claims of individuals are legitimated by ideologies grounded in a transnational community, through international codes, conventions and laws on human rights, independent of their citizenship in a nation state. Hence, the individual transcends the citizen. This is the most elemental way that the postnational model differs from the national model.

If my assertions about a trend towards postnational membership and declining significance of national citizenship are correct, how can we make sense of the unfolding episodes of world and European politics in the 1990s? Here I am referring to the reinventions and reassertions of national identities in eastern but also western Europe, or the violent vocalization of anti-foreigner groups throughout Europe, accompanied by demands for restrictive refugee and immigration policies. As citizenship matters less, national identities are articulated in new ways, either in exclusionary narratives, or as search for new national identities.

How can we account for these contradictory propensities? In order to untangle these trends, I suggest that we go back to the very first point that I made: increasing decoupling between rights and identity. In the post-war era, if one facet of the discourse and praxis of immigration is the closure of national polity, the other is the expansion of the same polity beyond national closure. While the first involves boundary construction through restrictive policy measures and national(ist) narratives, the other is about 'border crossings' (Rosaldo 1989): the constant flux of people, extension of rights of membership to foreigners, and narratives of multiplicity. This apparent paradox is only intelligible if we take into consideration the organizational rules and ideologies embedded in the post-war global system.

I would argue that the contradictory propensities reflected in the post-war international migration emanate from the institutionalized duality between the two normative principles of the global system: national sovereignty and universal human rights. The same global-level processes and institutional frameworks that foster postnational membership also reify the nation state and its sovereignty.

The principle of human rights ascribes a universal status to individuals and their rights, undermining the boundaries of the nation state. The principle of sovereignty, on the other hand, reinforces national boundaries and invents new ones. This paradox manifests itself as a deterritorialized expansion of rights despite the territorialized closure of polities. The post-war period has witnessed a vast proliferation in the scope and categories of the universalistic rights. Human rights have expanded beyond the conventional list of civil rights to include social and economic rights such as employment, education, health care, nourishment and housing. The collective rights of nations and peoples to culture, language and development have also been recodified as inalienable human rights. Women's rights have become 'women's human rights' of freedom from 'gender violence' and freedom from traditional practices, cultural prejudices and religious extremism.

Incongruously, inasmuch as the ascription and codification of rights move beyond national frames of reference, postnational rights remain organized at the national level. The world is still made up of territorially configured political units; implementation and enforcement of global rules and norms lie with national political structures. Simply put, the exercise of universalistic rights is tied to specific states and their institutions. Even though its mode and scope of action are increasingly defined and constrained by the wider global system, the sovereign nation state retains the formally and organizationally legitimate form venerated by the ideologies and conventions of transnational reference groups such as the UN, UNESCO, European Union and the like.

Expressions of this duality between universalistic rights and the territorially bounded nation state abound. Faced with a growing flux of asylum-seekers in the 1990s, western states have defensively reconsidered their immigration policies. Regulation of immigration is often articulated as elemental to national sovereignty, and several host countries have initiated restrictions. On the other hand, the category of the refugee has broadened to encompass new definitions of 'persecution'. For example, Canada's Immigration and Refugee Board has begun to grant asylum to women persecuted because of their gender; cases involving rape, domestic violence and state restrictions on women's activities qualify for asylum. France recognized 'genital mutilation' as a form of persecution in granting asylum to a west African woman. So, even as the western states attempt to maintain their boundaries through quantitative restrictions, the introduction of expanding categories and definitions of the rights of personhood sets the stage for new patterns of asylum, making national boundaries more penetrable.

The paradoxical connection of human rights and the sovereign nation state is also manifest in the German government's attempts to control the flow of refugees. In 1992, the German government decided to repatriate Gypsies, 'who do not qualify for asylum', to Romania. However, to 'compensate' for human rights, Germany pledged financial aid to help the Gypsies 'reintegrate' into Romanian society. Thus, while acting in its 'national interest' by denying entry to potential refugees, the German state simultaneously extends its responsibilities beyond its national borders by 'providing for the welfare' of the deportees.

Again, in 1993, Germany revised its constitutional provisions which guaranteed automatic right to asylum (like other European countries, Germany now has a quite restrictive asylum policy); but at the same time the government eased the naturalization procedures for second-generation Turks, by significantly disrupting Germany's 'lineage-based' citizenship codes.

These seemingly paradoxical affinities articulate an underlying dialectic of the post-war global system: while nation states and their boundaries are reified through assertions of border controls and appeals to nationhood, a new mode of membership, anchored in the universalistic rights of personhood, transgresses the national order of things.

I would argue that the explosion of nationalisms can also be construed as an exponent of the underlying dialectic of the post-war global system. More and more collectivities are asserting their 'national identities' and alleging statehood on the basis of their acclaimed 'nationness'. These claims are fed and legitimated by the institutionalized principle of political sovereignty and self-determination, which promises each 'people' an autonomous state of its own. Thus, even when previous nation states are dissolving (for example the Soviet Union and Yugoslavia), the 'emerging' units aspire to become territorial states with self-determination, and the world political community grants them this right. The new (or would-be) states immediately appropriate the language of nationhood, produce anthems and flags, and, of course, pledge allegiance to human and minority rights.

The principle of self-determination further reinforces nationalisms, since, for a sovereign statehood, a nationally bounded and unified population is imperative. Therefore, collectivities that have been previously defined simply as ethnicities, religious minorities or language groups, reinvent their 'nationness', accentuate the uniqueness of their cultures and histories, and cultivate particularisms to construct their 'others' (see Hobsbawm 1990).

At another level the collective right to self-determination, as well as to political and cultural existence, is itself increasingly codified as a universal human right. Claims to particularistic identities, cultural distinctiveness and self-determination are legitimated by reference to the essential, indisputable rights of persons, and are thus recast as world-level, postnational rights. This recodification is, in fact, what Roland Robertson (1992: 100) calls 'the universalization of particularism and the particularization of universalism'. What are considered to be particularistic characteristics of collectivities – culture, language, and standard ethnic traits – become variants of the universal core of humanness. In turn, as universal attributes and human rights, they are exercised in individual and collective actors' narratives and strategies.

Framing political self-determination and collective cultural rights as universalistic rights occasions ever-increasing claims and mobilizations around particularistic identities. An identity politics – energized by narrations of collective 'pasts' and accentuated cultural differences – becomes the basis for participation and affords the means for mobilizing resources in the national and world polities. If one aspect of the dynamism generated by identity politics is relegitimization and reification of nationness, the other is its fragmentation, displacement of its meaning, and hence its delegitimization.

A growing tendency toward regionalisms (sometimes separatisms) and their recognition by the central states fragments the existing nations and nationalities into infinitely distinct ethnicities and cultural sub-units. In Europe, for instance, more and more groups seek economic and linguistic autonomy on the basis of their regional identities: Bretons, Corsicans, Basques and Occitans in France; Scots and Welsh in Britain; Lombards and Sardinians in Italy. And European states, even those that have long resisted linguistic and cultural diversity, increasingly accommodate autonomous entities (as in Spain) and provide for regional languages (as in France and Italy). The multiplication of particularisms and subsequent fragmentation disrupt the presumed contiguities of nationness and undermine the territorial sanctity of nation states.

Furthermore, as particularistic identities are transformed into expressive modes of a core humanness, thus acquiring universal currency, the 'nation' loses its 'charisma' and becomes normalized. The idea of nation becomes a trope of convenience for claims to collective rights and identity. Even groups that may not fit the classic definitions of a nation refer to themselves as such: gays and lesbians claim a 'Queer Nation'; the Deaf define themselves as a national subgroup with its own cultural peculiarities and language; and indigenous peoples request to be called not a tribe but a nation and seek a voting seat in the United Nations. In this universalizing flux, 'the ways of "doing" identity' (Robertson 1992:99) become a standardized exercise, with common modes of presentation and themes. At the centre of this activity lies the construction of official taxonomies, with reference to routine markers and attributes of culture; that is, the placid images of cuisines, crafts, life-styles, religious symbols, folklores and customs.

In the context of this normalizing trend, national identities that celebrate discriminatory uniqueness and 'naturalistic' canonizations of nationhood become more and more discredited. It is, for instance, increasingly difficult to protect and practice a code of nationality that inscribes 'blood' or 'lineage' as its primary principle. Note the widespread reaction to Germany's lineage-based citizenship and naturalization laws, and the German government's decision to overhaul these laws, which were called 'outdated' even by Chancellor Helmut Kohl. Similarly, national canons that valorize ancestral warmaking and symbols of patriarchy are increasingly less enticing as vehicles for doing identity. It has been truly amazing to observe the remaking of the 'Vikings', from warrior forefathers to spirited long-distance traders.

All these recontextualizations of 'nationness' within the universalistic discourse of human rights blur the meanings and boundaries attached to the nation and the nation state. The idea of the nation persists as an intense metaphor, at times an idiom of war. However, in a world within which rights, and identities as rights, derive their legitimacy from discourses of universalistic personhood, the limits of nationness, or of national citizenship for that matter, become inventively irrelevant.

Our dominant theories and conceptualizations of citizenship, nation state membership have yet to catch up with these changes in national citizenship. Until then we will continue to have anomalies in existing paradigms, models that do not work, and incongruities between official rhetoric and institutional actualities.

NOTE

1 Parts of this chapter are reprinted from Yasemin Nuhoğlu Soysal, *Limits of Citizenship: Migrants and Postnational Membership in Europe* (Chicago: University of Chicago Press, 1994).

REFERENCES

Bendix, Reinhard (1964) *Nation-Building and Citizenship*, New York: Wiley.
Brubaker, Rogers (1992) *Citizenship and Nationhood in France and Germany*, Cambridge, Mass.: Harvard University Press.
Dumont, Louis (1994) *German Ideology. From France to Germany and Back*, Chicago: University of Chicago Press.
Hobsbawm, Eric (1990) *Nations and Nationalism since 1780: Programme, Myth, Reality*, Cambridge: Cambridge University Press.
Marks, Gary and McAdam, Doug (1993) 'Social Movements and the Changing Structure of Political Opportunity in the European Community', paper presented at the annual meeting of the American Political Science Association, Washington, DC.
Robertson, Roland (1992) *Globalization*, London: Sage.
Rosaldo, Renato (1989) *Culture and Truth: The Remaking of Social Analysis*, Boston, Mass.: Beacon Press.
Schmitter, Philippe C. (1992) 'Interests, Powers, and Functions: Emergent Properties and Unintended Consequences in the European Polity', unpublished paper, Department of Political Science, Stanford University, Stanford, Calif.

Soysal, Yasemin Nuhoğlu (1994) *Limits of Citizenship: Migrants and Post-national Membership in Europe*, Chicago: University of Chicago Press.
Turner, Bryan S. (1986) 'Personhood and Citizenship', *Theory, Culture, and Society* 3:1–16.
Weber, Max (1968) *Economy and Society*, G. Roth and C. Wittich (eds), Berkeley: University of California Press.

3

THE LEGAL FRAMEWORK OF CITIZENSHIP OF THE EUROPEAN UNION

Elspeth Guild

INTRODUCTION

On 1 November 1993 the Treaty on European Union (the Maastricht Treaty) finally limped into force after suffering a thorough mauling in many member states of the Union.[1] On that day every citizen of a member state of the Union became also a citizen of the European Union.[2] In legal terms, this represents a very significant and interesting step in the development towards European Union. It might also be said that despite the significance of the development contained in the Maastricht Treaty many European citizens remain profoundly unaware or unmoved by it.[3]

This may come as something of a surprise considering the substantial debate which has and continues to take place in some member states regarding dual citizenship. In Germany, most notably, much discussion has occurred on this issue.[4] However, the sudden acquisition of a second citizenship by all nationals does not appear to have caused a moment's anxiety as regards, for instance, the spirit of the Council of Europe Convention of Reduction of Cases of Multiple Nationality.[5] There are two possible explanations: first, everyone knows that citizenship of the Union is not really a citizenship at all, but just some fancy words on a piece of paper; second, if it is more than some fancy words it does not confer on the holder any rights which he or she did not already have.

In this chapter the legal concept of citizenship of the Union will be examined under the following headings:

1 What is citizenship of the Union? What rights and obligations does it carry? This will include some consideration of whether or to

what extent citizenship of the Union may properly be described as a citizenship and to what extent it may also have the characteristics of a nationality.

2 Acquisition and loss of citizenship of the Union. The rules of acquisition and loss of any citizenship provide the parameters within which the question of who 'belongs' to a society and to whom does a society 'belong' is played out.

3 International human rights obligations relating to nationality: the UN Declaration of Fundamental Rights and Freedoms and the European Convention on Human Rights create obligations on contracting parties relating to nationality. If citizenship of the Union is also a nationality what implications do these obligations have?

CITIZENSHIP OF THE EUROPEAN UNION

The Treaty on European Union amended the EC Treaty, *inter alia* by introducing into it a new Part Two (Citizenship of the Union) Article 8. It commences with the creation of citizenship of the Union by baldly stating that henceforth it is established.[6] It provides that 'Every citizen holding the nationality of a member state shall be a citizen of the Union'. Article 8(2) goes on to state that citizens of the Union shall enjoy the rights conferred by the treaty and shall be subject to the duties imposed thereby. The EC Treaty establishes the four fundamental freedoms: the free movement of goods, persons, services and capital. These rights are therefore now attached to citizenship of the Union, whereas previously they attached exclusively to citizenship of a member state. At the moment these two categories are identical, so the enjoyment of the rights by virtue either of national citizenship or of citizenship of the Union does not appear material. Whether this will remain the situation is unclear.

While the rights of the treaty as regards persons are normally considered in the context of free movement,[7] which will be considered below, there are also other rights, such as freedom from discrimination on the basis of sex,[8] rights of job security on transfers of undertakings[9] and consumer protection rights.[10] These rights too, presumably now attach to citizenship of the Union as well as nationality of a member state. As the treaty provides that citizens of the Union shall enjoy the rights conferred by the treaty[11] there does not appear to be any reason why those rights are limited to those set out in Article 8 EC itself. Indeed, the wording clearly suggests that all rights conferred by the treaty, in whichever chapter, are conferred on citizens of the Union.

In accordance with the changes introduced by the Treaty on European Union, these rights have been extended to include certain civic rights: to vote and stand for election in certain circumstances and protection by the diplomatic or consular authorities of any member state on the same conditions as nationals of the state. These rights, which define the relationship between the individual and the state in respect of participation in public life and the individual *vis-à-vis* other states, approach a convergence between the concepts of citizenship and nationality as understood in a number of member states.[12]

No simple answer exists to the question of whether citizenship and nationality are the same thing or different and, if different, in what way.[13] In the UK, the British Nationality Act 1981 creates British citizenship but does not create or define British nationals. UK nationals are defined exclusively in terms of the European Union.[14] Therefore a division may be perceived between citizenship as regulating the position *vis-à-vis* the state of citizenship, and nationality in relation to other states: in the case of UK nationals, other member states. However, this is by no means universally accepted or applied in UK law.[15]

The International Court of Justice attempted to clarify the definition of nationality as the legal bond having as its basis a social fact of attachment, a genuine connection of existence, interests and sentiments, together with the existence of reciprocal rights and duties. Nationality is the juridical expression of the fact that the individual upon whom it is conferred, either directly by law or as a result of an act of the authorities, is in fact more closely connected with the population of the state conferring the nationality than any other state.[16] This definition creates a number of difficulties that limit its practical use.[17]

In many member states the concepts of citizenship and nationality are not clearly distinguished. However, where a delineation has occurred nationality has come to mean the affiliation of an individual with a state from the point of view of international law, while citizenship implies the host of rights domestically attached to that affiliation.[18] Elsewhere, nationality has been described as a term denoting the quality of political membership of a state.[19] Perhaps a more practical definition is that of Close, for whom nationality 'is the external face of a complex concept which also possesses an internal face which is citizenship'.[20]

Such a division of meaning between the two terms would appear to hold true for citizenship of the Union. As every national of a member state is a citizen of the Union, the quality of nationality appears to be the international law relationship of the individual as participant in a member state to the Union. It is the relationship of the individual *vis-à-vis* a member state (i.e., for domestic purposes as a citizen) which creates his or her international law status in respect of the Union (i.e., as a national). But the creation of a link between the individual and the Union which is that of citizenship implies a host of rights attaching to the Union exercisable by the individual. There is suddenly a direct link between the Union and the individual.

If citizenship and nationality are two sides of the same coin, the one determining the individual's status as regards the domestic affairs of a specific state and the other determining the individual's status as regards the international community, what is the 'citizenship' and 'nationality' content of citizenship of the Union, if it exists at all? To put the question otherwise, do the rights, including both active and passive civic rights, which attach to citizenship of the Union fulfil the criteria of a 'citizenship'? Does the European Union have an identity capable of sustaining a nationality and, if so, does citizenship of the Union have a nationality aspect?

Citizenship: rights and duties in the Union[21]

First, on the question of citizenship there is no clearly established list of rights or duties which must apply in order for a status to qualify as a citizenship. The position is governed primarily by municipal law. Rather, it is recognized that the detailed content of citizenship is likely to vary depending, *inter alia*, on the nature of the state and the ideology on which it is based.[22] None the less, the essence of citizenship remains the constitutional arrangements made for participation by a defined category of individuals in the life of a state.[23]

A classic definition of citizenship is formulated by T. H. Marshall as follows:

> The civil element is composed of the rights necessary for individual freedom – liberty of the person, freedom of speech, thought, the right to own property and to conclude valid contracts, and the right to justice. The last is of a different order from the others because it is the right to defend and assert all

one's rights on terms of equality with others and by due process of law. This shows us that the institutions most directly associated with civil rights are the courts of justice.

By the political element I mean the right to participate in the exercise of political power, as a member of a body invested with political authority or as an elector of the members of such a body. The corresponding institutions are Parliament and the councils of local government.

By the social element I mean the whole range from the right to a modicum of economic welfare and security to the right to share to the full in the social heritage and to live the life of a civilised being according to the standards prevailing in the society. The institutions most closely connected with it are the education systems and the social services.[24]

This is not as helpful as might first appear, as many of the characteristics attributed by Marshall to citizenship would now be considered attributes of more general human rights that could not be denied resident non-citizens.[25] None the less, the definition may be seen as something of a 'high water mark' of the rights which may be ascribed to citizenship.

A recent study by the Institute for Citizenship Studies and the British Institute of International and Comparative Law compares the attributes of citizenship in the twelve European Union jurisdictions and concludes there are eighteen hallmarks of citizenship.[26] Table 3.1 provides a summary of the extent to which citizenship of the Union compares against those hallmarks. However, in view of the variations among member states as regards the presence or absence of the hallmarks[27] they cannot be considered definitive as regards citizenship of the Union.

Turning to citizenship of the Union, then, to what extent is a holder of this citizenship entitled to participate in the life of the state and, for that matter, which state or part thereof?

Residence

Generally, in order to participate in the life of a state the first step is to enjoy a right to live in such part of the state as may be desired. In an attempt to provide further particularity to the rights of citizens of the Union, Article 8A(1) EC states that every citizen of the Union shall have the right to move and reside freely within the territory of the member states, subject to the limitations and conditions laid down in the treaty and by the measures adopted to give it effect.

The right of free movement for economic purposes across European Union borders is fundamental to the Union and has existed from the Community's inception. It has been extended to include three categories of economically inactive persons: pensioners, students and persons with sufficient means so that they do not become a burden on the member state's social assistance schemes.[28] The right to move for an economic purpose includes a right of residence for the same purpose.[29] A right of residence may found a right to family reunion.[30] These rights contained in Articles 7, 48–66 EC and supplemented by the directives on the economically inactive create an entitlement to cross the borders of the member states and to remain on the other side. The group of persons most notably excluded from the exercise of free movement rights is the unemployed and apparently unemployable who are reliant on state social assistance benefits. There is no right or protection for these persons to move across the Union in search of better social assistance benefits. However, citizens of the Union do have a right to move to another member state in search of work and may have a right to assistance for an initial period while looking for work.[31]

Article 8A(1) EC now adds a new element: the right to move and reside freely within the territory of the member states. It is a principle of Community law frequently upheld by the Court of Justice that rights of free movement cannot be invoked in respect of situations which are wholly internal to a member state, i.e., where there is no factor connecting them to any of the situations envisaged by Community law.[32] However, if there is a right freely to reside within the territory of the member states it would appear that this may include a right to move within a member state. This question arose in the matter of a challenge to an exclusion order against Gerry Adams. Although the matter was referred to the Court of Justice, the reference was withdrawn following a settlement. However, it is of interest that the referring judges found:

> the words of Article 8A(1) are wide. It provides that 'every citizen of the Union shall have the right to move ... freely within the territory of Member States.' Depending on the precise shade of the meaning of the concluding words, it may be said that Mr Adams is prohibited from moving freely throughout 'the territory of the Member States' [by reason of an exclusion

order under the Prevention of Terrorism (Temporary Provisions) Act 1989]. It must also be borne in mind that the Report of the European Commission to which we referred emphasized that the status of the relevant rights under Community law have now been fundamentally altered ... Bearing in mind the context of a direct political link between citizens of Member States and European Union, which previously did not exist, we regard the submission on behalf of Mr Adams as seriously arguable.[33]

It is of particular interest to note here that the referring judges viewed the creation of a direct political link between citizens of the Union and the Union itself as intrinsic to the question of residence rights. This goes to the heart of the meaning of citizenship, the right to reside on any part of the territory of the state in which the individual enjoys participation in public life.

Expulsion/exclusion

The right of residence in Article 8A(1) EC is subject to the limitations and conditions laid down in the treaty and by the measures adopted to give it effect.[34] The right of free movement has been subject to limitation on grounds of public policy, public security and public health.[35] How does this proviso on public policy grounds apply to citizens of the Union? If citizens of the Union have a right to live in any part of the territory of the Union then the application of this proviso excluding them from part of the Union must be akin to an internal restriction on movement. In the UK such a restriction exists in the Prevention of Terrorism (Temporary Provisions) Act 1989.

The public policy proviso has been limited by the European Court of Justice in respect of member state nationals exercising economic rights outside their country of nationality as follows:

1 a member state relying on the public policy proviso must show that the measure in question is justified on the basis of some objective which forms part of public policy,[36]

2 the public policy proviso must be an exception to the general principle of free movement and construed restrictively;[37]

3 exclusion can only be justified where the person's presence or conduct constitutes a genuine and sufficiently serious threat to public policy,[38]

4 a member state may exclude a national of another member state on public policy grounds even though it cannot place a similar restriction on its own nationals.[39]

All of the decisions of the Court of Justice on which the above summary is based pre-date the establishment of citizenship of the Union. The Court of Justice specifically noted that it is a principle of international law, which the EC Treaty cannot be assumed to disregard in the relations between member states, that a state is precluded from refusing its own nationals the right of entry or residence.[40]

The creation of a direct political link between citizens of the Union and the Union itself has already been highlighted as a potentially fundamental change to the status quo.[41] It is by no means clear what consequence this may have for the power to expel a national from one part of the Union to another. However, at the very least, it would appear likely that the test on expulsion and the test in the member states on internal restrictions such as contained in the Prevention of Terrorism (Temporary Provisions) Act 1989 must be consistent as manifestations of the same power.

Political participation

The right to exercise political rights both actively by voting and passively by standing for election is granted to citizens of the Union by Article 8B EC. Article 8B(1) establishes that every citizen of the Union residing in a member state other that of which he is a national shall have the right to vote and to stand as a candidate at municipal elections in the member state in which he or she resides under the same conditions as nationals of that state. Article 8B(2) provides that citizens of the Union residing in a member state of which he or she is not a national shall have the right to vote and stand as a candidate in elections to the European Parliament in the member state in which he or she resides under the same conditions as nationals of that state.

Therefore, through Articles 8B(1) & (2) citizens of the Union are entitled to full participation in the political life of their state of residence on two levels: municipal and European. Arrangements are made for transitional adjustments and implementing measures. Participation in political life at national level in a state of which the individual is not a national is intentionally excluded from the rights attaching to citizenship of the Union.

Remedies against maladministration

Finally, on the issue of the bundle of rights attaching to citizenship of the Union, the Maastricht Treaty introduced a right for every citizen of the Union to petition the European Parliament and to apply to the Ombudsman established under Article 138D EC.[42] This Ombudsman, also a child of the Maastricht Treaty, in fact may receive complaints from any natural or legal person residing or having a registered office in a member state.[43] The tension between the two provisions of the treaty, Article 8D and Article 138D as regards who may have access to remedies against the administration, reflects the uncertainty that permeates the question of rights attaching to citizenship as opposed to fundamental human rights, which must be available to all persons irrespective of citizenship. Article 8D may be considered to echo the classic position as set out by T. H. Marshall[44] whereby the right to judicial protection is a defining prerogative of the citizen. Article 138D represents the alternative perspective that equality before the law (including access to remedies) is a fundamental right which must be available to all persons on the territory.

The Ombudsman's remit is to conduct inquiries into instances of maladministration in the activities of the Community institutions or bodies with the exception of the Court of Justice and the Court of First Instance acting in their judicial capacities.[45] This role is rather curious, as it limits the right of the Ombudsman to protect the citizen of the Union (and others) from maladministration in respect of the institutions of the Community rather than those of the Union (i.e., the two new pillars, common foreign and security policy and justice and home affairs are excluded).

The concept of allegiance has not here been considered in respect of citizenship of the Union or indeed of citizenship generally in view of the increasingly difficult correlation between the two which has been noted elsewhere.[46] Suffice it to say that the ideas relating to the duties attendant on citizenship are in a state of substantial flux. Beyond a rather nebulous concept of a duty to be 'loyal', which must none the less be compatible with the right to free speech and the much more concrete duties – where they exist in some member states – to vote and to undertake military service, there is little agreement on what the 'duty' side of citizenship might include.

Nationality: the external dimension

If nationality is the mirror image of citizenship which defines the individual in international law (i.e., to which state does this individual belong), to what extent can citizenship of the Union be considered to have such an identity? This external aspect of citizenship of the Union is much less developed than the inward focus considered above. In order for an individual to have a status which may be recognized externally as belonging to a state, the state itself must have such an identity. First, then, does the Union consider that it has such an identity itself?

Statehood: the Union's view of itself

The most comprehensive analysis of the statehood of the Community divides the issue into four components:

1 the power to communicate with other governments and 'persons' in international law

2 the power to take internal autonomous measures within the territory that affect other states, other states' nationals and companies

3 the power to contract treaties and take part in international organisations

4 the power to carry out international obligations[47]

The pivotal power is the third, which presupposes the exercise of the first and fourth. The second power may be regarded as the fruit of the acceptance of the other three powers by the external world. The development of this theme in depth is beyond the scope of this chapter. Suffice it to say here that the judicial development of this aspect of Community competence has not been uncontentious within the Community.[48]

From its inception, the Community has had the power to conclude agreements with one or more states or international organisations.[49] Such agreements are specifically permitted to establish an association involving reciprocal rights and obligations, common action and special procedures.[50]

The negotiation of such agreements was, until the provision was amended by the Treaty on European Union, undertaken by the Commission and concluded by the Council after consultation with the European Parliament.[51] The scope of operation of the Commission in the field of negotiation of agreements with third countries or international organizations has been limited by amendments to Article 228 EC. However, the power to negotiate as if a sovereign state continues to exist and agreements concluded by the Community are binding not only on the Community's own institutions but also on the member states.[52]

By securing performance of the undertakings arising from such agreements made by the Community institutions, member states fulfil an obligation not only to the third country or international organization concerned, but also and above all to the Community itself, which has assumed responsibility for due performance of such agreements.[53] Further, the Community nature of the provisions of such agreements means that their effects cannot be allowed to vary in the Community according to whether their implementation in practice is the responsibility of the Community institutions or member states and, in the later case, according to the attitude taken by the law of each member state regarding the effects produced in their internal system.[54]

The framework established by the treaty and interpreted by the Court of Justice is thus one within which the Community perceives itself as a single entity, where in pursuance of the competences of the treaty it negotiates agreements either with third states or international organizations. There exists a 'self-regulating' system to ensure uniform interpretation and execution of obligations. The Community has state-like powers to negotiate and to ensure compliance in international matters, but to what extent may the member states choose to adopt alternative arrangements in international negotiations?

The Court of Justice has held that the Community has exclusive competence to enter into international commitments to the exclusion of the member states where this authority flows even by implication from measures adopted by the Community institutions within the framework of the treaty provisions or the acts of accession.[55] Further, the existence of such a competence arising from the treaty excludes any competence on the part of the member states which is concurrent with that of the Community, in the Community sphere and in the international sphere.[56] The Court of Justice has added, for the sake of clarity, that in all areas corresponding to the objectives of the treaty, Article 5 EC[57] requires the member states to facilitate the achievement of the Community's tasks and to abstain from any measure which could jeopardize the attainment of the objectives of the treaty.[58] Therefore, it is clear that the Community considers itself to have an identity in international law. The member states, which have ceded sovereignty to permit the Community to acquire such an identity, are under a duty not to undermine that identity so long as it is limited to the objectives of the treaty.

Is the external manifestation of citizenship of the Union an objective within the treaty? The preamble to the Treaty on European Union which introduces citizenship of the Union states that the member states are resolved to establish a citizenship common to nationals of their countries. It goes on to state that they are similarly 'resolved to implement a common foreign and security policy including the eventual framing of a common defence policy, thereby reinforcing the European identity and its independence in order to promote peace, security and progress in Europe and the world'.[59]

This is picked up in Article B setting out the objectives of the Union, *inter alia*:

> to assert its identity on the international scene, in particular through the implementation of a common foreign and security policy including the eventual framing of a common defence policy which might in time lead to a common defence;

> to strengthen the protection of the rights and interests of the nationals of its member states through the introduction of a citizenship of the Union.

By the inclusion of citizenship of the Union in the EC Treaty by way of its amendment the member states have placed it within the competence of all the Community institutions. The common foreign and security policy forms its own 'pillar' in the terminology of the treaty and is not subject to the jurisdiction of the Court of Justice. The objective of a common foreign policy may include measures taken in respect of the international community *vis-à-vis* citizens of the Union.

Article 8D EC provides that every citizen of the Union in the territory of a third country in which the member state of which he or she is a national is not represented, shall be entitled to protection by the diplomatic or consular authorities of any member state on the same conditions as nationals of that state. In this way a collective Union-wide responsibility for citizens of the Union abroad is established. It is of course limited to circumstances where the state of nationality is not represented. Nonetheless, the principle may be seen as a form of subsidiarity, in that the Union has devolved onto the member states' representatives abroad responsibility for protection of the Union's citizens.

As Union citizenship includes increasing elements of nationality so it must have a state to which to attach. If the Union is a state, the objectives of its citizenship must be sufficiently closely attached to its external persona that the nationality side of its citizenship is within its competence. Indeed, it is difficult to imagine how things could be otherwise.

The question of statehood of the Union is certainly open. Some commentators have come to the conclusion that citizenship of the Union cannot be a nationality because the Union lacks statehood.[60] However, it is possible that the development of statehood and citizenship proceed hand in hand. As the Union absorbs an increasing number of the elements of statehood so its citizenship must acquire attributes of nationality. Indeed, the dynamic between the two may be interdependent.[61] The decisions of the Court of Justice referred to above certainly seem to indicate some justification for the position of Professor Bleckmann that the Community as an entity itself possesses personal jurisdiction.[62]

So far, however, I have only considered what the Union thinks of itself. For statehood as with citizenship there is the other side of the coin: how is the Union perceived from outside?

Statehood: the external world's view of the Union

The treaty-making power of the Community certainly at this point in time causes relatively little angst amongst the third states with which treaties have been concluded.[63] Even the treaty which extended full free movement rights for persons and businesses of the Union into the territory of a number of third countries caused more concern for the Court of Justice than the contracting states.[64] A possible exception to this acceptance of the competence of the Community is the Association Agreement with Turkey, which required ratification by all member states rather than just the Community.[65] This exception may be explained by the period when the Agreement was under negotiation (1963) and the subsequent development of what Professor Bleckmann terms the 'personal jurisdiction' of the Community.[66]

The power to conclude agreements with international organizations has also not recently presented the external world with real difficulties. The Community is a Contracting Party of the GATT subject to the jurisdiction of the GATT Panel in respect of the interpretation of that agreement.[67] In the negotiation of the Uruguay Round, the Commission had exclusive competence to negotiate on behalf of the member states, a matter which caused some internal struggles in the Community but as a principle few problems for the other negotiating parties. However, a number of aspects of the agreement which concluded the Uruguay Round have caused the Commission to seek clarification of its jurisdiction from the Court of Justice.[68]

A different approach was adopted by the International Chamber of Commerce as regards a competition matter which raised a question about the breach of a distribution agreement in 1964.[69] *Inter alia*, the tribunal found itself competent to interpret the EC Treaty. It may be that the decision was extraordinary and a product of its time.

Accordingly, the outside world appears willing to acknowledge the 'nationality' of the Community as regards the power to enter into treaties and as regards their enforcement. The non-Community tribunals established to interpret such agreements have not by and large challenged this position.

The approach of the European Commission of Human Rights on the issue of the Community's status is illuminating. On the one hand the Commission of Human Rights has held consistently that it is not competent to examine proceedings before or decisions of the Community's institutions as it is not a party to the Convention on Human Rights.[70] This of course begs the question whether the Community could become a party.[71] In respect of a petition against a member state for enforcement of a judgment of the Court of Justice, the European Commission of Human Rights considered that the member state's authorities acted as Community organs and are to that extent beyond the scope of control exercised by the Convention organs.[72] However, the Commission of Human Rights did not stop there. It went on to note that the legal system of the Community not only secures fundamental rights but also provides for control of their observance. It made specific reference to the Court of Justice's caselaw according to which it is called upon to control Community acts on the basis of fundamental rights, including those enshrined in the ECHR.[73] This might be considered recognition by the European Commission of Human Rights that the Court of Justice 'has turned the Treaty establishing the Community into a quasi-constitutional document with distinct federal characteristics, even though the institutional structure is anything but federal'.[74]

A final judgment on whether the Community has sufficient statehood on which to balance a nationality cannot yet be given. However, it is clear that the Community enjoys many attributes of statehood and is recognized by the world at large as competent to exercise them. When the Treaty on European Union augmented the Community with foreign and security policy structure within the European Union, attributes of statehood increased. The pratical test of external acceptance of Union nationality will occur when a British citizen of the Union is deported from, say, Turkey to Greece (perhaps on grounds that this is cheaper than sending the person to the UK) because as a citizen of the Union Greece must accept the person.

ACQUISITION AND LOSS OF CITIZENSHIP OF THE UNION

According to Article 8(1) EC every person holding the nationality of a member state shall be a citizen of the Union. Therefore, the question of who is a citizen of a member state remains a matter exclusively of domestic law.[75] For example, by virtue of a Declaration on accession the UK defined who were 'nationals' for the purposes of Community law.[76] This definition of nationals was not the same as the definition for the purposes of UK domestic law.[77] On the reworking of British nationality law in 1981, when a new Declaration was made for Community law purposes, a rather heterogeneous group of persons with British status were included.[78]

This status quo is reinforced by a Declaration to the Treaty on European Union (now merged into the EC Treaty) on Nationality of a Member State. So that there could be no doubt about national sovereignty over citizenship questions it states 'the question whether an individual possesses the nationality of a member State shall be settled solely by reference to the national law of the member State concerned'.[79] Just so that indecisive states like the UK could change their minds about who their nationals are from time to time the Declaration goes on to state 'Member States may declare, for information, who are to be considered their nationals for Community purposes by way of a declaration lodged with the Presidency and may amend any such declaration when necessary'.[80] It may be assumed that it is a matter for the Member State to decide when it is necessary to amend its declaration.

When presented with the question of the value of national citizenship before the creation of citizenship of the Union, the Court of Justice held that a member state was not entitled to refuse to recognize a person as a national of another member state.[81] However the

44

Court did add a proviso, almost as a footnote, that this national competence must be exercised with respect for Community law.[82] It remains a matter for speculation what this proviso may mean.

Therefore, the national laws of the member states as regards acquisition and loss of citizenship, which vary dramatically from state to state, create the parameters of citizenship of the Union. It is within the exclusive domain of the member states to decide to whom the Union belongs and who belongs to it. The member states alone through the configuration of their nationality laws permit or deny political participation in the Union to its residents. Or do they?

INTERNATIONAL HUMAN RIGHTS OBLIGATIONS RELATING TO NATIONALITY

Article 15 of the Universal Declaration of Human Rights provides that everyone has the right to a nationality and that no one shall be arbitrarily deprived of his nationality or denied the right to change his nationality. Protocol 4 of the European Convention on Human Rights provides, at Article 3, that no one shall be expelled, by means either of an individual or of a collective measure, from the territory of the state of which he is a national. It further states that no one shall be deprived of the right to enter the territory of the state of which he is a national.

If citizenship of the Union is indeed a nationality, or is in the process of becoming a nationality as the Union becomes a state, then the special place of human rights obligations, as enshrined first and foremost in the European Convention[83] but also in the Universal Declaration of Human Rights,[84] must be observed by the Union in respect of that nationality. The Court of Justice noted before the establishment of citizenship of the Union that a national of a member state enters and resides in the territory of the home state by virtue of the rights attendant upon his or her nationality and not by virtue of those conferred on the person by Community law. It also noted, however, that as is provided by Article 3 of the Fourth Protocol of the European Convention on Human Rights, a state may not expel one of its own nationals or deny him or her entry to its territory.[85]

Depending on the meaning of Article 8A EC discussed above, the territory of the Union may be indivisible for the purposes of this provision. If this is the case then the prohibition on expulsion applies to citizens of the Union in the whole of the Union. Of course, Article 3 of the Fourth Protocol ECHR does not prevent internal restrictions on movement where justified.[86] Therefore the expulsion of citizens of the Union from one part of the Union to another to be compatible with Articles 2 and 3 of the Fourth Protocol would need to be justified on the grounds of Article 2(3). Should this be the case, then the right of unemployable citizens of the Union to move within the territory of the Union may no longer be restricted by the provisions of Community law as set out in the treaty and arising therefrom.

Further, if the laws on loss of nationality of a member state result in the loss of citizenship of the Union then these laws must indeed be a matter of concern to the Court of Justice. The Union is bound to respect human rights and the Court of Justice must protect those rights in the field of application of Community law.[87] If a national rule on loss of nationality that will deprive the individual of citizenship of the Union as well is contrary to the obligations on nationality contained in the Universal Declaration and/or the ECHR, then the Court of Justice may, by its own formulation of its duties *vis-à-vis* human rights protection, have to protect the individual. Whether this would take the form of interference in the exercise of national rules on loss, or a divorce of citizenship of the Union from nationality of a member state, or some other form is a matter of speculation only.

None the less, it must be within the Court's competence to ensure that such rules do not offend against those human rights principles which it has already found itself obliged to uphold in the field of application of Community law.[88]

Table 3.1 Citizenship of the Union: Hallmarks of citizenship

Hallmarks of citizenship	Comparison with citizenship of the EU
1 Right to vote in national and local elections	Art. 8B EC confers the right to vote in local elections and European Parliament elections. No right to vote in national (state) elections
2 Eligibility to stand as a candidate in national and local elections	Art. 8B EC confers the right to stand for election in local and European Parliament elections
3 Right to petition and vote in referenda	Art. 8D EC confers the right to petition the European Ombudsman; access to bring a complaint to the European Parliament Committee of Petitions also exists. No specific provision as to referenda exists
4 Right to assemble/to form associations	Art. 11 of the European Convention on Human Rights enshrines this right. The Court of Justice has held that Article 11 ECHR has its specific manifestation in Community law[89]
5 Access to public office/service	Art. 48(4) EC excludes employment in public service from the non-discrimination provision as regards nationals of other member states. However, this is strictly limited to circumstances where the worker would otherwise exercise state power[90]
6a Access to justice: civil claims, administrative matters; entitlement to legal aid	Art. 6 EC prohibits discrimination on the basis of nationality within the field of application of the treaty. Therefore the right of access to justice must be available on the same basis as for 'own nationals'
6b Jurisdiction of the courts: domicile, applicable private law	as above
7 Obligation to undertake military/alternative service	There is no Union competence in this field. The new pillar on common foreign and security policy may develop this area

Hallmarks of citizenship	Comparison with citizenship of the EU
8 Freedom of movement; right to reside, to travel freely within the territory, to leave, to enter	Art. 8A(1) EC provides that citizens have the right to move and reside freely within the territory of the member states. Art. 2 of Protocol 4, ECHR which requires states to permit liberty of movement, residence and the right to leave has been considered as applicable to Community law by the Court of Justice[91]
9 Right to a passport	No right to a passport exists. A unified document was introduced[92] requiring uniform design but issue and withdrawal conditions apparently remain a national prerogative
10 Right to ownership of property/ use of property	Art. 6 EC, the non-discrimination provision, applies here. Where 'own nationals' are entitled to these rights so must citizens of the Union
11 Entitlement to welfare benefits (including the right to housing)/ obligation to contribute to social security systems	Art. 51 EC provides for the approximation of rules on social security so that migrant citizens of the Union are not penalized as regards social security rights by reason of their movement. Social security here means risk-related benefits. Social assistance benefits designed to keep people from poverty are not included.[93] However, social assistance benefits must be made available on a non-discriminatory basis once the citizen of the Union has worked.[94] Citizens of the Union are entitled to non-discrimination in respect of housing at least where they are exercising economic activities[95]
12 Liability to taxation	The Community tax, VAT, exists. As a tax on goods and services changing hands in the Union it applies to all persons in the Union

Hallmarks of citizenship	Comparison with citizenship of the EU
13 Freedom to exercise profession of choice/right to work	This is a fundamental Community freedom limited only by the exercise of state power (see above)
14 Allegiance to country of citizenship	Indeterminate in Union law
15 Right to education/vocational training	Citizens of the Union are entitled to move to pursue studies;[96] where they are exercising economic activities their family members are entitled to education and vocational training as are they themselves if unemployed on the same basis as 'own nationals'[97]
16 The right to medical treatment/ old age care	Where the citizen of the Union is engaged in an economic activity he or she must be entitled to equal treatment in this area; the general right of residence, the right of residence for pensioners and the right of residence for students are subject to a requirement to be covered by sickness insurance[98]
17 Linguistic rights, including the right to use mother tongue in the exercise of other rights	For citizens of the Union this is part of the non-discrimination right in the exercise of Community rights; this may extend to the right to use a mother tongue in criminal proceedings[99]
18 Fundamental rights including right to information and the right not to be discriminated against	There is no provision of Community law relating directly to the question of public access to information though this issue is before the Court of Justice at the moment.[100] As regards a general prohibition of discrimination based on nationality this exists in Art. 6 EC though the extent to which it may also prohibit discrimination on grounds other than nationality is uncertain. A specific non-discrimination provision as regards sex is contained in Art. 119 EC.

NOTES

1 In addition to the two Danish referenda, see also three cases before superior courts in member states regarding the constitutionality of the Treaty: *Re: Ratification of the European Union Treaty* (1993) CMLR 939 (France); *R v Secretary of State for Foreign and Commonwealth Affairs ex parte Lord Rees-Mogg* 1993 CMLR 101 (UK) and *Brunner v the European Union Treaty* (1994) CMLR 57 (Germany).

2 Article 8 EC (all references are to the EC Treaty as amended by the Treaty on European Union).

3 European Access, 1994 No. 3 p. 37.

4 See for instance: Information of the Federal Interior Ministry 4.9.92 Nr V/1992; the proposal to the Bundesrat on amendment of citizenship law of 27.2.92; and, for the broader political context, the contributions of Fulbrook and Schönwälder in this volume.

5 Convention of Reduction of cases of Multiple Nationality, 1963, Council of Europe. The principle of the convention is that where persons of their own free will acquire a second citizenship they will lose their former citizenship.

6 Article 8 (1) EC.

7 The rights attaching to citizenship of the Union have also been examined primarily from the perspective of freedom of movement with some additional comment on new rights conferred by the Treaty on European Union, see C. Closa, 'The Concept of Citizenship in the Treaty on European Union', in David O'Keeffe and Patrick M. Twomey (eds), *Legal Issues of the Maastricht Treaty* (London: Chancery Law Publishing, 1994); *Common Market Law Review* (*CML Rev*) 1137, 1992; David O'Keefe, 'Union Citizenship' in O'Keefe and Twomey (eds), *Legal Issues of the Maastricht Treaty*.

8 Article 119 EC.

9 Council Directive 77/187/EC.

10 Council Directive 85/577/EC; see also the decision of the Court of Justice *Paola Faccini Dori v Recreb Srl* C-91/92 of 14 July 1994.

11 Article 8 (2) EC.

12 C. Closa, 'Citizenship of the Union and Nationality of Member States', in O'Keefe and Twomey (eds), *Legal Issues of the Maastricht Treaty*, p. 114.

13 C. McCrudden, 'Citizenship and Law: The Structure of the Green Paper Identifying the Hallmarks of Citizenship', in J. P. Gardner (ed.), *Hallmarks of Citizenship: A Green Paper* (London: British Institute of International and Comparative Law, 1994), p. 16.

14 See the UK Declarations regarding UK nationals for the purposes of Community law.

15 See, for instance, the undifferentiated use of the term 'national' in their Lordships' judgment *Oppenheimer v Cattermole* [1975] 1 All ER p. 572.

16 *Liechtenstein v Guatemala* [1955] IJC Rep p. 15.

17 See G. Close, 'Definitions of Citizenship' in Gardner (ed.), *Hallmarks of Citizenship*. Also, H. U. J. d'Oliveira, review of the Micheletti case, *CML Rev* 30, 1993, p. 632. In the case the International Court found

that while it accepted that the individual had acquired the nationality of the relevant state under its domestic law, his links to that state were not sufficient to recognize this nationality under international law.

18 Closa, 'Concept of Citizenship', p. 114.
19 *Halsbury's Laws of England* (4th Edition, London: Butterworth & Co.), Vol. 18, para. 1613.
20 Close, 'Definitions of Citizenship', p. 6.
21 The Treaty on European Union created the 'Union', which consists of three segments, commonly called pillars: (1) the Community (the EC as it existed before the Union Treaty) (all references to the Community in this chapter are therefore to this 'first pillar'); (2) the Common Foreign and Security Policy which is controlled by the European Council; (3) Co-operation in the Fields of Justice and Home Affairs, again under the control of the European Council and fundamentally an institutionalization of previous inter-governmental processes. Reference to the Union here includes all three pillars and the territory of the member states.
22 A. C. Evans, 'Nationality Law and European Integration', *International and Comparative Law Quarterly* 16 (30), 1981 p. 20.
23 Ibid., p. 199.
24 T. H. Marshall and T. Bollomore, *Citizenship and Social Class* (London: Pluto Press, 1991 p. 25.)
25 For example, access to the law on terms of equality is a fundamental principle contained in Article 7 of the Universal Declaration of Human Rights 1948 and crops up over and over again in almost all human rights conventions and treaties.
26 Gardner, 'Hallmarks of Citizenship'.
27 Ibid., pp. 105–46.
28 Directives 90/364 (on the general residence right), 90/365 (on pensioners) and 93/96 (on students).
29 *Kus v Landeshauptstadt Wiesbaden* [1993] 2 CMLR 887.
30 *Re Students' Rights: European Parliament v EC Council* [1992] 3 CMLR 281.
31 *R v Immigration Appeal Tribunal ex parte Antonissen* [1992] 2 CMLR 373.
32 *Moser v Land Baden-Wurttemberg* [1984] ECR 2539.
33 *R v Secretary of State for the Home Department ex parte Gerard Adams* Court of Appeal, 29 July 1994.
34 Article 8A(1) EC.
35 Article 48 (3) EC and Directive 64/221.
36 *Rutili v Ministry of the Interior* [1975] 1 CMLR 140.
37 Ibid.
38 *R v Bouchereau* [1977] ECR 1999.
39 *Van Duyn v Home Office (No 2)* [1974] ECR 1337.
40 Ibid.
41 See note 33.
42 Article 8D EC.
43 Article 138D EC.
44 See note 24.
45 Article 138E EC.

46 See L. Fransman, 'A Future Citizenship Policy for the UK' in S. Spencer (ed.), *Strangers and Citizens: A Positive Approach to Migrants and Refugees* (London: Rivers Oram Press, 1994), pp. 282 *et seq.*

47 E. Stein, 'External Relations of the European Community', in *Collected Courses of the Academy of European Law* Vol. 1, Book 1: 'Community Law', 1990.

48 Ibid., p. 144 for, *inter alia*, discussion of the ERTA doctrine.

49 Article 238 EC.

50 Ibid.

51 Article 228 EC before amendment by the Treaty on European Union.

52 Article 228 (7) EC.

53 *Hauptzollamt Mainz v C A Kupferberg & Cie KG*, [1983] 1 CMLR 1.

54 Ibid.

55 *Kramer and Others* [1976] ECR 1279.

56 *Opinion 2/91*, European Court of Justice, OJ C 109/1 of 19.4.93.

57 'Member States shall take all appropriate measures, whether general or particular, to ensure fulfilment of the obligations arising out of this Treaty or resulting from action taken by the institutions of the Community. They shall facilitate the achievement of the Community's tasks.

They shall abstain from any measure which could jeopardise the attainment of the objectives of this Treaty'.

Article 5 EC is the 'good faith' requirement of the member states and is assuming an increasingly important role in the jurisprudence of the Court of Justice.

58 *Opinion 2/91*, see note 56.

59 Preamble paragraph 9, Treaty on European Union.

60 Close, 'Definitions of Citizenship', p. 11.

61 A. Bleckmann, 'The Personal Jurisdiction of the European Community', *CML Rev* 17, 1980, pp. 475.

62 Ibid.

63 See for example the Europe Agreements with the Czech Republic, Hungary, Poland and Slovakia.

64 The European Economic Area Agreement, *Opinion 1/91* [1992] 1 CMLR 245.

65 The Turkey EC Association Agreement 1963, Ankara, Art. 31 and the Additional Protocol 1970 Brussels.

66 Bleckmann, 'The Personal Jurisdiction of the European Community pp. 467–85.

67 See for instance *Re Refunds on Exports of Sugar: Australia v the European Communities* [1980] 2 CMLR 238; *Re Imported Wines and Spirits: EEC v Japan* [1989] 3 CMLR 230 or *Re the Dupont de Nemours/ AKZO Dispute: EEC v USA* [1989] 1 CMLR 715 which exhibit three different circumstances: a third country against the Community, the Community against a third country, a dispute between companies which becomes an 'interstate' dispute with the Community on one side.

68 *Opinion 1/94*, reported in *ECJ Bulletin* No. 14/94.

69 *Markenwaren v Riccadonna* [1967] CMLR part 26 p. 141.

70 See No. 8030/77 *CFDT v European Communities* Dec 10.7.78, Decision 10.7.78; No 13539/88, *D v European Communities*, Decision 19.1.89.

71 The Council of Ministers has recently sought the Opinion of the Court of Justice as to whether according to Community law it could become a party to the ECHR. *Opinion 2/94*, reported in *ECJ Bulletin* 14/94.

72 *M & Co v Federal Republic of Germany* Appl. No. 13258/87 Yearbook 1990 p. 144.

73 Ibid., p. 145.

74 Stein, 'External Relations of the European Community', p. 129.

75 *MV Micheletti & Ors v Delegacion del Gobierno en Cantabria* [1992] ECR 1–4239.

76 (1972) (Cmnd 4862); later replaced by (1983) (Cmnd 9062) published 28.1.83 OJ C p. 1.

77 British Nationality Act 1948: not all citizens of the UK and colonies, the then single and indivisible citizenship, were defined as 'nationals' for the purposes of Community law under the Declaration.

78 British Nationality Act 1981 and Declaration see p. 63. Specifically, three types of British 'national' were included for Community law purposes into the definition: British citizens, British subjects with the right of abode in the UK (this category had formerly been called British subjects without citizenship) and British Dependent Territories citizens who acquired that citizenship from a connection with Gibraltar. This definition excludes British Overseas citizens, British subjects without the right of abode, all British Dependent Territories citizens without the Gibraltar connection, British Nationals (Overseas), etc.

79 Declaration on Nationality of a Member State, Treaty on European Union.

80 Ibid.

81 *Micheletti v Delegacion del Gobierno en Cantabria* [1992] ECR I-4239.

82 See H. U. J. d'Oliveira, review of the Micheletti case, CML Rev 1993, 30, p. 632.

83 *Elliniki Radiophonia Tileorassi EA (ERT) v Demotiki Etairia Pliroforissis* [1994] 4 CMLR 540.

84 *Prais v EC Council* [1976] 2 CMLR 708.

85 *R v IAT & Surinder Singh ex p Secretary of State for the Home Department* [1992] 3 CMLR 358.

86 Article 2, Protocol 4 ECHR permits restrictions to be placed, *inter alia*, on the liberty of movement and choice of residence on grounds of national security or public safety, for the maintenance of public order, for the prevention of crime, for the protection of health or morals or for the protection of the rights and freedoms of others.

87 *Elliniki Radiophonia Tileorassi EA (ERT) v Demotiki Etairia Pliforissis*.

88 Ibid.

89 *Rutili v Minister of the Interior* [1975] ECR 1219.

90 *Commission v Belgium* [1980] ECR 3881.

91 *Rutili v Minister of the Interior; R v IAT & Surinder Singh*

92 Resolution, 23.6.81, OJ 1981 C 241/1.

93 Regulation 1408/71 and *Hughes v Chief Adjudication Officer* [1992] 3 CMLR 490.

94 Art. 7 (2) Regulation 1612/68 and *Centre Public D'Aide Sociale v Lebon* [1989] 1 CMLR 337.

95 Art. 10 Regulation 1612/68.
96 Directive 93/96.
97 Art. 12 Regulation 1612/68, *Gravier v City of Liege* [1975] 3 CMLR 1.
98 Directives 90/364, 90/365 and 93/96.
99 *Ministere Public v Mutsch* [1985] ECR 2681.
100 *Carvel & Ors v Council* T-194/94 reported in ECJ Bulletin 17–94.

Part II

CITIZENSHIP, NATIONALITY AND THE CONSTRUCTION OF NATIONAL IDENTITY

4

THE CHANGING CHARACTER OF CITIZENSHIP AND NATIONALITY IN BRITAIN

David Cesarani

It is virtually axiomatic that of all the European states Britain has the most benign reputation for constitutional stability and an unproblematic national identity. The historical absence of large-scale xenophobic movements or systematic legal discrimination against ethnic minorities is commonly attributed to this vaunted political calm and settled sense of nationhood. Elsewhere, as Rogers Brubaker has shown with respect to France and Germany, political upheavals and concordant variations in the concept of the nation have had a crucial effect on modes of citizenship. In these cases, political volatility and insecure national identity are credited with periodic, destructive assaults upon citizens as well as strategies to exclude, and discriminate against, aliens.[1]

Yet the dynamic that Brubaker observes in France and Germany is by no means absent from Britain. In recent decades the makeshift character and consequent weakness of British constitutional arrangements have become painfully obvious.[2] At the same time, the fragility of British national identity has been cruelly exposed. There is a connection. Current debates on the need for a British Bill of Rights and devolution reflect questions about citizenship that are inextricably tied up with nationality, national identity and immigration. As Ann Dummett and Andrew Nicol have written:

> We [the British] lack a clear-cut nationality, or citizenship with rights and duties attached to it which are easily ascertainable. This is partly because we do not have, as most countries do, a single-document constitution or basic law listing rights and

duties; partly because our constitutional theory does not envisage some British nation, or a sovereign people, of which individuals are members; partly because nationality in the British empire was handled in a haphazard and uncertain manner, leaving a legacy of confusion; and finally because nationality law since 1962 has been entangled with, and at last come to be based upon, the law of immigration.[3]

This paper will look briefly and schematically at the history of British nationality and the confused development of British citizenship. It will attempt to explain how shifts in national identity impelled certain changes in the privileges/rights and duties/obligations of British subjects/citizens. It will also endeavour to show some of the causes of these shifts: the rise and fall of empire; war; immigration; and internal and, most recently, global economic and social transformations. In Britain, debates about citizenship and nationality must be seen against a deep historical background as well as in the contemporary context of immigration and responses to it.

I

The concept of citizenship has a notoriously weak presence in English history. Under the feudal system membership of the nation and the status of subject rested almost exclusively upon a person's birthplace. The land was the foremost component of the nation; ownership of the land and ultimate loyalty to the crown as the chief landlord and ruler of the nation comprised the other determinant of subjecthood. So, persons born in England owed personal allegiance to the English monarch. According to the principle of *jus soli* they were English subjects by virtue of birth within the realm of the English crown. Due to the English Reformation and the identification of the crown with the national church, allegiance and subjecthood later acquired a confessional dimension, which was to have repercussions for both naturalization and the acquisition of political rights.[4]

During the seventeenth century, the feudal notion of allegiance was challenged by political thinkers in Scotland and the American colonies who advocated a voluntary, contractual allegiance to a community defined by territory. In the struggle between crown and Parliament the contractual model was deployed against the mediaeval model. But the debates about sovereignty did not lead to any enlargement of the rights of subjects. On the contrary, the spectre of large masses of people claiming political rights and power impelled the political élite of the country to associate political rights with the possession of property rather than regarding them as the birthright of every person. The victory of Parliament over the crown emphatically did not entail the recognition of popular sovereignty. Rather, sovereignty became vested in the Parliament, later the crown-in-Parliament, and the status of subject was preserved. Since the crown and Parliament were the symbolic core of the nation, a limited and passive concept of the subject was inscribed on national identity. The conservative settlement to the constitutional contest in seventeenth-century England ensured that arguments over membership of the nation and right of citizenship continued to be dominated by issues of property, religion and, later, gender, for the next two centuries.[5]

The French Revolution paradoxically dealt a blow to those in England who wished to develop the concept of citizenship. In the course of the wars against revolutionary France, patriotism became allied to a narrow and reactionary idea of the privileges and duties of the subject. Change came only slowly, through a number of processes. Historical memory of movements for popular sovereignty and the notion of an Englishman's birthright continued to animate reformers. The industrial revolution created a proletariat that came to see political rights as a route to social and economic improvement. Widespread education facilitated the extension of the franchise and eroded objections to this step. Concepts of citizenship imported from France and Germany gave a convincing rationale for expanding political rights and creating an active citizenship.[6]

For mid-nineteenth-century liberals active citizenship was seen as a form of civic and moral education. The state was considered to have a duty to confer this benefit on its members. The idea of citizenship as a device for improvement was, however, threatened by the impoverished and ignorant condition of the potential, active citizenry. Hence it led shortly to the elaboration of social citizenship according to which the state was obliged to enable all its members to participate effectively in the civic and political sphere by extending welfare provision. Liberalism thus gave birth to the welfare state, and one type of citizenship was conjoined with another.[7] However, large-scale immigration would expose the question of who had access to this form of citizenship.

II

Contrary to popular belief, the potential of immigration to expose the nerve of national identity and raise questions about nationality is deeply rooted in British history. It stems, in part, from the late arrival of the British nation and the precarious sense of artificial nationhood. The Act of Union in 1707 set in train the process of 'forging' the nation. Confessional allegiance was a key element of this process. As Linda Colley states, 'Protestantism was the foundation that made the invention of Great Britain possible.' The enjoyment of full political rights, such as election to municipal or national office, rested on conformity to Anglicanism and declaring oaths of supremacy and allegiance to both the crown and the state church.[8]

The nexus between British national identity, political rights or citizenship, and Protestantism was vividly illustrated in 1753–4, when there was a popular outcry against an Act to enable the naturalization of foreign-born Jews. The agitation against the 'Jew Bill' pitted stereotyped notions of Britishness, intimately bound up with Protestantism, and the 'Briton's freeborn rights' against foreign Jews – who were tarred with the same brush as Catholic countries, which lacked the freedoms allegedly native to Great Britain. Hence the cry 'No Jews, no wooden shoes', which associated Jewish naturalization with Catholic France and poverty. An exclusive Britishness, defined against immigrants, was already engraved on the boundary markers of the nation and determined who might become a British subject.[9]

The union with Ireland in 1801 rendered untenable the continued exclusion of Catholics from full civil rights and led inexorably to Catholic emancipation in 1829. This step dislocated the identification of the Anglican Church with the British nation, but ended up reinforcing the popular conviction that Britain was a Christian state. If the Anglican supremecy no longer sufficed to unite the nation and provide the moral undergirding for its constitution and laws, then this function would have to be performed by a broadly defined Christianity.[10]

Consequently, Catholic emancipation made the resistance to Jewish emancipation even more intense. A profound concern with the nature of Britishness and the relationship between citizenship and nationality, expressed in terms of confessional allegiance, ran through the emancipation debates from the 1830s to the 1860s. According to the opponents of Jewish emancipation, Britain was a Christian country governed by a Christian legislature. They held it virtually inconceivable that non-Christians could be admitted into full citizenship. Religion, citizenship and nationality were tightly bound together. In the end, the Jews could be emancipated and allowed to enter the political nation precisely because it was so strongly Christian. Aside from the argument that Jewish emancipation would benefit the nation, opponents of emancipation were assuaged by the assurance that the accession of a few Jews could do the nation no real harm. The Christian legislature of a Christian nation could absorb a few Hebrews without losing its integrity.[11]

Jewish emancipation arose as an issue in mid-nineteenth-century Britain because of past waves of immigration, albeit relatively small ones. The sublime self-confidence that facilitated the extension of civic parity to Jewish subjects governed attitudes and policy towards subsequent immigration. For most of the mid- to late nineteenth century a confident mode of British identity made immigration largely unproblematic. Britain was the 'workshop of the world' and the torch-bearer of liberalism in both political and economic spheres. The pre-eminence of *laissez-faire* ideology dictated the free movement of goods and labour, while a feeling of innate superiority and security negated any sense of threat that this traffic might have posed. Furthermore, because British national identity was formed in opposition to foreign countries that were considered repressive and 'backward', the continued free entry of refugees, political exiles and economic migrants was a matter of pride. In any case, immigration was small scale and took place in the context of an expanding economy. Although British nationality law was 'a peculiar jumble of old and new elements' in which, astonishingly, Britishness was never even defined, there seemed to be no cause to tamper with it.[12]

This situation altered dramatically in the last quarter of the nineteenth century. From the late 1870s Britain began to experience serious economic competition and geopolitical rivalry from other states; the country suffered a drastic loss of imperial confidence. At this moment of introspection thousands of Jews from eastern Europe began to pour into Britain each year. This was Britain's first experience of sustained mass immigration from beyond the British Isles (as against the influx of Irish people that occurred under quite different circumstances). Jewish mass immigration between 1882 and 1905 coincided also with periodic economic depressions and phases of high unemployment. At the same time, and for not unconnected reasons, free trade was being challenged by protectionist doctrines. Calls to restrict the importation of cheap goods, or the labour that could manufacture them in Britain, found a sympathetic hearing amongst workers who blamed unemployment, low wages and bad working conditions in certain industries on the influx of poor, foreign Jews. Simultaneously, the intensification of economic and diplomatic conflict between Britain and other European powers provoked a heightened sense of Britishness. It acquired a sharp, exclusivist edge due to racial ideas and found a convenient 'Other' in the immigrant Jews who flowed into London's East End.[13]

Jewish immigration became a subject of controversy and political argument. Citizenship was central to this discourse. Could alien Jews be good citizens? Could they have a place in a Christian country? What stake could poor, propertyless immigrants have in their country of adoption? To what welfare provisions were they entitled? How quickly and under what conditions could they be permitted to vote? The immigration debate thus revived and repeated many of the arguments about Jewish emancipation that had been heard in the mid-nineteenth century. It revealed the same dyad of national identity and citizenship as obtained in France and Germany.[14]

In 1905, following twenty years of campaigning, the first legislation was passed to restrict immigration into Britain. The 1905 Aliens Act established an immigration control bureaucracy with powers of exclusion and enabled courts to recommend 'undesirable aliens' for deportation. It provided a model that was to be elaborated by subsequent Aliens Acts.[15] The 1914 Act created controls over the movement of aliens and obliged them to register with the police. These measures were perpetuated into peacetime under the 1919 Aliens Restriction (Amendment) Act. This Act was a product of war-fuelled chauvinism and the fear of revolution inspired by Bolshevik Russia. It struck at former 'enemy aliens', who were denied the right to sit on juries or take government service even if they had long been naturalized. Non-naturalized aliens could be deported for industrial or political 'subversion'. It was no accident that the Act's chief victims were Jews who were popularly associated with Germany and international finance capital on the one hand, and with Russia and revolutionary internationalism on the other.[16]

The aliens legislation of the post-war years went further and temporarily abrogated the principle of *jus soli*. The British-born children of non-British-born parents, even if the parents were naturalized, were barred from employment in the civil service, and from educational and housing entitlements. This limitation of rights and entitlements was possible because the rights of British subjects were defined by the state in its own interests, and were not something inherent to a concept of citizenship or defensible by appeal to a Bill of Rights or written constitution. The systematic discrimination against British-born subjects of non-British-born parentage, the obstacles placed in the way of the naturalization of aliens and their consequent vulnerability were underpinned by the common racist assumptions that these groups did not or could not fully belong to the nation. British nationality was conceptualized and constructed in legal terms so as to exclude a racialized Other, be it Russian Jews, Chinese or Black seamen.[17]

III

The narrowing of 'Britishness' to a white, Christian, Anglo-Saxon identity and the tighter control over access to British nationality were prefigured by the desire of the dominions to establish their own nationality and to control immigration into their territories. At this point the imperial dimension plays a role in reshaping British national identity, nationality and citizenship.

In 1914 the immigration policies of Canada and Australia obliged the British Government to re-examine the archaic, muddled and multiple forms of nationality that prevailed throughout the British Empire. The intention was to formulate a common category of belonging that would, nevertheless, enable Britain and the dominions to restrict access into their territories by people from other parts of the Empire, notably the native populations of colonies in Africa and Asia. The 1914 British Nationality Act declared that all inhabitants of the dominions and colonies owed allegiance to the crown and were, therefore, British subjects; but not all British subjects had the right of entry into a particular dominion or colony.[18]

The transmogrification of empire into Commonwealth after the Second World War impelled further mutations in British national identity and modalities of belonging. The next rethink of British nationality and the rights of British subjects was necessitated, first, by Canada's determination to establish its own citizenship and, second, by the partition of India. These events led to the 1948 British Nationality Act, which created two main categories: citizens of the UK and colonies, also known as British subjects, and citizens of Commonwealth countries. Both had the status of British subjects and carried the entitlement to settle in Britain. In most other respects, British nationality was hopelessly confused and did not entail a uniform set of rights throughout the former empire. It achieved the purpose of preserving the Britishness of the Commonwealth, but this gesture acquired unforeseen significance with the burgeoning of immigration from the colonies and, subsequently, the New Commonwealth countries.[19]

After 1945, Britain's global situation was radically amended. The end of empire and straitened economic circumstances both involved mass immigration into Britain. National identity, nationality and citizenship were increasingly inflected by global patterns of migration and movements of the international economy, notably Britain's relative decline and the formation of the European Economic Community.[20]

Labour shortages and anxiety about population decline prompted the post-war Labour Government to favour the immigration of east Europeans under a variety of schemes. Between 1947 and 1951, over 200,000 east Europeans were successfully settled in Britain. These immigrants were to some extent 'racialized', but positive stereotypes were deployed in their case. They were cast as valuable additions to Britain's Anglo-Saxon 'stock'. Deemed to be 'assimilable', they were given ready access to British nationality by means of naturalization.[21]

By contrast, West Indians seeking work in Britain – such as the 500 Jamaicans who arrived at Tilbury on board the *Empire Windrush* in June 1948 – were considered 'problematic'. Although there is evidence of a mixed response to non-white immigration into post-war Britain, the Government chose to heed the vocal, racist element that found spokesmen in parliament. Officials and politicians needed little convincing that unrestricted non-white immigration would cause a backlash. In short, Blacks were the heirs to centuries of anti-Black racism, the end result of which was their irredeemable difference and the assumption that their successful assimilation would be difficult if not impossible. So non-white people who were British subjects with a perfect right to enter Britain were constructed differently to white people who were technically alien, but whose Otherness was less threatening.[22]

The spectre of escalating popular hostility to non-white immigration from the colonies and the New Commonwealth challenged the continuity of the slack and confused definition of British nationality under the 1948 Act that made this influx possible. Pressure on successive governments to curtail immigration and, if necessary, change the definition of nationality, was held in check for more than a decade by several considerations. Although many Conservative

Members of Parliament opposed 'coloured immigration', a larger number defended the doctrine of *'civis Britannicus sum'*, the notion that the people who dwelled in the Commonwealth possessed a common citizenship binding them together and facilitating free movement within it. British governments were afraid of alienating the newly independent Commonwealth countries by imposing controls on the migration of their citizens to the 'mother country'. Finally, the Government was inhibited by the embarrassment of appearing to act in a racist manner. Instead, efforts were made to restrict the influx of New Commonwealth immigrants by informal means.[23]

Ameliorative strategies failed to reduce immigration. Meanwhile, the 1958 Notting Hill riots turned 'race' into a major public issue. Sections of the press and a phalanx of Conservative MPs demanded immigration controls even though they would compromise the status of British subjects in British colonies. This clamour finally resulted in the 1962 Commonwealth Immigration Act, which dramatically qualified the rights formerly inherent to the status of British subject. The Act established that 'citizens of the UK and colonies' were subject to immigration controls and could only enter Britain under certain circumstances, such as for purposes of study or to take up a job obtained under a schedule of work vouchers. 'Citizens of the UK and colonies' born in the UK or who held British passports would be exempt from controls. The key factor of discrimination was who held or could obtain British passports: this was limited to persons born in the UK or of British descent and, therefore, embraced the white dominions or white settlers in the colonies. Citizens of newly independent Commonwealth states did not, in most cases, have British passports since they became citizens of these new countries.[24]

Subsequent immigration and nationality legislation further narrowed the right of entry to Britain from the New Commonwealth rendering this form of 'citizenship of the UK and colonies' virtually meaningless. The 1965 White Paper cut down the number of work vouchers available to the New Commonwealth countries and tightened frontier controls. In 1967–8, 'Africanization' measures in Kenya led to the economic persecution of Asians who were 'citizens of the UK and colonies', prompting Asians with British passports to settle in the UK. Afraid of a 'backlash', the Labour Government passed the 1968 Commonwealth Immigration Act, which summarily deprived Kenyan Asians of the right to settle unconditionally in the UK. The Act established that the status of British subject was obtained by descent from parents or grandparents born in Britain, thereby excluding non-whites in the former Empire from the right of settlement in the UK. The Commonwealth was undergoing a process of bifurcation into white and non-white parts. British national identity, increasingly exclusive, related to the Old, or white, Commonwealth only. The Kenyan Asians crisis was a traumatic illustration of how a shift in the definition of nationality, reflecting changing conceptions of national identity, could destabilize citizenship with tragic human consequences.[25]

The erosion of Commonwealth citizenship and the drive for an exclusive Britishness was powered by the apparently implacable and widespread popular hostility to immigration to which successive governments since 1962 had paid obeisance. The 1971 Immigration Act set out to appease this racist sentiment by terminating 'primary' immigration from the Commonwealth, even though in reality the influx of single, job-seeking immigrants had been virtually throttled by previous legislation. In essence the Act grasped the nettle that earlier legislators had avoided and finally cast adrift those who previously held 'citizenship of the UK and colonies'. Henceforth, UK citizenship would belong to 'patrials' – that is, anyone born in Britain or with a British-born or naturalized parent or grandparent. The non-white citizens of the Commonwealth lost the right to enter Britain while the white 'kith and kin' who populated the Old Commonwealth could still do so. In detail the Act was a good deal more complex and bequeathed a legacy of confusion as well as distress.[26]

The 1971 Immigration Act and the politicization of race and immigration that led up to it cannot be understood outside the framework of a nation and a national identity undergoing prolonged crisis. During the late 1960s Enoch Powell MP popularized a notion of Englishness as ethnic and hereditary. In November 1968 he proclaimed that a West Indian born in Britain could never become an Englishman. The new salience of Englishness reflected the coterminous upsurge of nationalism in Scotland and Wales and the unrest in Northern Ireland. By the mid-1970s, British national identity was in question and efforts to define it inevitably impacted upon immigrants and aliens (as well as Britain's new partners in the European Economic Community, albeit in a very different sense).[27]

Immigration controls and the loss of an effective citizenship harmed thousands of people in the Commonwealth. But immigration laws also stigmatized settlers already in the country and had a negative effect upon their lives. This was demonstrated most clearly by the obstacles placed in the way of family reunion and, later, the imposition of visas on visitors from several New Commonwealth countries. The 1981 Nationality Act exceeded all previous legislation in sweeping away the ancient structure of British nationality and the rights of the British subject by abrogating the principle of *jus soli*. It stipulated that from 1986 only the British-born children of British-born or naturalized British people would inherit British citizenship.[28]

In other respects, the 1981 Act left British nationality in as chaotic a condition as ever. Over time, as clarifications became necessary, its racialized character acquired a clearer outline. For example, under the 1981 Act the people of Hong Kong and those of the Falkland Islands were categorized as British Dependent Territories citizens, which carried no right of entry to the UK. In 1983, full British nationality was retrospectively extended to Falkland Islanders, while in 1990 only a privileged and wealthy section of the Hong Kong population was considered for the same status.[29] The 1988 Immigration Act removed the right of certain British citizens to be joined in the UK by their spouse. Clearly, this was a regulation that hit most directly at recent settlers with close ties to their countries of origin where for social, ethnic and religious reasons they would be likely to seek a marriage partner.[30] Such legislation exposed the racialized character of British nationality, reflecting the bitterly polarized and, at one extreme, racist understanding of national identity in the mid-1980s.[31]

IV

The dynamic relationship between national identity, nationality and citizenship in Britain can be explained in various ways. Englishness and Britishness have had changing components depending upon the territorial expanse of the state and its dominant religion. In medaieval times there was a need to define who owed allegiance to the monarch and who was an alien. Initially this differentiation was determined by birthplace, but it was overlaid by an emergent sense of English nationhood, burnished in the course of wars against France and reinforced by religion after the Reformation. The Union of England and Scotland required the construction of a common, British national identity. Britishness was then defined against France, again, the Irish and Catholics in general, and the Jews. Mass immigration by east European Jews, which occurred when national identity and self-confidence were in crisis, provoked the first restrictions on immigration. The 1905 Aliens Act formalized the distinction between British subject and alien more starkly than ever before.[32]

In tandem with the creation of a domestic empire, Britain created a global empire. The mutations of the empire reacted with the national identity of the 'mother country'. In order to differentiate and control the movement of populations within the British Empire, borders and identities had to be drawn more tightly. The racialization of identity was central to this process. The dominions were the first to experiment with citizenship and nationality that discriminated on grounds of 'race'. Eventually the concept of *'civic Britannicus sum'* collapsed and the 'mother country' erected barriers based on racialized identities, too.[33]

Of course, without 'race' there could have been no racialization process. 'Race' legitimated imperial domination. During the late nineteenth century 'race' coalesced with national identity and served to differentiate aliens and Britons ever more pointedly. Racial stereotypes were deployed against each wave of immigration, from the Jews onwards, and used to justify the regulation of immigrant flows.[34]

Racial thinking operated in many areas, especially population policy. Concern about the size and 'quality' of the population of the British Isles forms another thread running through national identity, nationality and immigration policy. Whenever population comes under scrutiny, immigration and 'race' are never far behind. The alleged 'degeneration' of the population was a factor in the opposition to unrestricted Jewish immigration at the turn of the century. Racialized concepts were central to the discussion of population in Britain in the 1930s and the 1940s. The 1948 Royal Commission on Population specifically recommended immigration as a means to replenish the depleted national stock, but emphasized that it had to be from a source that was compatible with, and assimilable to, the existing 'Anglo-Saxon' population.[35]

While the operation of racism in the definition of national identity has been heavily researched, less attention has been paid to the role of war in the twentieth century. Yet war as a contemporaneous experience has played a neglected role as a catalyst for the reassessment of nationality and national identity. Military service accentuated the sense of difference between subjects/citizens and immigrants/aliens. Anti-alienism, xenophobia and racism flourished in the First and Second World Wars. During both, foreigners were subjected to mass internment on flimsy pretexts, but really as concessions to chauvinism and sheer racial viciousness. It is important to note that this pattern was repeated during the Gulf War, when British Muslims were characterized as a 'Fifth Column' and threatened with internment. Indeed, over 200 Arabs in Britain were interned.[36]

War as embodied in national memory is no less important. The resonances of war in British national identity continue to divide the population along racial lines. Thousands of West Indians and Indians served in the British armed forces in 1939–45, but this fact hardly registers in public memory of the war. Although the 1962 Commonwealth Immigration Act actually includes a special category for veterans from the British colonies, the war continues to exert a divisive rather than an inclusive influence.[37] Paul Gilroy has noted that the compulsive reference back to Britain's 'finest hour' and the round of wartime anniversaries in the 1990s all focus on an England that was white. The war is taken to evoke the British at their best, the qualities of Churchill's 'island race'. This is mythological nonsense, but it helps construct a sense of nation and nationality that excludes the bulk of post-1945 immigrants. They were not there; they did not share in Britain's greatness; as a result, they are somehow inferior citizens. It is possible that a faint echo of the doctrine of the arms-bearing citizen may even be heard in this refrain.[38]

Nazism and the 'Final Solution' temporarily stigmatized racial–biological thinking after 1945. However, the 'New Racism' that emerged in the 1970s evaded the opprobrium of biological racism and eugenics by superficially relocating difference away from phenotype and genes and on to culture. This has had a dramatic effect on the nature and appearance of racism in Britain. By camouflaging hereditary qualities as a cultural inheritance, it became possible for mainstream politicians to inject racism back into debates about nationality and citizenship. The 'New Racism' has made citizenship itself the site of struggle over conceptions of the nation and national identity.[39]

In the new discourse of racism, culture was taken to define the differences between the British and non-white immigrants. Ethnicity, religion, language and customs were held to render immigrants unassimilable without it ever being necessary to mention racial types. The shifting locus of racism reflected the new realities in British society: the virtual cessation of primary immigration after 1971 on the one hand, and the consolidation of ethnic minority communities on the other. These communities, on their own and assisted by certain race relations legislation, as well as policies of central and local government, began to assert their identities and ethnic agendas. The spear-carriers of white, ethnic nationalism found a new battlefield in multiculturalism. Cultural differences relocated the arena of conflict away from the margins of the nation and to its very core: the constitution, law, education and national religion. Citizenship, no less than national identity and nationality, has now acquired racially polarized meanings.[40]

The rhetorical construction of the good citizen is increasingly becoming a code for the white citizen. Stuart Hall, Paul Gilroy and John Solomos have catalogued and analysed the racialization of crime and the criminalization of young Blacks in Britain's inner cities. They have connected policing against Black youth with the exploitation of the law and the British constitution as long-established vessels of national identity.[41] The current emphasis on the family as the training ground for citizenship and a building block of the nation has racial implications, too. Black family life has been systematically stigmatized and declared inadequate. The implication is that dysfunctional or incomplete Black families produce bad citizens – members of the 'underclass'. Hence, citizenship again becomes a divisive, racial concept rather than an inclusive, universal one.[42]

Overt linkages between nation, culture, religion and race are present in education policy, too. The 1988 Educational Reform Act prescribes the teaching of British history to all pupils and places on schools an obligation to provide an act of Christian worship. Successive ministers responsible for recent education policy have depicted this as necessary for the creation of a homogeneous population of loyal citizens. Conversely, Muslim schools are characterized as a breeding ground for dual loyalty and Fifth Columns as well as an alien fundamentalism.[43]

This dangerous recasting of citizenship in the light of a changing sense of nationhood and national identity has not been ameliorated by Britain's entry into Europe. Rather, party politics have led to an accentuation of national chauvinism and the reiteration of a narrow sense of Britishness defined against a farcically demonized 'Europe'. Recent British governments have sought to project on to the European Union their own restrictionist immigration policies and have supported an exclusive, Eurocentric definition of European identity and membership. Sadly, it seems as if the idea of a Europe of diversity is giving way to the notion of European homogeneity behind closely guarded frontiers. British politicians may yet succeed in making a 'Little Europe' in the image of 'Little England'.[44]

NOTES

1 Rogers Brubaker, *Citizenship and Nationhood in France and Germany* (Cambridge, Mass.: Harvard University Press, 1992).
2 The constitutional mess has been given salience by Charter 88.
3 See Geoff Andrews (ed.), *Citizenship* (London: Lawrence & Wishart, 1991) on the constitutional crisis, with particular respect to citizenship, and Tom Nairn, *The Break-up of Britain* (London: Verso, 1981, first published 1977) which heralded a wave of analyses and publications on the theme encapsulated in the title. Ann Dummet and Andrew Nicol, *Subjects, Citizens, Aliens and Others. Nationality and Immigration Law* (London: Weidenfeld & Nicolson, 1990), p. 2.
4 Dummet and Nicol, *Subjects, Citizens, Aliens and Others*, pp. 21–55, 56–9.
5 Ibid., pp. 64–70.
6 Derek Heater, *Citizenship. The Civic Ideal in World History, Politics and Education* (London: Longman, 1990), pp. 49–71.
7 Ibid., pp. 71–80.
8 Linda Colley, *Britons. Forging the Nation* (New Haven: Yale, 1992), pp. 11–54; Dummet and Nicol, *Subjects, Citizens, Aliens and Others*, pp. 56–9, 77.
9 On the 'Jew Bill', T. W. Perry, *Public Opinion, Propaganda and Politics in Eighteenth Century England* (Cambridge, Mass.: Harvard University Press, 1962); Dummet and Nicol, *Subjects, Citizens, Aliens and Others*, pp. 77–9.
10 Colley, *Britons. Forging the Nation*, pp. 325–34.
11 David Feldman, *Englishmen and Jews. Social Relations and Political Culture, 1840–1914* (London: Yale, 1994), pt 1; Israel Finestein, 'Some modern themes in the emancipation debate in early Victorian England', in Jonathan Sacks (ed.), *Tradition and Transition* (London: Jews' College 1986), pp. 135–40.
12 Bernard Porter, *The Refugee Question in Mid Victorian Politics* (Cambridge: Cambridge University Press, 1979) and Bernard Porter, ' "Bureau and Barrack": early Victorian attitudes towards the Continent', *Victorian Studies* 26(1), 1982, pp. 407–33; Dummet and Nicol, *Subjects, Citizens, Aliens and Others*, pp. 86–7.
13 See John Garrard, *The English and Immigration: A Comparative Study of the Jewish Influx 1880–1910* (London: Oxford University Press, 1971) and Bernard Gainer, *The Alien Invasion. The Origins of the Alien Act of 1905* (London: Heinemann, 1972).
14 Feldman, *Englishmen and Jews*, pp. 28–48, 370–8. More generally, Dummet and Nicol, *Subjects, Citizens, Aliens and Others*, pp. 92–100.
15 Dummet and Nicol, *Subjects, Citizens, Aliens and Others*, pp. 103–7.
16 David Cesarani, 'An Alien Concept? Anti-alienism in Britain before 1940', in David Cesarani and Tony Kushner (eds), *The Internment of Aliens in Twentieth-Century Britain* (London: Frank Cass, 1993), pp. 25–52; Dummet and Nicol, *Subjects, Citizens, Aliens and Others*, pp. 107–12, 145–52. For the background see Panikos Panayi, *The Enemy in Our Midst: Germans in Britain During the First World War* (Oxford:

Berg, 1991) and Sharman Kadish, *Bolsheviks and British Jews* (London: Frank Cass, 1992).

17 Dummet and Nicol, *Subjects, Citizens, Aliens and Others*, pp. 145–50 160–9; David Cesarani, 'Anti-alienism in Britain after the First World War', *Immigrants and Minorities* 6(1), 1987, pp. 4–29.

18 Ibid., pp. 115–30.

19 Ibid., pp. 134–41.

20 For the global context, see Stephen Castles and Mark J. Miller, *The Age of Migration* (London: Macmillan, 1993), ch. 3.

21 D. Kay and R. Miles, *Refugees or Migrant Workers? The Recruitment of Displaced Workers for British Industry 1946–1951* (London: Routledge, 1992); Robert Miles, *Racism After 'Race Relations'* (London: Routledge, 1993), ch 6; David Cesarani, *Justice Delayed* (London: Heinemann, 1992), ch. 7.

22 Bob Carter and Shirley Joshi, 'The role of Labour in creating a racist Britain', *Race and Class* 25(3), 1984, pp. 53–70; Ken Lunn, 'The British state and immigration, 1954–61: new light on the Empire Windrush', in Tony Kushner and Ken Lunn (eds), *The Politics of Marginality* (London: Cass, 1990), pp. 161–74. For the background to attitudes towads Black people in Britain, see James Walvin, *Black and White: The Negro in English Society, 1555–1945* (London: Allen & Unwin, 1973); Douglas Lorimer, *Colour, Class and the Victorians: English Attitudes to the Negro in the Mid-Nineteenth Century* (Leicester: Leicester University Press, 1978); Peter Fryer, *Staying Power. The History of Black People in Britain* (London: Pluto, 1984).

23 Zig Layton-Henry, *The Politics of Immigration* (Oxford: Blackwell, 1992), pp. 28–41; Zig Layton-Henry, *The Politics of Race in Britain* (London: George Allen & Unwin, 1984), chs 1–3.

24 Dummet and Nicol, *Subjects, Citizens, Aliens and Others*, pp. 183–8; Layton-Henry, *The Politics of Immigration*, pp. 71–7.

25 Ibid., pp. 196–205.

26 Ibid., pp. 216–23

27 Ibid., pp. 224–26. In general, see John Osmond, *The Divided Kingdom* (London: Constable, 1988)

28 Ibid., pp. 241–51

29 Ibid., pp. 249–52 Layton-Henry, *The Politics of Immigration*, pp. 208–9.

30 Dummet and Nicol, *Subjects, Citizens, Aliens and Others*, pp. 253–4

31 Layton-Henry, *The Politics of Immigration*, pp. 187–210.

32 Dummet and Nicol, *Subjects, Citizens, Aliens and Others*, chs 2–4.

33 Paul B. Rich, *Race and Empire in British Politics* (Cambridge: Cambridge University Press, 1986).

34 Miles, *Racism After 'Race Relations'*, ch. 3; Colin Holmes, *John Bull's Island: Immigration and British Society, 1871–1971* (London: Macmillan, 1988); Michael Howard, 'Empire, race and war in pre-1914 Britain', in Hugh Lloyd-Jones et al., *History and Imagination. Essays in Honour of Hugh Trevor-Roper* (London: Duckworth, 1981), pp. 340–55. Rich, *Race and Empire in British Politics*, pp. 12–27.

35 Layton-Henry, *The Politics of Race in Britain*, ch. 2; Miles, *Racism After 'Race Relations'*, pp. 152–69.

36 David Cesarani, 'An embattled minority: the Jews in Britain during the First World War', in Kushner and Lunn (eds), *The Politics of Marginality*, pp. 61–81; Cesarani and Kushner (eds), *The Internment of Aliens in Twentieth Century Britain*.
37 See, for example, M. Sherwood, *Many Struggles: West Indian Workers and Service Personnel in Britain, 1939–45* (London: Karim Press, 1985).
38 Paul Gilroy, *Small Acts* (London: Serpents Tail, 1993), pp. 20–2, 52–3; Patrick Wright, *On Living in an Old Country* (London: Verso, 1985), pp. 23–4, 45–8, 81–7.
39 Miles, *Racism After 'Race Relations'*, pt 1, discusses how 'new' this form of racism really is. cf. Paul Barker, *The New Racism* (London: Junction Books, 1981); Gill Seidel, 'Culture, nation and "race" in the British and French New Right', in Ruth Levinas (ed.), *The Ideology of the New Right* (London: Polity, 1986), pp. 107–35.
40 Centre for Contemporary Cultural Studies, *The Empire Strikes Back: Race and Racism in the 1970s* (London: Hutchinson, 1982); Layton-Henry, *The Politics of Immigration*, chs 6, 8; Paul Gilroy, *There Ain't No Black in the Union Jack* (London: Hutchinson, 1987), ch. 3.
41 Gilroy, *There Ain't No Black in the Union Jack*, ch. 3 and Gilroy, *Small Acts*, pp. 22–7, 80–4; John Solomos, *Race and Racism in Contemporary Britain* (London: Macmillan, 1989), chs 3–7.
42 See ibid.
43 Gilroy, *Small Acts*, ch. 3; Philip Lewis, *Islamic Britain* (London: I. B. Tauris, 1994), pp. 145–69.
44 For trends in Europe see John Wrench and John Solomos, *Racism and Migration in Western Europe* (Oxford: Berg, 1993).

5

NATIONALITIES AND CITIZENSHIPS

The lessons of the French experience for Germany and Europe

Patrick Weil

Translated by George Lavy and Josh Gibson

The Maastricht Treaty is said to have established a European citizenship. The rationale of the leaders meeting at Maastricht in December 1991 was to correct or disguise the overly economic and financial nature of the treaty. But by instituting suffrage for nationals of the European Union in local and European elections without first reconciling each member state's laws regarding nationality, the Union accepted the notion – probably false – that there are essential and unavoidable differences between the national traditions of each country. The method chosen by the leaders, far from creating a feeling of citizenship or allowing for the emergence of a true European citizenship, rather had the effect of upsetting the basic conditions for the integration of resident immigrants.

POSSIBLE CONVERGENCE OF NATIONAL LEGISLATION

The primary obstacle to the creation of European citizenship is the belief shared to a great extent in France as well as in Germany that the traditions of the different countries would be too difficult to reconcile. However, a more detailed socio-historical analysis of the origin of these nations and their legislation regarding nationality would have allowed the leaders to determine similarities among the laws and to emphasize these similarities.

In this chapter I will dispute the flawed assumption of the leaders in a somewhat backwards manner by first analysing the preconceptions of the French tradition and then comparing the French and German systems.

In France, those who are trying to define the specificity of the French national identity focus on two points: the first is that the French nation is held together and in fact exists through the free will and consent of the people. This notion comes from the text of a lecture delivered by Ernest Renan: 'A nation ... is the consent, the clearly expressed desire to continue communal life ... The existence of a nation is a daily plebiscite.'[1] This notion contradicts the German ethnic self-conception defended by Strauss, a philosopher, in a debate in which he participated with Renan.

The second assumption is that the tradition of *jus soli* (the law of the soil) was established in 1889 by the French Republic, as opposed to the German tradition which is based on the *jus sanguinis* (the law of blood).[2]

But nowadays, 95 per cent of all the French have never been required to explicitly express their desire to be of French nationality, to be considered as French. This leads one to ask, if this is the case, where does this myth of 'free will' and 'consent' come from? And, furthermore, it is important to note that the criteria for determining who is of French nationality, as they were defined in 1889, and as are still in effect today, have many points in common with the definition of French nationality that existed in the jurisprudence of the courts of the *ancien régime* (the *parlements*) throughout the eighteenth century and up until the first days of the French Revolution.

The following period, which began with the issuing of the Code Napoléon in 1804 and continued through the adoption of a key law regarding nationality in 1889, seems then, in the history of the definition of 'Frenchness', to be unique. For this was the only period in French history when, as in contemporary Germany, the *jus sanguinis* had precedence over the *jus soli*.

An explanation of the origin of the myth of free will and consent, as well as why and how the previously dominant criterion of *jus sanguinis* came to be progressively replaced by the *jus soli*, might then allow a possible means of achieving Franco-German and European agreement on this issue.[3]

To understand this return to the *jus soli*, one must first examine the history of French nationality. Like all other legislation involving nationality, ever since the seventeenth century the French tradition has been based upon a mixture, or a blend – as in a painting, several colours are mixed to achieve the desired effect. In the case at hand, two of these 'colours' are always mentioned: first, the birthplace, or *jus soli*, the fact of being born in a territory over which the state extends, has extended, or possibly wishes to extend its sovereignty; and, second, family/blood ties, or *jus sanguinis*, that is to say the nationality of one or both parents.

However, two other 'colours' are often forgotten or neglected. The third is marital status, for to be married to a citizen of a certain country can lead to ties of citizenship with that country. Lastly there is past, present, or future residence, considered at any given moment for a duration, extended or otherwise, in the past or supposedly in the future, within the borders of the country.

The mixture of these four basic 'colours' on the different legal 'palettes' that have evolved over the centuries determines what one must do in order to be granted French nationality.

Among these four criteria, the *jus soli* was dominant prior to the French Revolution; throughout the *ancien régime* the *jus soli* was the primary requirement for the attribution of French nationality. And although, beginning in the seventeenth century the *jus sanguinis* could independently be used to access French nationality, it is important not to be mistaken on this point – birth on French soil still took precedence over birth by French parents (regardless of birthplace) as a legitimate criterion for determining French nationality.

The proof of this can be seen through an example provided by Jean-François Dubost: during this period, children of French parents born outside France and residing on French territory needed to request from the king a letter of naturalization in order to confirm their French status.[4] Children born in France of foreign parents would not have needed to do this.

It is important to take into account the major changes that were brought about by the French Revolution. First, the constitution of 1791 created a uniform nationality code – prior to this time, requirements for attributing French nationality varied by *parlement* and therefore by region. Second, the Revolution allowed non-Catholics, and notably Jews, access to French nationality. Lastly, the Revolution led to the emergence of the modern notion of citizenship – that is to say, individual participation in national sovereignty. It was this last transformation which would upset the construction of the definition of 'French' developed under the *ancien régime*.[5]

For the responses to the question of which of the monarchy's subjects (then named 'passive citizens') could become active citizens of the Republic vary greatly between 1789 and 1804. With the rapid succession of rule changes, the characteristics of loyalty and allegiance to the new regime were constantly sought after. Those who drafted the 1793 constitution believed that, considering the conditions of that time, a link, even tenuous, with the newly created French Republic (for example, residence in Paris with an active social presence – although many Frenchmen fought against the Revolution from outside French territory) would suffice to demonstrate this allegiance. A few weeks later, the Convention decided that, on the contrary, foreign origin constituted a threat to the Republic – so foreigners were imprisoned. Finally, in 1804, it was decided, against the will of Napoleon, that birth within the borders of the country was not enough to guarantee the loyalty of the children of those foreigners born in France. Legislators warned of the danger the country could face if it forced these people to call themselves French against their will. The civil code thus rejected the simple *jus soli* and instituted a monopoly on the automatic transferral of French citizenship through a father's direct blood line. Beginning in 1804, this new right of citizenship based on blood ties, temporarily stabilized, would be tested in practice.

This legislation very rapidly produced unanticipated social consequences that E. Rouard de Card presented in this way:

> A few years after the Code Civil had been instituted, it was observed that numerous individuals who had been born on French territory, even though they belonged to families who had lived on French territory for an extended period, were in no hurry to formally request their French citizenship ... They would take advantage of the benefits of our social state by passing themselves off as French citizens while avoiding any public responsibilities by claiming to be foreigners.[6]

Long before 1889 and the creation of the Third Republic, which would only accelerate the progression that was already underway, the *Assemblée Législative* decided to require a number of these individuals to become French, regardless of their individual will. A first effort to write this into law in 1831 did not come to fruition. Then, a law passed on 7 February 1851 stated that an individual born in France of a foreign parent who was also born in France would be considered as French from birth. However, such an individual could

still avoid this designation by indicating, upon reaching legal adult-
hood, a desire to be considered as a foreigner. A law enacted on 16
December 1874 reinforced the restriction, stating that an individual
as described above could only renounce French citizenship by pro-
ducing a statement prepared by the 'original' country that indicated
that the person in question 'had maintained his original nationality'.
A law passed in 1889 finally removed all opportunity for a child
born in France of foreign parents born in France to renounce French
citizenship.

When the judiciary commission of the *Chambre des Députés* proposed in 1889 to impose once and for all the *jus soli*, it was because,
for them, a child born in France of parents who themselves were
born in France was 'French from the point of view of spirit, incli-
nation, habits, and morals'. The Chambre des Députés made no
reference to public schools or the army (which, of course, would
later play an important role in the socialization of the children of
foreigners), as if to say that this socialization could have taken place
without the assistance of these institutions. But the Chambre des
Députés's decision to leave out these references was also in the best
interest of the state: first, because between 1851 and 1889 mass immigration had developed, particularly in border regions, and second,
because the recent French reacquisition of the Savoie and of Nice
and the presence of a large Italian colony in Algeria made it quite
urgent to react to this extent or even further, more in the name of
public order than for reasons of equality.[7]

If in 1804 the hesitation in providing children born in France of
foreigners born in France with French nationality (and therefore
potentially with 'active' citizenship) was based on a fear of their
individual disloyalty, in 1889 the acknowledgement of their assimilation as well as the fear of their collective separatism justified the
shift of citizenship laws in favour of the *jus soli*. Thus, from that
time, French nationality was transmitted by foreign parents themselves born in France to their children just as it was transmitted
to the children of French parents. This reform also represented a
compromise between the opinions of several social groups, as Gérard
Noiriel indicates: in favour of the change, were

> representatives of French industry, with a vital need for workers,
> elected officials from industrial areas seeking to stop foreign
> competition, and those in the military, who wanted to rebuild
> a powerful army. Those opposing the change were the defenders

of the French race and identity, who were massively recruited from the French aristocracy.[8]

Thus, with the institution of the *jus soli* in 1889, the Third Republic was not creating it, but was merely re-establishing it. It had then taken a century, from 1789 to 1889, to clarify the relationship between nationality and citizenship, as well as to incorporate the definitions of these words into the minds of the French.[9] The current rules regarding French nationality that were reintroduced into the civil code in 1993 have changed very little since 1889 – the most important of these changes was the equalization of men's and women's rights of access to and transmission of French nationality.

If any judicial innovation took place in 1889 it was not the institution of the *jus soli* but rather the Republic's total and complete reversal in the handling of an often neglected factor in the attribution of French nationality: the criterion of residence. In the time of the *ancien régime*, the criterion of residence was very important: when recognition of French nationality could only be based upon French parents giving birth abroad or foreign parents giving birth in France, the parlements required that current and future residence be established within the kingdom. This was the sign of personal allegiance, both present and future, to the king. However, over the course of the nineteenth century, the requirement of current and future residence changed to become instead a requirement of past residence. In the shift from loyalty to the king to loyalty to the nation, this loyalty would no longer be judged on individual ties but instead on a person's socialization and education in French culture – and past residence on French territory was in some ways the guarantee of these qualities.

The 1889 nationality law thus made a child socialized in French culture French by law, whether born in France of foreign parents and educated in French society or born abroad to French parents and raised in the French language and culture. Access to French nationality is automatic if at birth the child has either a direct blood tie with a French parent or a double *jus soli* with France (two generations born on French territory). Some examples are a child born in Columbia of a 'Franco-Chinese' couple (Art. 17) or a child born in France of an Algerian parent born in Algeria before 1962 (when Algeria was still a French territory). Acquisition of French nationality is almost automatic for a child born in France of foreign parents, but the acceptance of French nationality only becomes binding when between the ages of 16 and 21 the child voluntarily declares his desire to become French.

For a foreigner without any birth ties to France to acquire French nationality, a formal link with France must be created, either through marriage or through an extended period of residence in the country and a formal request for citizenship.

If the link with France that is used to become a French citizen is marriage to a French man or woman, the state imposes a check, albeit weak and *a posteriori*, on the request for acquisition of French nationality (Art. 37–1). The request is made using a 'declaration', which constitutes, for those who meet the criteria laid out by law, a right. Therefore, all that is needed to claim French nationality is that the desire to claim it be formally expressed. The state bureaucracy must content itself with checking to see that the necessary legal requirements have been satisfied.

If the link used is an extended period of residence in France, the state exercises a much more powerful and a priori control, through the process of naturalization. Today, naturalization is granted fairly freely to those requesting it (80 to 90 per cent of requests are granted, although the average wait is 18 months), although relatively strict socialization criteria are expected of the applicant (a minimum of five years spent in France, knowledge of the French language, stable financial resources, current residence in France). These rules differentiate the French from the American or the German traditions. A child born in the United States of foreign parents becomes American even if he has not lived in the United States and has therefore not been educated there; a child born in Germany of foreign parents will often remain a foreigner, while the great-grandchild of a German raised abroad, to the east of Germany, without any ties to German culture, could claim German nationality simply by deciding to live in Germany. The law of 1889 thus, in reintroducing into law the principal of the *jus soli* and altering the role of residence legitimated the concept of socialization. And it is this fusion of socialization and passive citizenship (previously referred to in law as 'nationality') which made French nationality law unique.[10]

Instead of contract-based or ethnic origin-based citizenship, this concept of nationality permitted, in its primary usages, to symbolize a unique legislation based on socialization; a process and therefore neither an ethnic 'given' nor a simple voluntary act. French republican law bases French nationality more on the acquisition of certain codes of sociability than on the expression of one's individual will, one's origin, or one's birthplace. In the end, these are nothing but tokens of this acquisition.

80

Thus, the concept that the French nation exists out of the free will and consent of individuals is a philosophical invention, based solely on circumstance, that originally served a strategic purpose: those who worked with Renan in 1882 and had as their primary objective the need to differentiate the French nation from the German nation to illegitimate the annexation of Alsace-Lorraine by the German Empire, regardless of the cultural and ethnic ties that could be seen as tying it to the Empire. For the residents of Alsace-Lorraine at the time, the desire to be French could well have been a daily plebiscite; but today 95 per cent of French people have never been required to state their individual desire to have the nationality that they have been assigned, just as virtually all nationality is assigned in the world – automatically and without any possibility of choice. As for those who can express such a desire, they can only do so under certain tangible social conditions (residence, marriage, knowledge of the language, etc.).

However, this logic, which bases nationality more upon codes of sociability and citizenship than on individual desire, does not allow French national identity to be readily defined. The French system, which presents several means by which to receive French nationality, fails to respond to a question which each individual must ask himself: who am I? In responding to this question, a German could still respond that he is German because his ancestors were German – a response that not all French people could give. The French Republic therefore responds to the requirement for a common identity, necessary for the unity of any human group and therefore any nation, with symbolic republican values: you are French because you adhere (that is to say sociologically you can adhere) to republican values; those same values which give French citizens the desire to live together. This political identity is not embodied in daily plebiscites, but rather in occasional ones, through the 'ceremony of voting'. The vote, a republican rite confirming that one belongs to the nation, was historically a means of symbolically identifying the members of the sovereign French nation. He who votes is French and a citizen. There is no differentiation in the French social imagination between identity, citizenship and nationality, between local and national citizenship. It is for this reason that the creation of a citizenship that is enlarged to include all foreigners or only Europeans (as envisioned by the Treaty of Maastricht) which would break the bonds between the vote, citizenship, nationality, and identity is still very hotly contested.

PATRICK WEIL

THE IMPLICATIONS OF THE FRENCH EXPERIENCE
FOR GERMANY

From this history of French nationality, is it not possible to discover for today's Germany an important consideration in the form of a question: can such an important democratic country, a country of welcome and refuge, continue to deny German nationality to the large majority of foreigners and their children who live in Germany?

All of the countries of Europe have become, willingly or not, countries of immigration where a foreigner who receives temporary authorization to live in the country for a short but undetermined period of time usually ends up obtaining either for himself or for his descendants the right to stay more or less permanently. And then what of their access to the nationality of the country in which they are living? It seems to me that the profound changes that have taken place since 1945 could help to highlight and to favour the similarities between German legislation and that of its European neighbours. Many of these possibilities come independent of German reunification, but the most important can be seen as having resulted from it.

The settlement of the question of territory: German reunification no longer left enough Germans outside German territory to justify that which had been the unique and central focus of German nationality law: that the right of nationality based on family ties maintains a bond between citizens who are dispersed over the territory of several states.

The intermingling of the citizens of East and West Germany which rendered null and void the myth which had previously structured German nationality: that of the community based on common origin. The West Germans waited for forty years to welcome their brothers from the East; but once the much-anticipated reunion took place, they often felt that despite their common ancestors, forty years of separation and of life in different societies had left them greatly different.

Then, in addition to this, there has been a mass immigration, notably of Turks, who are foreign by law but in reality more and more integrated, sociologically quasi-German in their activities and their social habits.

Next, a political reality has imposed itself since 1949, that of a vibrant German democracy that the West Germans gradually took for their own, founded on shared social habits and on values that the foreigners residing in the country shared. The bonds that had developed between the West Germans and the resident foreigners are such that those in the latter group often seem sociologically more to be citizens than do the East Germans.

Lastly, maintaining the status quo could in the end seem to be the most dangerous option to those strongest conservatives who are concerned above all with the security of the German state. The continued presence of those of a foreign nationality and thus under the judicial authority of a foreign country, a population born and raised in Germany, determined to live and to grow old there, could be seen (as was the case in France in 1889) as more of a risk than would be a progressive integration of this group into the German nationality.

Thus, objective social and political realities put into question, in Germany, the concept of national identity based on the *jus sanguinis*. Often, however, objective social and political factors only lead to modifications of powerful and legitimate historical traditions when they are brought about as a result of a shocking event which reshapes dominant representations based on new points of reference. Lawrence Fuchs reminds us that the shift in the balance of power in American society on the question of black civil rights was the result of the Second World War, which saw GIs of all colours and origins fighting in the same army for the freedom of the American people.[11] This positive jolt was accentuated by the negative shock of the revelation of the atrocities of the Nazi regime. Lastly, the Cold War created a context that was favourable to the unification of all Americans and in general the questioning of the principle of 'separate but equal' which had been the standard since the end of the Civil War. The events that have recently taken place in Germany would seem to have been an example of this kind of traumatic and restructuring shock – this is possible but not certain.[12] French political and historical experiences provide reasons that allow us to hope that this is in fact the case.

THE RISKS OF MAASTRICHT

These reasons for hope are found to a much lesser extent in the current method for the construction of European citizenship developed by the Maastricht Treaty. Up until now, a central debate in Europe has been between partisans of a local citizenship attributed to all foreign residents on the one hand and, on the other, the defenders of the strong, traditional relationship between nationality and citizenship that is very prevalent in France. The Treaty of Maastricht brings this debate to closure and proves both of these parties to be wrong.

In France, the partisans of reform believe that reform will only take place through a process of equalization of rights – after receiving social and then civil rights, resident foreigners will then receive political rights, all the more legitimate since these foreigners pay local taxes. This will require mayors to distribute more equitably the resources of their towns in favour of the neighbourhoods with the highest immigrant populations.

Those in favour of the status quo consider that, on the contrary, there is no direct relationship between integration and the right to vote. This right, provided without any consideration to socialization, could even have the opposite result: the leaders of different communities could, as in Great Britain, negotiate collective votes in exchange for the creation of strong ethnic communities.

An advantage of the strong relationship between nationality and citizenship is that it permits an open conception of the nation. Socialization into French culture rather than blood relations is the principal criterion for membership in the nation. Once blood relation has become but one criterion among several (birth in the country, marriage, or extended residence) for the attribution of French nationality, citizenship and its corollary, the vote, are the means of identifying and unifying the members of the national community – he who votes is a citizen and is French. The creation of a local citizenship, in breaking the link between citizenship perceived as a whole and nationality, risks over the long term justifying a redefinition of nationality around an ethnic conception of the 'original' or 'true' French.[13]

Partisans of a local right to vote and defenders of the republican tradition disagree on this point, but solely in terms of means and not in terms of their objective: their common goal is the integration of resident foreigners into French society, without any distinction based on national origin. The Treaty of Maastricht institutes a citizenship based on inequality and national origin which creates a distinction among resident foreigners. This does not come without risks.

First, this new European citizenship is based on inequality because, according to the place of birth, a child educated in the European Union either will or will not become a citizen. In effect, one becomes a European citizen by receiving the nationality of one of the states of the European Union. As a result of the differences between the fifteen sets of laws regarding nationality (the Treaty of Maastricht reaffirmed that they would continue to be determined sovereignly by each of the fifteen member states of the European Union), near-absurd conditions of inequality have been created.

Let us examine the case of two brothers, who, with their wives, emigrated from Turkey in 1970 – one to Paris and one to Frankfurt. Let us say that the following year, each of the wives gives birth to one child. If, after the ratification of the Treaty of Maastricht in 1992, the child born in Paris decides to live with his uncle in Frankfurt, for example to find a job there, he could theoretically vote in Frankfurt's city elections, despite being unable to speak German and unfamiliar with Germany and the problems of the city of Frankfurt. However, his cousin, born in Frankfurt, raised in German society and possibly able to speak only one language – German – would not be able to vote in this same election. The first child would have become French at 18 and would therefore have voted there as a French citizen; the child born in Germany would not have become German as a result of refusing to make a formal request for naturalization, which would have necessitated his repudiation of his Turkish nationality.

Above all, not being a citizen of one of the fifteen member states of the European Union becomes, among foreigners living in France, a factor of discrimination. Real-life situations, extent of integration, and length of residence are not taken into account: a Québecois or Polish person who has lived in Paris for twenty years has now fewer rights than a Greek or Irish person who has just arrived in France. It is important not to delude oneself – it is as shortsighted to think that giving the right to vote to all Europeans from the European Union would be an initial step towards giving this right to all resident foreigners as it was in the past to think that the right to be different could aid or lead to integration. The text of the constitutional reform adopted by the French Congress leaves little doubt on the subject – the Maastricht Treaty represented a closure and not an opening.

Additionally, as put into practice without any amendment, the creation of this kind of European citizenship could have as its first result the exacerbation of social and political tension related to immigration in France and Germany. Those in France who, in the debate over integration of resident foreigners, create a distinction between Europeans (the 'assimilatable') and non-Europeans (the 'non-assimilatable') will be comforted by the current framework for European citizenship. This reform will legitimate their fight for the restriction of access to French nationality on the basis of European origin (previously referred to by former French President Valéry Giscard d'Estaing or by the Front National), to the detriment of the republican tradition.

German law evolves slowly. Very recently, legislation was modified so as to make it easier for the children of those born and educated in Germany to acquire German citizenship. None the less, a large number of foreign immigrants are neglected by this integration into German nationality. The Treaty of Maastricht continues and accentuates the marginalization of those who are not citizens of the fifteen member states of the European Union, primarily those from Turkey and the former Yugoslavia. This increases once again the risk of conflict and inter-ethnic confrontation on the local level.

And finally, why was the task of separating voting and non-voting immigrants left to the municipalities – thus taking the risk of further burdening local governments, possibly beyond what is bearable, when they are already responsible for the integration of immigrants without having the necessary means even for this? The creation of a legitimate European citizenship should take place more through strengthening the controls the citizens of the fifteen members of the European Union have over the supra-national bodies of the Union than by the creation of a local citizenship.

CONCLUSION

What safeguards have been neglected on the road to European monetary union? How many experts have been consulted, how many commissions created and ministerial meetings convened? How many late-night negotiations regarding the range of fluctuation of various currencies within the framework of a 'snake' and then a European monetary system have been debated hotly – to the nearest 0.25 per cent? How many steps will be judged necessary before the co-ordination of the various economic and budgetary policies will be assured? By the time it is complete, all this will have taken a minimum of twenty years.

Citizenship, nationality, collective identity, inter-ethnic relations – these are probably more delicate questions than money and economics. With what speed, if not offhandedness, have decisions on these subjects been made, without seeking to learn from past experience, without taking the time to study similarities in nationality law in the fifteen member states? Mistakes made in economic policy quickly show themselves through indicators such as increases in inflation, the unemployment rate, the deficit and the national debt. In matters of collective identity or inter-ethnic relations, however, mistakes are often noticed only much later, by their heavy cost in human, social, and political terms. Now that the Treaty of Maastricht has been adopted, the fifteen countries of the European Union should, as a matter of priority, reflect with caution on how best to put European citizenship into practice.

NOTES

1 This debate is reproduced in Ernest Renan, *Qu'est-ce qu'une nation?* (What is a nation?) and other texts (Paris: Presses Pocket, 1992).
2 This thesis is specifically defended by Rogers Brubaker in *Citizenship and Nationhood in France and Germany* (Cambridge, Mass. and London: Harvard University Press, 1992), p. 272.
3 On the history of French immigration and nationality policy, see Patrick Weil, *La France et ses étrangers – L'aventure de la politique française de l'immigration de 1938 à nos jours* (Paris: Folio/Gallimard, 1995), p. 592.
4 Cf., Jean-François Dubost, 'Significations de la lettre de naturalité dans la France des XVIe et XVIIe siècles', *Working Paper HEC No. 90/3*, European University Institute, San Domenico, Italy, October 1990.
5 The constitution of 1791 institutes that an active citizen will be a French male, at least 25 years old, paying a direct contribution equal at least to the value of three days' work, and having taken the civic oath.
6 E. Rouard de Card, *La nationalité française* (Paris: Pedone et Gamber, second edition, 1922), pp. 37–8.
7 Ibid., pp. 66–7.
8 G. Noiriel, *La tyrannie du national* (Paris: Calmann-Lévy, 1991), p. 88.
9 On the theoretical links between the two, cf. Jean Leca, 'Nationalité et citoyenneté dans l'Europe des immigrations', in J. Costa-Lascoux et P. Weil, *Logiques d'Etats et Immigrations* (Paris: Kimé, 1992), pp. 13–57.
10 On this point, see G. Noiriel, 'Le mirage des mots', *Le monde des débats*, July/August 1993.
11 Cf., Lawrence H. Fuchs, *The American Kaleidoscope* (Hanover and London: Wesleyan University Press, 1987), pp. 87–109.
12 Cf. Claus Leggewie, 'La pression des faits', *Le monde des débats*, July/August 1993.
13 Even during the upheaval of the French Revolution, the link between nationality and citizenship, which at that point had to be defined, was never broken. In the Constitution of 1791, the foreigner achieved citizenship through nationality, whereas in the constitution of 1793 it was citizenship which allowed him to acquire nationality. If that constitution had lasted, a law would have been necessary to formally lay out the rules of access to nationality (passive citizenship) for children and women. These were not established in the 1793 constitution.

6

GERMANY FOR THE GERMANS?

Citizenship and nationality in a divided nation

Mary Fulbrook

The division of Germany in 1949 provides an extremely interesting test case for theories of citizenship definition and national identity construction. Initially founded as 'temporary', impermanent entities, products of the emergent Cold War, the Federal Republic of Germany and the German Democratic Republic over time became widely accepted as apparently permanent features of the geopolitical land-scape of divided post-war Europe. Concepts of national identity were transformed as a result of a wide range of processes, including the changing social and economic context, the passage of generations, and a number of political considerations, not least the changing relations between the two Germanies themselves. The German case highlights particularly the dissonance between a number of aspects of citizenship definition and identity construction which suggest a growing dispar-ity between official conceptions of citizenship and popular concep-tions of nationality and belonging.

WEST GERMAN CITIZENSHIP: THE ETHNIC GERMAN *VOLK* AND THE WEST GERMAN NATION

The Basic Law (*Grundgesetz*), or 'temporary' constitution of the Federal Republic of Germany when it was founded in 1949, retained a remarkably ethnic concept of citizenship, based on the Reich Citi-zenship Law of 1913. Refusing to recognize the legitimacy of the post-war division of Germany or the loss of former German territor-ies east of the Oder–Neisse boundary, the West German constitution sustained an essentially 'blood-right' notion of German citizenship: Article 116 of the Basic Law bestowed automatic rights of citizenship and residence in West Germany on those who were, or were the spouses or descendants of, citizens of Germany in the boundaries of 1937. In order to repeal Nazi amendments to citizenship entitlement, Article 116 also included those persons who had been deprived of citizenship on political, racial or religious grounds between 1933 and 1945 and their descendants.

As critics have pointed out, it was in practice easier for 'ethnic Germans' in eastern Europe to claim rights to citizenship in West Germany if they had documents proving that their parents or grand-parents had been members of the NSDAP, the SS, or other Nazi organizations, than if they had been murdered in Auschwitz and all their property and documentation destroyed. Be this as it may, the unresolved legacy of the Third Reich not only entailed an official unwillingness to recognize the revised central European political borders of the post-war era; it also, however ironic this may have been for a democracy which sought utterly to denounce its Nazi past, imparted an ambiguous aftertaste in its definition of citizenship. The principle of ancestry – blood-right – was clearly prioritized over the principles of birth or residence. Although the word 'Aryan' might have been dropped for ever from the acceptable political vocabulary of the Federal Republic, the political uncertainties of the Cold War era were accompanied by massive population movements, which essentially concentrated the German *Volk* on West German soil.[1] In much reduced geographical boundaries, and under totally different political colours, this was in effect a policy of *Heim ins Reich* ('home into the Reich'). The implicit assumption that an ethnic German nation could be clearly defined, and that it should be gathered together in a homogenous area of territorial settlement under a common political framework, remained a constant, unexamined but underlying guiding force throughout the post-war era.[2]

The strength of commitment to this notion allowed West Germany to overcome massive challenges with respect to the migration of millions of people in the aftermath of the war. In the first decade and a half after the defeat of Hitler's Germany, the territory which became the rump West German state was able to integrate between 10 and 12 million people migrating westwards from eastern Europe. Volker Berghahn estimates that there were around 10 million refugees and expellees entering the western zones of Germany in the first couple of years after the war, with the 'flood of people', as he puts it, beginning to abate in 1947.[3] Two conservative authorities on West Germany, Dennis Bark and David Gress, state that: 'By 1950 about 12 million expellees, as they were called, were living in various degrees of poverty in the Federal Republic.'[4] The US High Commissioner for Germany produced figures in 1950 suggesting that the native population of the area which became the Federal Republic of Germany was 38,167,600, while the number of refugees and expellees totalled 9,250,100 and the number of displaced persons was 248,900.[5] By 1961, an additional 3 million or so people had left the GDR for West Germany. Many of the early refugees had fled from their homelands in the closing months of the War as the Red Army closed in. The large number of 'expellees' were subsequently forcibly expelled from areas which were taken over by the Soviet Union and Poland following the cessation of hostilities; others fled westwards from the Soviet Zone of Occupation, which in 1949 became the German Democratic Republic, while it was still possible to escape prior to the building of the Berlin Wall in 1961.[6]

This massive population migration was accompanied by a very high degree of personal trauma and tragedy at the time, and undertaken under very much less than optimal social and economic conditions.[7] The devastated landscape of defeated Germany, with the ruined skylines of bombed towns and cities, the lack of adequate food, shelter, or communications, hardly constituted ideal conditions in which millions of homeless people possessing at most a cartload of personal possessions and suffering varying degrees of malnutrition, ill-health, and psychological disorientation could be integrated. The most remarkable feature of the post-war wave of population migration is perhaps the way in which the assimilation of these millions of post-war refugees in the compact territory of West Germany was accomplished with a degree of successful silence. Integration was so complete that there was little or no talk of being 'swamped', of 'floods' of migrants, of a 'foreigner problem' – largely because the concept of the ethnic German *Volk* readily encompassed those who often spoke in very different dialects and practised very different customs.

In the occupation period, there were in fact many tensions between refugees and native communities in western Germany. There were basic material conflicts over housing and food, as refugee families, often suffering from illness and exhaustion, had somehow to be accommodated and fed in conditions of acute housing shortage and inadequate food supplies in the west.[8] In the harsh winter of 1946–7 there were very real fears that there would be mass famine in Germany: the Americans were sufficiently worried that they took to monitoring the average weights of Germans in their zone of occupation. Everywhere, the black market predominated, with cigarettes, chocolate and stockings becoming more coveted units of exchange than the official currency, while *hamstern* ('scouring the countryside for food') and *fringsen* ('illicitly stealing coal', named after Archbishop Frings, who suggested in a sermon that such stealing might not be entirely reprehensible in the circumstances) became prevalent and widely condoned practices, often far more remunerative than spending one's days in an ordinary job for worthless wages.[9]

In addition to the material strains in conditions of totally inadequate resources, there were cultural clashes between native and refugee populations. For centuries, the German lands of central Europe had been characterized by a wide degree of religious, cultural, social, linguistic, political and economic diversity. The 'Holy Roman Empire of the German Nation' was a very loose framework for an extraordinarily rich variety of patchwork states. Following the religious and political strife unleashed by the sixteenth-century Reformation, and the ensuing conflicts of the Thirty Years War (1618–48), the Peace of Westphalia (1648) essentially enshrined an agreement to differ. The political map of 1648 left its traces in the religious and cultural patterns of different regions of German-speaking central Europe right into the mid-twentieth century.[10] But the population movements unleashed by Hitler's war dramatically altered all this. After 1945, communities which for centuries had spoken their own regional dialects and engaged in relatively uniform religious practices (whether Catholic or some variant of Protestantism) suddenly found themselves exposed to the effective invasion of wholly different cultures. The 'traditional' homogenous local community became a myth of the past in what rapidly became a far more diverse and mobile society.

One might have grounds for thinking that, under the constrained material circumstances, the attempt to integrate millions of migrants from different geographical and cultural backgrounds was doomed to fail. Conflicts over scarce resources, combined with cultural tensions between people barely able to understand each other's dialects and lifestyles, should have led, on most models, to inevitable mutual hostility. Yet this was, after the early period, not the case. Within less than two decades, erstwhile refugees had become fully integrated into the new, materially successful and future-oriented society of West Germany.

The 'Equalization of Burdens Act' of 1952 made considerable (if inadequate) efforts at economic restitution to refugees and expellees. The political activities of the rather right-wing party representing this constituency, the *Bund der Heimatvertriebenen und Entrechteten* (BHE) (League of Refugees and Expellees), which scored considerable electoral success in Schleswig-Holstein in 1950, ensured the salience of refugees' concerns as a factor on the conservative political agenda; by the later 1950s, their views and votes had been largely absorbed by the ruling conservative party, Chancellor Konrad Adenauer's CDU. The process of cultural assimilation was overlain by changing social and cultural currents and a more open, cosmopolitan atmosphere in the era of the 'Americanization' of West Germany. Regional and local diversity was exposed to a degree of national and international homogenization, through the growth of communications – autobahns, expanding car ownership, increased cultural penetration by radio and television – and through the economic and political processes associated with emergent European integration. From being an initial drain on resources, the relatively cheap and mobile labour of often highly qualified and well-trained refugees became a component factor in the extraordinarily rapid economic growth – the 'economic miracle' – of the 1950s. By the 1960s, the increasingly affluent and mobile society of West Germany had successfully integrated migrants amounting to around one-fifth of its population.

How was this extraordinarily successful, yet virtually invisible, integration effected? First, no salient, let alone adverse, distinctions were made between 'Germans' from one place of origin rather than another. Whether born in Königsberg or Breslau, Danzig or Halle, 'German' migrants to the Bonn Republic became part of an ever more cosmopolitan and western-orientated consumer society that became the stereotypical face of 'Germany' to the western world. There were few, if any, visible differences between Germans of different areas of origin which could form the basis of continuing social and political discrimination; nor was there any desire to identify features which might form the basis for in-group and out-group formation. Cross-regional ties of class (the German aristocracy, the Junkers of yore), historical ties of experience and unexamined assumptions about the ethnic nation transcended any local and regional differences. Second, there was massive political will to welcome and absorb these migrants in the Cold War era, when the very flood of refugees itself served to confirm the black and white imagery of 'West is Best, Communism is Worst'. Third, and intimately associated with the first two points, the migrants enjoyed immediate political rights and status; their concerns were articulated in the formal political arena, their views were represented, and the government responded rapidly to demands and grievances that were perceived as entirely legitimate and justified. Fourth, although the immediate social and economic circumstances after the war were very severe, the 1950s saw impressive rates of economic growth in West Germany, averaging 8 per cent per year; in the circumstances of a rapidly growing economy, the growth of population was more readily absorbed and even beneficial.

Thus, for all the material frictions and local tensions between native populations and refugees in the early post-war period, there was at a wider level a shared set of assumptions about belonging together as members of a common nation. However politically discredited the concept of 'nation' might be, however impossible it was for Germans in the shadow of Auschwitz to express any sense of patriotism or admit to any easy sense of national identity, it nevertheless lived on as a very real if silent phenomenon in this unprecedented feat of population assimilation.

The same was not true of another, economically equally valuable, group of migrants to West Germany. Following the erection of the Berlin Wall, the supply of cheap refugee labour from the east dried up: at a time of continued labour shortage, the West German government sought instead to attract 'guest workers' (*Gastarbeiter*) from the southern regions of Europe. These foreign residents, in contrast to their 'German' predecessors, were never fully accepted as an integral part of a culturally diverse society. It was at first assumed that individual foreign workers would stay for a while, working for relatively low wages in often disagreeable and non-unionized conditions, would contribute their taxes without being any drain on the education or social security systems, and would eventually return to their countries of origin before becoming a burden by drawing a pension from the funds to which they had, as employees, contributed.[11] In the event, however – and quite predictably – many *Gastarbeiter* stayed and settled, married, had children and grandchildren. But the presence of those 'foreign' residents, for many of whom Germany was more home than the less familiar country from which their parents or grandparents had come, was never fully accepted by the majority of their German 'fellow-citizens' (*Mitbürger*) – a term which, however well-meant, was in any event a misnomer. With the growing economic recession following the oil crises of 1973 and 1979, the status of

Gastarbeiter became ever less welcome. In 1982, nearly two-thirds (62 per cent) of West Germans thought that there were 'too many foreigners' in West Germany; and 50 per cent of West Germans thought that 'foreigners' should be sent back to their countries of origin.[12]

In contrast to the earlier 'ethnic German' migrants to the Federal Republic, these migrants had not enjoyed automatic citizenship entitlement, nor the associated rights of political participation and representation. While it was not in principle impossible for *Gastarbeiter* to apply for and ultimately be granted citizenship, the constraints and hurdles were in practice very high.[13] Length of continuous residence and valid work permits, 'commitment' to German culture and mastery of the German language, possession of economic means and adequate domestic conditions (even requirements stipulating minimum floor area per family member) as well as lack of any record of infringements of the law were criteria which virtually none of the earlier refugees and expellees could have possibly hoped to meet. In addition, the lack of provision for dual nationality provided a further factor deterring applications from *Gastarbeiter* for German nationality. And while the 'German' refugees and expellees from Pomerania, Silesia, East Prussia and elsewhere were encouraged to maintain the customs of their provinces of origin in cultural associations which often played a powerful, if somewhat veiled, role in the conservative politics of the Federal Republic, the concept of multi-cultural integration without total assimilation appeared not to be a politically viable option for the *Gastarbeiter*.

In the west, the official notion that citizenship was effectively rooted in a homogenous ethnic and cultural community persisted. The notion of a *Volksgemeinschaft* as enshrined in the official definition of citizenship entitlement was a more lasting legacy of the Third Reich than many West German democrats who utterly abhorred the Nazi heritage might care to admit. Yet at the same time, any popular sense of common German identity was, ironically, declining. There was considerable evidence that, by the 1980s, younger generations of West Germans had little interest in or knowledge of the 'Germans' on the other side of the Wall. Reunification was viewed as an ever-receding chimera, a shibboleth to be repeated on certain occasions for purely political reasons but with little hope of realization in the foreseeable future. Those who raised seriously the issue of the lost homelands in the east were treated as beyond the acceptable political pale, while even the ethnic German 'resettlers' from the east who began once again to migrate to West Germany in larger numbers in the mid-1980s were treated to less of a welcoming reception than their predecessors of the late 1940s and 1950s.[14] There was a growing dissonance, in other words, between popular conceptions and official policies with respect to assumptions of citizenship or 'who belonged'. At the official level, the ethnic notion encompassed ethnic Germans in the east as well as those resident on West German soil, but did not extend to long-term 'foreign' residents of the Federal Republic; in popular conceptions, the assumption of ethnic homogeneity was overlain by an even more restrictive cultural notion, by the 1980s beginning to see even 'resettlers' from the east as 'not really German'. For all the difficulties over defining a West German identity, for all the spilt ink and public agonizing of the intellectuals, at grass roots a fairly robust notion of West German ('national'?) identity appeared to have developed, excluding not only long-term foreign residents but also ethnic Germans from further east. The full implications and social reality of an emergent West German identity only became fully apparent with the new tensions between *Ossis* and *Wessis* once they began to get to know each other better after the fall of the Wall in 1989.

THE EAST GERMAN *VOLK* AND THE NEW COMMUNIST CITIZEN?

If there was an emerging dissonance between popular and official conceptions in what was in reality a multicultural state in the west, in a rather different direction there was a comparable dissonance in the far more homogenous, mono-ethnic German Democratic Republic in the east. Despite official attempts from the early 1970s onwards to make a break with precisely the ethnic definition of German nationality espoused by the West German state and to create a sense of a new GDR nationality, the underlying assumption of a common German nation defined in ethnic terms proved remarkably resilient among the population. While tensions between East Germans and the very small minority of foreign workers present on East German soil seem to have been endemic throughout the existence of the GDR, undermining any alleged notion of the international solidarity of the working classes, the concept of one German nation remained very much alive among those forced to live on the wrong side of the Wall. *Wir sind ein Volk* became the rallying cry of many East Germans, once the Berlin Wall had been breached and the parameters of the

German question irreversibly changed in the winter of 1989–90. The assertion of common citizenship played a key role both in the collapse of communist rule in the GDR and in the rush to German unity the following year. Why was the attempt to develop a separate GDR nationality so unsuccessful? And how can the very real differences in identity between *Ossis* and *Wessis* be explained?

For the first twenty years of the GDR's existence, the SED (Socialist Unity Party, the ruling communist party) officially maintained the line that it was the West German imperialists who were obstructing any possibility of German reunification. Only with the process of western recognition conceded in Willy Brandt's *Ostpolitik* of the early 1970s did the official East German interpretation change. While the West Germans now formally recognized that there was 'one German nation in two German states', the SED view was that there were not only two states, but also two nations. Rejecting the ethnic theory of nation, the East German communists became proponents of a new 'class theory' of the nation. In contrast to the 'bourgeois nation' in the west, strenuous efforts were made by the SED in the 1970s to propagate new notions of a GDR national identity. With the somewhat more permeable inner-German border after the relaxations on communications and travel restrictions entailed by *Ostpolitik*, the GDR government adopted a policy of proactive cultural demarcation or *Abgrenzung*. The original constitution of the GDR had undergone major revision with a new constitution in 1968; this was again revised in 1974 to expunge references to 'German' and to emphasize the GDR's closeness to the USSR. At the same time, of course, there were official references to 'socialist internationalism'.

Such appeals seem to have had very little impact on the ground. For one thing, the West German consumerist democracy remained a permanent point of ultimate comparison for many East Germans, although the patterns of comparison were perhaps more realistic and differentiated than westerners used to like to believe. For example, East Germans realistically judged the GDR to guarantee more security of employment and basic social welfare, while considering the standard of living to be higher in the West.[15] East Germans were sharply aware of the Wall and the legacies of defeat, occupation and division in a way that younger generations of West Germans increasingly were not, or at least did not need to be. The 'national question' remained alive in the East in a manner quite incomparable to the West. Effectively imprisoned in their part of the country, prevented from travelling west and subject to constant, if often muted, political pressures at home, eking out a passable but hardly luxurious existence with long hours of work and little by way of long-term consumer goods or variety of foodstuffs, and yet able nightly to watch western television and see, if only in two-dimensional media refraction, what was attainable elsewhere, the East Germans could never entirely ignore the west. Even those East Germans who were ideologically committed to building socialism and who legitimized the shortcomings of the present as the necessary means to achieve Utopia in the future could not afford to ignore the west, for they knew it was the Achilles' heel of their uncomfortable political project. The paranoia of the East German leadership, even at the apparent height of its powers – as in the late summer of 1987, when Honecker made his official visit to the Federal Republic – was a constant factor in the forty-year history of the GDR. A sense of the ethnic unity of the German nation remained alive in the GDR in a way which was quite asymmetrical with that of the Federal Republic: an official position with ever-declining popular resonance in the west, it was officially rejected in the east but sustained among the people by the political pressures and material miseries of everyday life.

The relations between indigenous Germans and resident foreign populations was also rather different in the GDR. The GDR had, in comparison with West Germany, a relatively small population of foreign workers who lived in somewhat segregated conditions. In 1973 there were, on the GDR's own estimates, around 35,000 foreign workers from around sixty different countries in the GDR.[16] At the end of 1989, it was estimated by the West Germans that there were 59,000 Vietnamese workers, 15,100 Mozambicans and 8,000 Cubans resident in the GDR.[17] Most foreign workers lived in separate hostels, and the main contact with East Germans was only in the workplace.

Although there is as yet no definitive study of the relations between East Germans and foreign residents in the period 1949 to 1989, there is evidence to suggest that, for whatever combination of reasons, there were many incidents of hostility between native and foreign workers. The Executive Committee of the official trade union organisation, the FDGB, remarked explicitly that the 78 incidents (*Vorkommnisse*) reported to the national committee in 1972 and the 96 incidents reported in 1973 represented but the tip of an iceberg; in Karl-Marx-Stadt alone, the local FDGB organization knew of at least a hundred incidents. Among causes of tension, there were not only problems relating to work discipline, accidents, theft, drunkenness, but also 'chauvinism and nationalism among some GDR workers'.[18] According to the FDGB, the figures of 'incidents' involving foreign workers in the early 1980s were: 1980 – 206; 1981 – 205; 1982 – 115; 1983 – 96; 1984 – 63. The numbers of workers involved in each 'incident' are not given. In relation to the 63 incidents reported for 1984, the report laconically notes that 'these incidents primarily concern . . . accidents, sometimes with fatal consequences, physical arguments relating to excess alcohol consumption, and suicides.' In two of the 1984 'incidents', 123 Mozambicans went on strike.[19] Similar reference to misuse of alcohol is made in the report for 1983.[20]

Whatever interpretation one reads into these reports, it is clear that a relatively large proportion of the small numbers of foreign workers in the GDR were, year in year out, involved in unpleasant situations of one sort or another, sometimes relating to conflicts over wages, working conditions, or discipline, and sometimes relating to difficult relations with the East Germans alongside whom they were working. Furthermore, reports from SED local party organizations suggest that, in the broader sphere of attitudes generally, long-standing German prejudices against their Polish neighbours persisted too, despite their allegedly new brotherly relationships as fellow communist states. Such prejudices coloured East German reactions to major political flashpoints, such as the upheavals in Poland in 1956 or the Solidarity movement of 1980–1.[21] Whichever way one looks at the emerging evidence, it is clear that East Germans both had relatively little exposure to anything approaching a multi-cultural society, and retained a very strong sense of an ethnic German nation.

In the 1980s there was a remarkable attempt on the part of the regime to reappropriate the German cultural heritage for the communist regime in the GDR, with the political rehabilitation of erstwhile historical villains such as Martin Luther or Frederick the Great. Such historical re-evaluations were part of a manipulative attempt to gain the emotional identification of the people with the GDR as not only their ethnic/cultural homeland but also the political culmination of the successive stages of history. While this may indeed have struck some chord with the people, it was not sufficient to overcome other serious problems concerning their identification with the regime: rising economic problems, ever more apparent environmental damage and destruction, the space for explicit dissent provided by the church/ state agreement of March 1978, all combined to produce a situation of heightened lability, accentuated (although not occasioned) by Mikhail Gorbachev's accession to power in the Soviet Union in 1985.

It was at the same time a major goal of the SED state to gain not only the pragmatic and partial recognition which they had won from the west in the early 1970s, but also full recognition of their citizenship and the renunciation of the West German claim to speak for all Germans. For all the tentative moves towards greater recognition in the course of the 1980s – the loan and credit agreements, the western visit of Honecker, the joint SPD-SED paper – this goal was never realized. The West German claim to represent all Germans remained a sticking point from which Chancellor Kohl's conservative government refused to budge. Had the SED been successful in this key strategy with respect to the mutual recognition of separate citizenship, an independent East German state might have been much more viable: the dramatic surge of westwards migration in 1989–90 would not have been so great, nor the political challenge to the legitimacy of communism and the economic undermining of its material foundations so effective, and the pressures on West Germany to respond would have been much less. Without the West German claim to common citizenship, in other words, the history of the GDR would have been very different. Had there been mutual recognition of two German citizenships, there might still be two German states.

TWO – OR MORE – NATIONS IN ONE STATE? CITIZENSHIP, NATIONALITY AND MIGRATION IN GERMANY SINCE UNIFICATION

A 'nation' is, as many commentators have pointed out, essentially an invention. It is a social construct, an imaginary community, which is both created by and sustained through a combination of conditions. When East and West Germans finally met, they were somewhat surprised at the differences that had emerged in terms of assumptions, attitudes, social profiles and patterns of behaviour over forty years of separation.[22]

The tensions between *Ossis* and *Wessis* – which gave rise to so many caricatures in the immediate months after the fall of the Wall – relate of course not only to the very real differences which had emerged in characteristic modes of being in the world under the preceding political conditions, but also to the new tensions and strains consequent on the unprecedented historical experiment of extraordinarily rapid social and economic restructuring in the east. Effectively colonized by the pattern of takeover by the west, people in the 'new eastern Länder' found themselves exposed to massive upheavals and existential uncertainties, overlain by political recriminations in the era of 'de-stasification'; while many West Germans grumbled that their comfortable, affluent society was, for the first time in many years, more at risk of recession, inflation, and increased taxes than they had initially been led to believe by the ever-ebullient 'unification Chancellor', Helmut Kohl.

At the same time, the fall of the Iron Curtain, the collapse of communism elsewhere in eastern Europe, and the break-up of Yugoslavia, led to further massive changes and population migration challenging the certainties of the previous four decades of frozen stasis in central Europe. Along with the influx of asylum-seekers and migrants came rising numbers of racial attacks and incidents of right-wing violence in Germany. In these circumstances, the whole issue of citizenship and nationality could not help but be pushed to the forefront of the explicit political agenda – although, from the perspective of many, the (West) German political leadership was remarkably slow to rise to the challenge, let alone be open to any far-reaching conclusions with respect to a fundamental rethinking of what it might mean to be 'German' in the new Europe. The German government effectively continued to cling, with limited and grudging concessions, to the old ethnic concept of German citizenship.

The German lands of central Europe have always constituted an area of population movement, from the great eastwards migrations and settlement of the mediaeval period onwards.[23] While German settlers went east, the heartlands of Germany often benefited from the inward migration of foreign labour, ranging from seasonal migration of agricultural labour in border areas to the more permanent influx of Poles to the Ruhr at a time of rapid industrialization. The foreign labour system of the Third Reich (in so far as it was not an integral part of Nazi policies of racial extermination) was clearly distinctive in the degree of coercion, exploitation and degradation of foreign workers, but the mere presence of foreign labour as an integral part of the German economy was in itself nothing new. Under rather more benign auspices, the *Gastarbeiter* from the 1960s onwards formed part of this long history of migration.

Yet the myth of the ethnically homogenous nation state remained. In contrast to states such as France or the USA, where the concept of 'nation' is an essentially populist concept constructed from a set of ideals to which 'the people' assent, and citizenship is a status which can be attained by birth rather than blood-right, the West German state adhered – both despite and in part because of the legacy of

Hitler, at least as far as the post-1945 settlement was concerned – to a peculiarly ethnic concept of nation. Because of the destruction of their territorial integrity, the West Germans retained what was in effect a notion of a *'Volksgemeinschaft'*: a homogenous, ethnically and culturally defined community, or a nation consisting of those with common ethnic origins, common language and culture. To state explicitly this underlying continuity in assumptions across the 'zero hour' of 1945 may be found disagreeable by undoubtedly sincere proponents of West German democracy; it is nevertheless true, and has been reiterated on numerous occasions since the unification of East and West Germany in 1990.

In March 1993, in the context of the heightened political debate about asylum-seekers, Wolfgang Schäuble, CDU fraction leader and right-hand man of Chancellor Kohl, asserted that 'We gain our identity, not from commitment to an idea, but from belonging to a particular *Volk*'.[24] And, in an accommodating response to the growth of right-wing parties threatening to draw away crucial marginal voters among the conservative electorate, Chancellor Kohl continued to emphasize in the run-up to the 1994 election that 'we are not a country of immigration'. What he meant, of course, was that the Federal Republic of Germany was not a country whose government, in the early 1990s, was prepared to countenance any shift towards a more multicultural notion of citizenship.

The immediate problem for the German government, following the collapse of the Iron Curtain in 1989–90, was the influx of political asylum-seekers from the ever more chaotic conditions of eastern and particularly south-eastern Europe, as well as elsewhere. The Basic Law had not only enshrined an ethnic definition of citizenship; in Article 16 it had also sought in some measure, however limited, to atone for aspects of Hitler's racism by uniquely generous asylum policies. This double legacy of the Third Reich meant, therefore, that while it was extremely hard to acquire rights of citizenship and political representation, it was conversely relatively easy to enter Germany as a refugee seeking political asylum. In the immediate aftermath of the upheavals associated with the collapse of communism and the break-up of Yugoslavia, hundreds of thousands entered Germany through the newly opened borders to the East. Between 1989 and 1992 a total of around 1 million arrived in Germany seeking asylum.[25] In addition, between 1989 and 1992 1.2 million ethnic Germans entered the Federal Republic.[26]

With rising racial hostility, and attacks on asylum-seekers' hostels,

101

a particular focus of right-wing extremism, as well as other incidents of racist violence directed against *Gastarbeiter*, Jews, and other targets of extremist hostility, the Government's response was double-edged. On the one hand, the government condemned right-wing violence and extremism as utterly reprehensible but, on the other, it also effectively conceded that the 'problem' was 'too many foreigners'. In May 1993, with the consent of the opposition parties, the asylum laws were amended to restrict entry and withhold the right to asylum from those who were seeking to enter the Federal Republic from all EU states and from 'safe third countries' with borders neighbouring Germany, thus effectively closing the doors to asylum-seekers by land routes on all sides.

While the generous entitlement to asylum was tightened up and restricted, apparent concessions were being made with respect to citizenship laws. In July 1993, restrictions limiting applications for naturalization were slightly eased: those aged between sixteen and twenty-three who had been legally resident in the country for at least eight years, had attended school in Germany for at least six years, who were prepared to give up their current citizenship and who had not been convicted of a major felony were entitled to apply for naturalization. Foreigners aged over 23 were entitled to apply if they had lived in Germany for at least fifteen years, were prepared to give up current citizenship, had not been convicted of a major felony and were able to support themselves and their families. Yet the implicitly ethnic notion of the German nation was merely underlined when, in the wake of the General Election of 1994, faced with a very narrow margin of electoral success, the CDU/CSU and FDP agreed a further amendment to the citizenship laws. A new notion was introduced under the curious linguistic formulation of '*Staatszugehörigkeit*', in contrast to the more usual concept of '*Staatsangehörigkeit*'. Under this new 'relaxation' of citizenship regulations, a third generation 'immigrant' child born in Germany and at least one of whose 'foreign' parents must also have been both born in Germany and resident in Germany for at least ten years, was to be entitled to this hybrid status as, effectively, a cuckoo in the German nest, until the age of 18 when a choice would have to be made between fully fledged German citizenship or the citizenship of the country of origin of the grandparents' generation.

Thus, for three generations of the presence of 'foreigners' as 'guest workers' on German soil, very little had changed. If they were not prepared to renounce distinctive cultural heritages and affirm full commitment to a 'Germanic' culture, if they had inadequate living conditions or unstable economic circumstances, they could not apply for citizenship. Permanent residents had no entitlement to vote in national elections, could neither stand as representatives themselves nor exert pressures on elected politicians. The latter had more of an eye to the demands of popular right-wing prejudices, when crucial votes might be lost to more extreme parties of the far right if concessions to an implicitly and sometimes explicitly nationalist sentiment were not made. The attempt to preserve the homogenous German *Volk* across the Cold War division of the German state had served to consolidate the ethnic assumptions and nationalist legacies, however dormant, of the past.

The 1990s pose new questions for the Germans, however. The Cold War is over; the processes of western European integration which had accompanied it have at the same time fostered new population movements within the EU. Anomalies between the voting rights of citizens of other EU states resident in Germany and those of long-term 'foreign' workers living in Germany have led to new demands for comparable rights for *Gastarbeiter*.[27]

Moreover, the rise of racist violence and neo-Nazi attacks – not only in Germany, but across Europe – have led to closer scrutiny of the importance of political representation for the protection of minority rights. The united Germany of the 1990s, having achieved arguably the closest it has ever come to being a 'nation state' – something of a mirage or chimera for the Germanic peoples in central Europe across the ages – must now seriously ask whether the concept of a putative German 'national identity' should not be divorced from that of citizenship entitlement and associated rights of political representation and participation. The protection of different cultural heritages – including of course the 'Germanic heritage' – should be seen as a realizable goal in what should finally be recognized as a persistent and long-term condition of cultural diversity. If the German *Volk* were prepared formally to recognize that Germany is not only – and never has been only – 'for the Germans', then the legacies of the past could, perhaps, be finally laid to rest.

NOTES

1 '*Volk*' is an extraordinarily difficult word to translate, because there is no exact equivalent in English. It does not imply 'folk' in the rather whimsical sense of the English word, but rather embodies a bundle of ethnic

and cultural features together. The Germans clearly have a sense of a really existing ethnic and cultural entity where the British do not.

2 When this is raised explicitly and in a critical fashion, a common official response of Germans is that it is quite comparable to the Jewish notion of a common, enduring Jewish identity wherever Jews may find themselves scattered across the world, and that the most racial definition of citizenship entitlement anywhere is to be found in the state of Israel. The subsequent discussion can easily become, for obvious reasons, more emotional than rational.

3 Volker Berghahn, *Modern Germany* (Cambridge: Cambridge University Press, 2nd edn., 1987), p. 177.

4 Dennis Bark and David Gress, *A History of West Germany, vol 1: From Shadow to Substance* (Oxford: Basil Blackwell, 1989), p. 305.

5 The map representing the geographical origins of these population movements is reprinted in ibid., p. 306.

6 For a quasi-biographical account, see for example: Christian von Krockow, *The Hour of the Women* (London: Faber and Faber, transl. Krishna Winston, 1992; orig. 1988).

7 For useful commentaries and selections of documents giving insights into the social, economic and political character of early post-war Germany, see for example Christoph Kleßmann, *Die doppelte Staatsgründung*, (Göttingen: Vandenhoek and Ruprecht, 1982).

8 See for example Rainer Schulze, 'Growing Discontent: Relations between the Native and Refugee Populations in a Rural District in Western Germany after the Second World War', *German History* 7 (3), Dec. 1989, pp. 332–49.

9 See the more general discussion in Mary Fulbrook, *The Divided Nation: Germany 1918–1990* (London: Fontana, 1991), ch. 6.

10 For a brief overview of these longer-term patterns of German history, see Mary Fulbrook, *A Concise History of Germany* (Cambridge: Cambridge University Press, 1990).

11 For a by now classic journalistic account of exploitation as a *Gastarbeiter*, see Günter Wallraff, *Ganz Unten* (Köln: Kiepenheuer and Witsch, 1985).

12 Figures cited in Nora Rätsel, 'Germany: one race, one nation?', *Race and Class* 32 (3) (1991): 31–48, p 38.

13 In 1991, only 27,295 persons without an ethnic claim to nationality were in fact naturalized. Given the hurdles, and the requirement of renunciation of one's previous cultural heritage and nationality, very few even sought to apply.

14 Between 1968 and 1984 a total of 652,897 persons in this category 'resettled' in West Germany; in 1985 the figure was 38,968; in 1990, with the opening of borders, it jumped to 397,073 and in 1991 it was 221,995. Press Release of the Embassy of the Federal Republic of Germany, 11 August 1994, p 6.

15 For SED opinion surveys, see for example: IfGA, ZPA, IV B 2/2.023/51, Institut für Meinungsforschung beim ZK der SED, 'Bericht über eine Umfrage zu einigen Fragen der sozialistischen Landwirtschaft (Bereich Tierproduktion)' 27.2.76 and 24.5.77; IfGA, ZPA, IV B 2/2.028/40, 'Bericht über eine Umfrage zum gesellschaftlichen Leben und zur Arbeit der

Nationalen Front in den Wohngebieten', 7.7.76. For further details on popular opinion in the GDR, see Mary Fulbrook, *Anatomy of a Dictatorship: Inside the GDR* (Oxford: Oxford University Press, 1995).

16 FDGB, Bundesvorstand, Büro Präsidium, 3023: 'Analyse über besondere Vorkommnisse 1973', p 11.
17 Report from the Embassy of the Federal Republic of Germany, 92/94, August 11, 1994, p 5.
18 FDGB, 207.3023, 'Analyse über besondere Vorkommnisse 1973', pp. 11–12.
19 FDGB, 201.5414, 'Information über vorliegende besondere Vorkommnisse im Jahre 1984'. 13.3.1985, pp. 5, 9.
20 FDGB, 'Information über die uns vorliegenden besonderen Vorkommnisse im Jahr 1983', VVS B 401/1 – 04/84, p. 5.
21 For further details, see Fulbrook, *Anatomy of a Dictatorship*.
22 See Mary Fulbrook, ' "Wir sind ein Volk"? Reflections on German unification', *Parliamentary Affairs*, 44, July 1991, pp. 125–40.
23 For the changing boundaries of 'Germany' through the centuries, see Fulbrook, *A Concise History of Germany*.
24 *Der Spiegel*, 47(11) 15 March 1993, p. 53.
25 The numbers of asylum-seekers by year are as follows: 1988 – 103,076; 1989 – 121,318; 1990 – 193,063; 1991 – 256,112; 1992 – 438,191; 1993 – 322,842. In 1992, Germany was the destination of 75 per cent of those seeking asylum in countries of the European Union. The two largest groups in 1993 were asylum-seekers from Romania and the rump Yugoslavia. Figures given in a Press Release of the Embassy of the Federal Republic of Germany, 11 August 1994.
26 Figures taken from a Press Release of the Embassy of the Federal Republic of Germany, February 1993.
27 See the example of the two cousins resident in Paris and Frankfurt, given in Patrick Weil's article, above, p. 85. At a meeting in Weimar in April 1993 of officials concerned with immigration matters, Frau Cornelia Schmalz-Jacobsen, the then Federal Commissioner for Foreigners' Affairs, argued that the 6.5 million 'foreign residents' in Germany should have comparable voting rights in local elections to migrant workers from EU countries such as Spain or Portugal. Report from the Embassy of the Federal Republic of Germany, Labour and Social Affairs, 64/93, no. 4/93, p 4.

7

ITALY BETWEEN EMIGRATION AND IMMIGRATION AND THE PROBLEMS OF CITIZENSHIP

Enrico Pugliese

INTRODUCTION

This chapter on the Italian situation will deal initially with the ways in which problems concerning citizenship in Italy are nowadays treated in the context of immigration. It will then deal with the history of migrations which affected Italy, and concentrate on the features of the present immigration flow. It will end by analysing recent migration policies and their implications concerning citizenship.

When talking about immigration in a given country, the citizenship issue can be addressed either in strictly legal terms (as a set of conditions and constraints for the acquisition or the maintenance of the right to be a citizen of a state) or in social terms as the possibility of enjoying all the rights, social and economic, envisaged in citizenship. Both aspects are important in this, and they are closely interrelated. The conditions for the acquisition and the maintenance of citizenship represent a topical issue of great importance in all European countries. It is obviously the more urgent the larger the number of people it affects, that is to say those seeking or applying for citizenship.

It is well known that in this field policies vary from one country to the next, but as the migration flow has increased (or there is an increase of migration pressure) there is a tendency, in the wealthiest countries, to restrict the conditions of entry, residence and eventually of citizenship (Adinolfi 1992; Collinson 1993). However, apart from a greater strictness and limitations that can be noticed on the whole front, some basic motives and requirements for citizenship can be identified. The *jus sanguinis*, or right by descendence, is still the main factor in Germany, whilst the *jus soli*, or right by birth in a country, is the basic principle in France, as well as in the United States of America. Obviously the possibility of awarding citizenship to those born in a country, regardless of their parents' nationality, represents a wider opening to the extension of citizenship. France has certainly been more open than other European countries to the immigration of people of different origin and ethnicity. In the United States, a country of immigrants, the right to citizenship for those born on American soil has continued also after the restrictions on entry. Both principles (the right of blood, and the right of the soil) can of course be applied with greater or less rigour. It is not by chance that in Europe there are limitations also on rights already acquired: for example, in France one can quote the case of those French people, born in France, but of Algerian origin. Originally they were citizens *tout court*, but now they have to reapply for citizenship when they are 18.

One should take into account the other criterion of access to citizenship in a legal sense, represented by residence in a country. But obviously in this case it is not a right automatically applied, and the level of discretion of those in charge of migratory policy is much higher. However important these issues are from a political viewpoint, they have not had and do not appear to have, in Italy, the importance they have in other developed European countries, such as Germany, France or Britain. One can easily understand the reasons for this situation, because Italy has always been historically a country of emigration: a provider of labour, rather than a receiver. The citizenship issue, like the one relating to the right of residence, affected Italians emigrating abroad. There has always been an immigration of foreigners to Italy, but in the past this used to have a molecular character, i.e., it affected a small number of people, whilst emigration was, especially in certain periods, a mass phenomenon affecting thousands of people every year. Moreover, there was also a class difference between the individuals involved in the respective flows. Italian emigrants belonged to the lower social classes, above all farm labourers, first from the north and then from the south, who represented the core of Italian emigration. The immigrants belonged to all social classes with a clear predominance of upper and middle classes. Even after political and military events which brought about changes in the borders and in population movements, the citizenship issue has not represented a big problem or a topic of discussion in Italy. There has been, on certain occasions, a problem of political or 'ethnic' refugees, but this never took the proportions it had in other European countries.

In conclusion: historically there have been few non-Italians who needed Italian citizenship. On the other hand there have been few non-Italian people resident or destined to settle permanently in Italy. Therefore the number of people seeking Italian citizenship has always been small. Even now, although the inflow of foreigners into Italy is considerable and Italy has taken on the features of an immigration country, the number of people seeking Italian citizenship is very small. One should, however, take into account that this last fact might be due to the great difficulties in obtaining Italian citizenship.

ITALY: A COUNTRY OF IMMIGRATION

Attention to the question of citizenship was brought by immigration itself, that is from the fact that there has been a significant influx of people looking for jobs and accommodation in Italy. The 1970s was a decade of great changes in Europe in the field of immigration. Countries which, up to a few years earlier, had only experienced emigration, were becoming immigration countries. Greece, Spain, Italy and, with numerous local qualifications, Portugal started to become the target of workers coming from countries of the southern Mediterranean shores and from even more distant areas (King 1990; Rocha-Trinidade 1993; Frey, 1991). Initially, male workers came to Italy from Morocco and Tunisia and later male and female workers came from other African countries. There were women from the Philippines or from the Green Cape islands. There are now also people from eastern European countries, mainly Poland.

It has not always been easy to keep track of these people in the statistics. The institutional statistical data gathered directly by the Central Italian Institute of Statistics (ISTAT) initially recorded ridiculously low numbers of nationals from Third World countries. Conversely – and this is still the case – the presence of Europeans and of foreigners coming from developed countries is recorded much more accurately. This very lack of statistical information is meaningful: since Third World immigrants live in a highly precarious way, it is difficult to collect systematic information about their situation. The only sources which could record their presence at mass level are police records. Residence permits are in fact issued by the Home Office – and at a local level (*Provincia* or 'district') by the Questura, the main Police office. The lists of residence permits can reveal the number of people living in Italy in a non-clandestine way (Birindelli and Bonifazi 1993; Natale, 1990). The only reliable information from other official statistics concerns citizens from developed countries, in particular from Europe. More recently, because of an increase in clandestine settlers, even police records are no longer reliable. Connected with this particular problem, which is only superficially neutral since it relates only to statistics, there is a series of misunderstandings concerning the extent and the quality of immigration. When immigrants are discussed in newspapers, or in political and scientific circles, one specific component of the foreign population is meant: immigrants from Third World countries. The great national debate, whether centred on the fear of an invasion or, in a more positive vein, on multicultural opening and on acceptance, has taken place with reference to such immigrants. But whilst most discussions concerning immigration deal with this specific group of foreigners, the figures mentioned are the ones for the whole foreign population, and this can only cause confusion. It is therefore necessary to distinguish two separate processes which help the increase of the foreign population in the national territory: the one due to the new role of Italy as a country of immigration (receiving labour from poorer countries) and the other due to the intensification of commercial, economic and cultural exchanges among different countries. The number of foreigners in Italy has therefore increased.

Another foreign component which has nothing to do with the immigration flow but is carefully recorded – in population censuses for example – consists of people who owe their 'foreign' nationality to having been born abroad of Italian parents. This concerns American citizens, in particular from South American states. It is a realistic hypothesis that the latter represent a kind of long-term return migration. Therefore the migration flows which affect Italy are various and have changed in time. The greatest novelty is that Italy, like other countries in southern Europe, after being a supplier of labour for a long time – i.e. a country of emigration – is becoming more and more a country of immigration as well – even with the rigorous policies of closure that we shall discuss. This fact that Italy is now a country of immigration does not exclude either the existence of large Italian communities abroad or the possibility that there may be still people leaving, although the migration balance is near zero or occasionally positive. But at present the fairly limited number of

109

emigrants is offset by a similarly limited, or occasionally slightly higher number of people returning.

ITALIAN EMIGRATION AND ITS DEVELOPMENT

Because of the interrelation between emigration and immigration it is useful to refer to Italian emigration abroad. As is well known, there have been two great migration waves from Italy: the first at the end of the nineteenth and beginning of the twentieth century whose main destinations were across the Atlantic Ocean, and the second in the golden era of the welfare state, during the period of Fordist industrial development, towards the more developed areas of Europe (Calvanese 1983; Reyneri 1980). To these two great economic migrations from Italy one should add smaller migrations, like the one towards Latin America in the period after the Second World War and other small movements into Italy made mainly by refugees in the Second World War. These were Italian nationals or people who identified themselves as Italians, whose movement was rather less significant than that in other European countries. Generally, writers on Italian migration have not dealt with the movements of these people in an extensive way, but they are important for the implications they have had on the citizenship issue.

We must also mention the substantial internal migration within Italy from the south to the north, which took place at the same time as the great emigration to Europe and continued with considerable intensity also during the 1970s, when the international movement had radically decreased. In both cases the balance was near zero. The virtually zero internal migratory balance is not due to the lack of people leaving or returning but rather to the parity between the number of people moving in both directions, even if both figures are now very small.

The main migratory flows affecting Italy have been outward-going. It was only in the 1970s that numbers of foreigners, not of Italian origin, started to come to Italy intending to settle there for a period of time.

Let us return to the main Italian emigrations and look at their basic features.

The 'great emigration'

The first emigration, at the turn of the century, has had an unparalleled impact in Italy. It was interrupted by a series of internal and external political circumstances. As far as the internal ones are concerned, the population policy of fascism and its ideology of ruralization must be mentioned. The increasingly heavy demographic pressure forced migration to the colonies on the basis of the ideology of the 'great and proletarian nation'. As far as external reasons are concerned, serious problems began with the introduction of the quota system in the United States and the effective closure of the channel to the States, with the exception of family reunions. The standard image of this great migration is that of a one-way process: a great final departure involving millions of people. As a matter of fact, although millions have settled permanently across the Atlantic, the large number of temporary and permanent returns that took place in this migratory wave was also quite impressive. Every year the enormous number of people leaving was counterbalanced by a slightly smaller number of people returning. Yet these were not, in the main, permanent returns.

The effects of this great emigration on the social and economic structure of the most affected regions were substantial, for example the erosion of large land ownership and the increase of small peasant farms (Rossi-Doria 1983). However, in the long run, the social, cultural and political implications were reduced because of the relatively sudden stopping of the flow in the 1920s. The transformation process, which had started with the emigration, came to a standstill as soon as the migratory flow ceased. The effects of the end of the migratory flow were made more serious by the social and political situation determined by the fascist regime. Rather than mass social transformations there were some considerable individual instances of social mobility. Some people did change status as individuals, but within a social structure hardly affected by changes.

We should add that there was a new migratory wave, mainly to South America and Australia, at the end of the Second World War. This is important because it caused problems of return immigration and of citizenship in a very broad sense. This concerns the Italian population in Argentina in particular (but it affects many other emigrants in Latin America). On the one hand there is the request to enjoy the Italian national social pension in the country of residence (Argentina in this case), on the other a tendency to obtain or

111

re-obtain Italian political citizenship, mainly with a view to returning to Italy to look for a job (Macioti and Pugliese, 1991).

Inter-European industrial migrations in the golden age of welfare capitalism

The last substantial mass departures towards countries across the Atlantic took place in the early 1950s. From that moment onwards Italian emigration was directed towards European countries, mainly Switzerland and Germany. In the case of the latter country this was a migratory process dominated mainly by industrial events: the immigration specific to industrial societies. As industrial production and employment requirements in industry grew, so did the number of foreign workers employed, in so far as the local supply of labour was not sufficient to satisfy the demand. Italy was the first country to contribute to a significant extent to the migratory flow, favoured in the early period by the fact of being – like Germany (importer country *par excellence*) – a member of the European Economic Community.

In the past decades scholars have devoted most of their attention to the immigration model of fully developed industrial countries (Boehning 1984; Castles and Kosack 1973). This is also the model around which interpretative attempts have been made concerning the position of immigrants (of the various immigrant waves in fact) in the employment and social structure of the destination countries. While the economy and the industrial production expand, local workers (and later the first waves of immigrants) go up in their socio-professional position, leaving the less sought after jobs to the latest arrivals. The latter obviously find in great part (even if not exclusively) work in industry, which is the productive area of greater expansion and expresses the greatest demand for labour. The productive model in this phase of development of industrial societies is based on Fordist and Taylorist principles. Without going into details which would not be relevant to citizenship, we could say that the Taylorist aspect of this model lies in the growing simplicity of the tasks performed in the factory, allowing the employment of workers with very low socialization and low skills in a short time. Therefore even immigrants recently arrived from rural areas can be employed in this way. The Fordist aspect lies in the fact that the tasks are generally highly paid, guaranteed in turn by trade union representatives on the shop floor. Another feature of this type of

112

employment is its effective stability, in contrast with the type of work which Third World immigrants tend to do now. Occupational stability, corresponding to settlement stability and therefore to a greater stability in social relations in the destination country, used to characterize the experience of emigrants (from an Italian point of view) or immigrants (from a German point of view) at the time of the great industrial migrations up to the 1970s.

At this point an important observation needs to be made. Germany used to define itself as a non-immigration country even when it received over 1 million foreign workers per annum. This was in line with the traditional principles underpinning Germany's immigration and citizenship policy based on the preference, according to the *Deutsche Bevölkerung*, awarded to people of German origin.[1] The immigration model chosen by Germany was the so-called rotating model. This meant that there was not going to be a permanent transfer of foreign immigrants (and of their families), but only a prolonged stay. At first this fitted in well with the migration project of Italian workers. They also did not foresee a permanent transfer. Moreover, the hope to return is generally widespread among first-generation immigrants. The German migration policy and the illusions of Italian workers have brought about a situation characterized by the absence of realistic projects and by the impossibility of planning for the future (in terms of returns or transfers). The workers hoped to be able to end their emigration when they were no longer needed. Rarely did the notion of a permanent transfer occur to them even when their stay in Germany – with longer or shorter interruptions – lasted for decades. This explains why the number of annual departures, like that of annual returns, has been very high – much higher than that concerning trans-oceanic migration. From the mid-1950s, and through most of the 1960s, 300,000 to 400,000 workers left Italy each year and slightly fewer (not less than two-thirds) returned. The rotation model was implemented on a large scale. This did not prevent a small minority from settling permanently in Germany. These workers formed one of the notable colonies of Italian workers abroad. It is for this reason that, although Italy has become an immigration country it continues being an emigration country as well. It is not by chance that two conferences took place in Italy within a year: the National Conference on Emigration (June 1989), and the National Conference on Immigration in June 1990 (Macioti and Pugliese, 1990).

ITALIAN IMMIGRATION

We can now turn our attention to immigration. Because it commenced during the 1970s, when the development model based on the large industrial concern started its crisis, as a result Italian immigration has new features with regard to the position of immigrants in the labour market. In conjunction with a reduction in industrial employment in large-scale firms, there is an expansion of employment in the secondary labour market (Piore 1979; Pugliese 1993). There is, in other words, a demand for precarious work: temporary and unprotected by the trade unions. Moreover additional employment opportunities concentrate in tertiary activities, above all in the service sector. Immigrants are no longer – as was the case in the great inter-European migrations – workers destined to a regular employment in industry, but workers precariously employed in various sectors, mostly in the informal economy.

It should be stressed that this new immigration model does not concern only the countries of new immigration like Italy. The expansion of the secondary labour market and the prevalent position of immigrants concerns also countries of traditional immigration: new employment prospects of immigrants are everywhere, above all in tertiary activities, frequently with low productivity and characterized by low wages and instability. This position of immigrants in the labour market has certain implications for the problems connected with citizenship. There is in fact instability as far as residence and the relationship with the local environment are concerned, together with potential instability in employment. As far as Italy is concerned there are differences between north and south, since it is less difficult in the north to find stable employment. In the south, instead, peddling and seasonal agricultural work continue to be particularly important (Frey 1991; Mottura 1992).

We are now facing a post-industrial immigration, in a two-fold sense: only a small number of immigrants finds employment in the industrial sector and the great integration institutions typical of industrial societies, in particular the trade unions, have by necessity a much reduced role. Another significant difference between present-day immigration in Italy (and the new migrations generally) and the preceding ones lies in the fact that present-day immigration is characterized by a very high number of immigrant nationalities. While in the 1950s, 1960s and 1970s immigration to Germany was made up of three or four main nationalities, all belonging to southern Europe (in addition to Turkey), at present the number of nationalities in Italian immigration is very high and is made up of people from all over the world. The high number of nationalities brings a high variety in the migratory project (Mottura 1992). The very socio-demographic composition of migration, which is so diverse, is an expression of the wide varieties of migration models and projects. The migratory model of a nationality (or a group of nationalities) is the outcome of the migratory project and its impact on the social and economic situation of the receiving country, and of its migration policy. The occupational location, the length of the migratory experience, the degree of stability, the presence or absence of the family and the type of migratory chain account for the character of the various migratory models. There is also a complication represented by the fact that immigrants have different positions within the various regions of Italy.

However, we can synthesize the main features of the immigrants' condition in Italy as follows (Amaturo and Morlicchio 1989):

(*a*) With reference to the labour market, immigrants are present in all areas of domestic work (above all in large metropolitan centres). This takes in a large quota of female occupations. Immigrants are also employed in seasonal work: agriculture, affecting tens of thousands of people, above all in the developing areas of the south, and services (catering and, to a lesser extent, hotels). Finally there is also a small, rather reduced presence in industry, concentrated mainly in northern regions.

(*b*) With reference to the ethnic and national composition of immigrants, besides the Mediterranean nationalities (Moroccans and Tunisians) there are Filipinos, who represent the third largest group. Among the larger groups there are people from Senegal, China, ex-Yugoslavia, Albania; among the middle-sized groups there are people from Bengal, Sri Lanka, Egypt, Eritrea, Somalia, Ghana, Nigeria, Green Cape, Poland and others whose numbers are difficult to estimate. There are also a great many other nationalities with a virtually insignificant presence. Each group has its own specific migration model, and it shows a strong correlation between country of origin, demographic composition of the migration flow and employment. Maghrebis are mainly male and are frequently pedlars, although many of them work in agriculture, which, especially in Sicily, also represents the main occupation for Tunisians. Filipinos, who were mostly female immigrants originally, are predominantly employed in domestic work. The 'ethnic' business (not only in restaurants but also in some industrial sectors like leather work) is typical of Chinese immigrants, who are a notable and expanding component (Carchedi 1995).

To conclude, we should add that the respective ethnic composition and nationalities tend to change: some groups, like those coming from Eritrea, Green Cape, San Salvador and Iran, who had a substantial presence and represented some of the main groups in the first phase of immigration (up to the mid-1980s), are now much fewer in number. There are still a number of people from eastern Europe, of whom Albanians are a notorious example. Two great waves of Albanian immigrants reached the Adriatic coast in the winter and late summer of 1992, in a very adventurous way on board overcrowded ships. While the first wave was made very welcome and the Albanians were granted visas for humanitarian reasons, the second wave was ill-treated, the refugees were concentrated in a football stadium under the control of armed police and finally they were mostly deported (Macioti and Pugliese, 1993).

As one can see, the picture of Italian immigration is an extremely complex and varied one, and it reflects not only changes in the economy and in the labour demand of Italy as an immigration country, but also and above all reflects pressures coming from events affecting Third World Countries. Italian immigration can be said to take place in a phase in which the 'push' effect is absolutely predominant, while the labour demand in the immigration countries which accounts for the 'pull effect', is in general very weak, except for informal employment. It is not by chance that borders are now closed in all developed countries, and Italy is certainly no exception.

ITALIAN IMMIGRATION POLICY

As we have said, the Italian migration experience is rather recent and therefore interventions in immigration policy are also recent (Adinolfi 1992; Veugelers 1994). If one tried to sum up the present Italian policy towards immigrants it could be said to be rather progressive in its principles and in the recognition of the rights of immigrants with a regular status. These principles, however, are frustrated or contradicted by the fact that the regular workers tend to be a minority of the total number of Third World immigrants and so the practical implementation of migration policies tends to move away gradually from such principles. The first important measure in migration policy in Italy goes back to 1986 with Act 943 (1986), encompassing the general framework of the migration policy and the rights of foreign

116

workers. The act deals with amnesty directives aimed at the regularization of the immigrants' position. In previous years, in fact, most
Third World immigrants had overdue residence permits, or were
without a permit, and were therefore in an illegal position. A significant aspect of this first measure is that it concerned only wage-
earners. This affected both the general issue of rights and duties as
well as amnesty rules. Only wage-earners, or those who were registered as unemployed, were able to regularize their position and enjoy
the benefits envisaged by the act. It is not a small matter, but an
important issue for its political implications, as well as being a manifestation of the cultural climate and the convictions prevalent at the
time.

In many ways the arrival of immigrants had given the impression
that Italy had entered an expansion phase in labour demand similar
to the one of immigration countries in the previous decade. It was
thought to be what was called 'industrial immigration'. It was
believed that the expansion in labour demand was not fulfilled by
local supply in the productive system and so attracted immigrants.
There was an assumption that this was an immigration of workers
destined to be employed by Italian firms. Therefore it was assumed
to be essentially an immigration determined by the 'pull' effect, and
as such it could be regulated according to the needs of the labour-
importing country. This had been mostly the case for immigration in
the most industrialized European countries at the time of the great
inter-European migrations. The amnesty was therefore believed to
allow a regularization on a large scale of irregular immigrants who
were already estimated, with considerable exaggeration, to be around
1 million.

During the first few months of the implementation of the amnesty
act there were surprising results: only a relatively small number of
immigrants from Third World countries, approximately 115,000, regularized their position. More than two-thirds of these were regularized as people looking for occupation, i.e. as unemployed. It is widely
known that first-generation immigrants (in Italy they are nearly all
first-generation immigrants) are nearly all working and it is unlikely
that there will be any unemployed among them. But most observers
found the number officially registered as unemployed out of proportion. In actual fact the massive registration as unemployed with
the labour office represented a device to obtain regularization. As
already mentioned, many immigrants work in the informal economy,
unregistered, and many have precarious jobs. Many precarious or

unregistered workers (especially in agriculture, building and services) were obviously unable to prove that they had a job and were therefore compelled to declare that they were unemployed. Moreover, since the legislation did not contemplate the possibility of regularizing their position as self-employed, many small pedlars also declared themselves as unemployed.

This contradiction was partly overcome by the more recent immigration Act 39 (1990), known as the 'Martelli Act', which envisaged the possibility of registering as self-employed. But even so the number of unemployed was too great, especially in southern regions, where illegal work is widespread. This data concerning the work position was used as an indicator of the divergence between the image of immigration widespread among the population at large and the actual picture, at an institutional level, of the migration phenomenon. The misunderstanding came from the widespread belief that immigrants were living with a stability and regularity much higher than was actually the case. The assumption of the Martelli Act was that, once a first phase characterized by natural difficulties of adaptation was overcome, immigrants would find a stable job and fixed accommodation. Funds were allocated for 'First Reception Centres', structures providing provisional accommodation for immigrants while waiting for their autonomous permanent accommodation. If the number of migrant workers is taken into consideration together with the lack of work stability for many of them, it is easy to understand that the problem is not that of a *first* reception, but that of an overall reception capacity.

Another poor aspect of the Italian policy on immigration – which is also linked to an inaccurate evaluation of its features – was the belief that it would be possible to programme each year the migration flow on the basis of the national labour market requirements. No serious consideration was given to the position of immigrants in the labour market and to the considerable weight of people employed in informal work (and in sectors in which it is difficult to forecast the labour demand). Therefore there has not been any planning of the migration flow on the basis of labour market requirements. The difficulties have been aggravated by the fact that present-day migrations are less migrations of labour and more migrations of people and families. Few legal immigrants have entered the country since 1990 except for family reunion.

In practice, from 1990 Italy has fully entered the European migration policy: a policy of closure which has rightly elicited the phrase 'Fortress Europe'. The borders in Italy are as closed as any in Europe. Meanwhile, however, a 'siege syndrome' is also affecting institutional policies. From the early 1990s in Italy attention has been shifted from social policies in favour of immigrants (which obviously continue to be bandied about in official statements) to the problems of monitoring inward flows; this change obviously reflects a more general European policy. The siege syndrome and the fear of invasion focus attention on the problem of clandestine and irregular immigrants (whose number, as we have seen, is increasing). But the great worry seems to be how to get rid of them and not how to favour their regularization. The fundamental contradiction of Italian migration policy consists in the fact that rights guaranteed to immigrants are limited to those in a regular position, while their numbers are decreasing because of restrictive policies of regularization and closing of borders. Moreover, the actual limited scope of social policies in favour of immigrants is leading some of them to a growing situation of social marginality. And this trend does not show any sign of abating. This, in turn, tends to worsen the siege syndrome. Most recently, we can say that Italian migration policy has been evolving from a benevolent attitude, even if lacking concrete initiatives, to a trend in which this very benevolent attitude is abandoned and the need for control takes priority over the one for solidarity.

CONCLUSIONS: IMMIGRATIONS AND SOCIAL RIGHTS OF CITIZENSHIP

It is understandable that in this context the expectations and the rights of immigrants tend to be frustrated in Italy. The main problem now is not legal citizenship, which still interests only a limited number of immigrants (this may, however, become a relevant issue in the future), but social and economic citizenship. Besides, this citizenship, as others have clearly illustrated, should be understood as postnational citizenship.[2]

The presence of foreign people, which is bound to continue, raises the problem of extending to them the rights of social citizenship in a Marshallian sense, which characterized the period of development of the welfare state. These rights consist of access to the benefits of the social policies concerning health, education, housing and, above all, social security. They were originally obtained by the national working classes and have been generally extended to immigrant workers. In the post-war period to the 1970s, during the period of

119

the great inter-European migrations, immigrants tended to settle in a definitive way in the immigration countries and many of them eventually became citizens. On the other hand the process of European integration extended at a supra-national level some of these social rights to all citizens of the European Union. Therefore Italian immigrants in other European countries, as citizens of an EU member state, could benefit from this process. The general Europen trend now is towards a greater generalization at a supra-national level of the rights of citizenship (at least formally), but at the same time towards restrictions against non-EU citizens.

However, the number of non-EU citizens is increasing in all countries, including Italy. In fact, the present immigration flow is composed mostly of people from the Third World, who have difficulties of access to citizenship and very often difficulties even in obtaining legal residence. The most relevant question now is therefore the access to these rights by people who are *de facto* resident, and, to a more limited extent, also *de jure* resident in the countries of immigration. Despite restrictive immigration policies, the process of internationalization of the labour market and the greater mobility of populations, workers and families cause an increase in the number of non-EU citizens who live and work in the European countries for a greater or smaller length of time. The access to the social rights of citizenship for these people cannot be conditioned by the access to legal citizenship. On the other hand, some of these rights (for example health and education for minors) are universally recognized by principles enacted by the UN.

In the specific case of Italy there is a contradiction between a tendency to recognize such rights in principle and difficulties of access to them. In fact, for immigrants, regularized status is an essential condition for being able to enjoy the rights provided by the Italian legislation and, as already mentioned, the non-regularization of immigrants frustrates the intention which is at the basis of the measures: granting citizenship rights to them. Therefore a first step of a policy aimed at expanding the rights of citizenship in a post-national sense lies in allowing immigrants to overcome clandestine status.

NOTES

1 An exaustive analysis of German immigration and immigration policy is carried out by K. Schönwalder in this volume, chapter 10.

REFERENCES

Adinolfi, A. (1992) *I lavoratori extracomuntari. Norme interne ed internazionali*, Bologna: Il Mulino.

Amaturo, E. and Morlicchio, E. (1989) 'L'Immigrazione straniera in Campania', *Critica Sociologica* 2.

Birindelli, A. M. and Bonifazi, C. (eds) (1993) *Impact of Migration in the Receiving Countries*, Geneva: CICRED IOM.

Boehning, R. W. (1984) *Studies in International Labour Migrations*, London: Macmillan.

Calvanese, F. (1983) *Emigrazione epolitica migratoria negli anni settanta*, Salerno: Laveglia.

Carchedi, F. (1995) *Una communità silenziosa: l'immigrazione cinese in Italia*, Turin: Edizioni Fondazione Agnelli.

Castles, S. and Kosack, G. (1973) *Immigrant Workers and the Class Structure in Western Europe*, London: Oxford University Press.

Collinson, S. (1993) *Europe and international migrations*, London: Pinter.

Frey, L. (ed.) (1991) 'Aspetti economici dell'immigrazione in Italia', *Quaderni di Economia del Lavoro* 43 (special issue).

King, R. (ed.) (1990) *Mass Migration in Europe: The legacy and the future*, London: Belhaven Press.

Macioti, M. I. and Pugliese, E. (1991) *Gli immigrati in Italia*, Bari: Laterza.

Mottura, G. (ed.) (1992) *L'arcipelago immigrazione*, Rome: Ediesse.

Natale, M. (1990) 'L'immigrazione straniera in Italia: consistenza, caratteristiche, prospettive', *Polis* 1, pp. 5–34.

Piore, M. (1979) *Birds of Passage*, Cambridge: Cambridge University Press.

Pugliese, E. (1993) 'Restructuring of the labour market and the role of Third World migrations in Europe', *Environment and Planning* 11, pp. 513–22.

Reyneri E. (1980) *La catena migratoria*, Bologna: Il Mulino.

Rocha-Trinidade, M. B. (ed.) (1993) *Recent Migration Trends in Europe*, Lisbon: Universidade Aberta.

Rossi-Doria, M. (1983) *Scritti sul Mezzogiorno*, Turin: Einaudi.

Veugelers, J. W. P. (1994) 'Recent immigration politics in Italy: a short story', *West European Politics* 17 (2) pp. 34–49.

Part III

THE POLITICIZATION OF 'DIFFERENCE'

8

THE SPICE OF LIFE?

Ethnic difference, politics and culture in modern Britain

Tony Kushner

The victory of Derek Beackon of the British National Party (BNP) in the Millwall council by-election, in London in September 1993, was greeted with both alarm and, it might be suggested, almost a curious sense of relief in liberal circles. There was genuine fear that a fascist party had tasted success in 'mainstream' British politics for the first time since the 1970s and concern that this was just the tip of the iceberg of a serious electoral presence of the extreme right. For some there was resignation to what they saw as the inevitable spread of racist politics across Europe eventually reaching Britain. The relief came out of the growing, if uneasy, recognition that racism in Britain was escalating in scale and intensity. The success of the BNP could then be equated with the growth in racial intolerance – the one blamed on the other. It has taken the period after Millwall for many in the media and beyond to realize that the BNP offers no electoral threat whatsoever on a national, or, with one or two minor (although not insignificant) exceptions, local level. In July 1994, when Parliament was discussing possible changes to the Public Order Act to include a new offence of racial violence, the *Guardian* announced to its readers that 'Race hate is not the exclusive preserve of the BNP in east London'.[1] This statement, actually presented as a remarkable discovery, contains a truth that, although actually banal, has still not been widely assimilated. Racism in Britain is persistently deemed to be the preserve of groups such as the BNP. If this were indeed the case, and ignoring the widespread evidence of racism beyond the limited realm of party politics, then the implications would be remarkable in the European context: Britain would be the exception in terms of the rise of xenophobia and racism. Even though the electoral threat of neo-nazi organizations in some European countries has been overstated, there has clearly been a growth of extreme right-wing organizations on the continent that has not occurred in Britain. Is the myth of a 'tolerant country' actually borne out by the failure of Britain's neo-nazis?[2]

So much attention has been paid to the alleged growth or revival of extreme right-wing groups in Britain in recent years, especially by anti-fascist organizations such as the Anti-Nazi League, that a basic detail that would have been provided by a historical overview has been missed. Membership figures, currently estimated at between two and three thousand, are at their lowest since British fascist parties came into being in the 1920s (if the period during the Second World War when such groups were banned is disregarded).[3] If an assessment of the politicization of difference were limited to a study of the far right, then an analysis would have to be made extrapolating wildly from the highly partial and to some extent temporary success of the BNP in Millwall, Tower Hamlets. This would be a dangerous and, it must be argued, ultimately limiting exercise. It would be hard to find a close parallel to the specific circumstances of the Isle of Dogs (where the Millwall constituency is situated) which involves unique factors such as the absolute and relative poverty and diminished life chances of many of its inhabitants in the presence of the opulent Docklands development; the continuation of incompetent and corrupt local politics that have characterized the area throughout the century; the existence of a Liberal Democrat council which limited the potential for a 'mainstream' protest vote; the implementation of racially discriminatory policies by the local council and encouragement by the party in control to play the 'race card'; and lastly, the existence of a strong local anti-alien tradition in the area (even if it had been one that had never before been successfully politicized by extremists).[4] Taken individually many of these factors exist elsewhere, although the proximity of extreme wealth and poverty so blatantly and massively displayed in the Isle of Dogs would be hard to find replicated anywhere in Britain or perhaps Europe as a whole. Taken together, however, they do suggest a uniqueness to the Millwall case – an accident almost waiting to happen. The inimitable features of Tower Hamlets and specifically the Isle of Dogs at a particular time (subsequently the Liberal Democrats lost control of the council thereby changing the nature of the 'protest vote') in respect of neo-fascist electoral success has been highlighted not only by Beackon's defeat in the same seat just over half a year later but also by the subsequent failure of his party to make anything like significant inroads at an electoral level. This was confirmed in later East End of London council by-elections in Shadwell and then Lansbury in the fifteen months after Millwall when the BNP finished third behind Labour and the Liberal Democrats. The BNP's low level of support since Millwall is even more striking given the prominence it has achieved in the media – especially as much of this has failed to expose the true nature of the organization.[5]

Whilst there is never any room for complacency when dealing with the far right (and the impact of the sustained efforts of anti-fascists in fighting the BNP after Millwall should not be minimized), it is difficult at present to conceive of any circumstances that would lead to a *significant* national success of the BNP or similar organizations. It is true that the current leadership of the far right is feeble and that their financial position is precarious. Improvements on either front could boost their status – yet the very fact that they cannot attract money, popular support or people of talent itself reflects the pariah status of fascists in British society. The untarnished war memory of Britain and the power of its patriotic anti-fascism has so far been an unsurmountable obstacle to far right organizations in Britain since 1945. As we move further from the conflict chronologically, the memory and myth of the war grows even stronger. It may not be impossible to imagine the situation in the middle of the 1970s being repeated if the Conservative party moved towards the centre and a moral panic over a refugee/alien influx occurred. Yet, even in the mid-1970s, the National Front never came close to winning a seat in the House of Commons and even the most 'favourable' proportional representation scheme would have kept them out of Parliament.

Today, the message of 'Millwall' is not that Britain is on the verge of a fascist electoral revival, but that race hatred and conflict *on their own* are not enough to win groups such as the BNP anything more than tiny pockets of local support. The BNP has desperately attempted to exploit the ethnic tension in areas such as West Yorkshire and the West Midlands but has failed almost totally. Is then the politicization of difference essentially now dead in Britain?[6]

This is the hopeful interpretation offered by Zig Layton-Henry. In his narrative of post-war race relations, the rhetoric and policies of Margaret Thatcher are presented as essentially killing off 'race' in British politics. He argues that her 'swamping speech' of 1978 and later campaigning destroyed the electoral chances of the National Front in the following general election. As Layton-Henry puts it:

'One major legacy of Mrs Thatcher's tough anti-immigration stance was the political annihilation of the National Front in 1979'. Since then there has been consensus between the two major parties on the need for 'firm but fair' immigration control. There may be some disagreement of what 'fair' consists of – especially from Labour MPs in seats dependent on ethnic minority votes – but this rarely becomes an issue of national focus. Layton-Henry concludes that immigraton was given little prominence in the 1992 general election and that the 'results of the election seemed to indicate that black candidates were more widely accepted by the electorate than ever before'. As part of this positive trend, the increase in black MPs rose from four in 1987 to six in 1992.[7]

There is another reading of modern Britain which suggests that rather than having ended the politics of 'race', Margaret Thatcher, with her nationalistic vision, gave it a new lease of life and actually brought race to the fore in a whole range of issues. Her concept of inward-looking 'Englishness', from which domestic and foreign policy stemmed, was essentially racialized. This incorporated key domestic policies, such as law and order and education, as well as those more blatantly addressing immigration and 'race', such as the Nationality Act of 1981. Critics have, in particular, pointed to the importance of culture rather than biology in the articulation of 'new right' opposition to minority groups such as Afro-Caribbeans and Asians. Utilizing cultural studies approaches, they have dismissed the focus on 'old-fashioned' racists such as the BNP as limiting because it fails to acknowledge the centrality of 'race' in mainstream politics.[8]

In this chapter I want to continue this debate but to offer a different perspective. Much of the existing literature on 'race' and racism in Britain and elsewhere is confined to an institutional and top-down approach. There is a focus on the government (but rarely the everyday state apparatus), political parties, racist and anti-racist bodies, the police and the media.[9] When dealt with at all, 'public opinion' is gauged through poll material carried out by organizations such as Gallup for newspapers or more occasionally 'race relations' organizations. The findings of such polls can appear startling. In surveys carried out in the 1980s over one in four of those interviewed supported the idea of repatriation for those of colour. Miles and Phizacklea in their study, *White Man's Country*, used these figures to support their labour market theory that now black workers were no longer needed (the post-war requirement for cheap, unskilled labour having passed) they could easily be disposed of by the capitalist state. Less pessimistically, a 1991 survey found that less than one in five white Britons would object to living next door to someone of a different race.[10] There are, however, grave dangers if these polls are regarded as giving a true representation of public opinion on such sensitive matters. Polls suffer from the problem of the interviewees giving the answers that they feel are expected of them or being pushed in a certain direction by loaded questions. The decrease in negative replies to the 'black neighbour' question from one in two in 1964 to less than half that by the early 1990s *could* be due to an increase in racial toleration. It might also be explained by the decline of respectability for public expressions of racist sentiment over this period. An alternative finding, from a poll carried out in 1993, that one in three black households feel threatened by racial harassment 'in or near their present homes' does indeed start to query the accuracy of the more positive assessment.[11] The other weakness inherent in opinion polls relates to their very nature. Ultimately, questions, even if refined and without any hint of bias, can only be answered on a yes/no basis. Those relating to such sensitive issues as race and immigration can lead to a crudity of responses which make no allowances for ambivalence – the key, as Homi Bhabha, Bryan Cheyette and others have suggested, to understanding such complex discourses. Polls inevitably also provide no depth or wider context in which to place the views of ordinary people.[12]

How is one to confront the dilemma of fairly representing public opinion in this area? The solution may be at least partially provided by the social anthropological organization, Mass-Observation. Originally formed in 1937 and wound down in the late 1940s, it was revived at the University of Sussex in 1980. The new Mass-Observation, unlike its predecessor, does not carry out investigations through paid observers, but maintains the use of directives to elicit opinions from a wide range of respondents. In spring 1990 a directive was circulated on 'Social Divisions'. It included questions on attitudes and contact with those of a different race and asked 'Is the plural society with cultural diversity a good thing?', as well as eliciting whether there really was a 'British character' or 'National Identity'.[13]

Criticisms have been levelled at the historical Mass-Observation which could be extended to the organization in its revived form. Its detractors argue that Mass-Observation's group of regular respondents in no way provides a representative sample of British society. In the case of the contemporary Mass-Observation writers this is undoubtedly the case. There is an obvious imbalance towards women and also a clear bias towards the professional middle classes. Politically the respondents are more left–liberal leaning than the population as a whole. The relative and absolute lack of Afro-Caribbean and Asian writers is more than noticeable and has obvious implications for the spring 1990 directive. The ethnic imbalance with respect to those of colour cannot be dismissed lightly, although it is compensated in part by recent and forthcoming surveys based on extensive interviews of Asians and Afro-Caribbeans in Britain carried out by the Policy Studies Institute which include questions such as how they feel about being British and whether they are accepted as British. It is important to add, however, that the shortcomings of the Mass-Observation directives do not extend to 'white' groups in Britain of Jewish, Irish, Italian, eastern European and other origins (minorities that are sadly absent in the PSI survey). Their large presence partly reflects the important but neglected tradition of immigration in British history, but their over-representation in the Mass-Observation project also indicates that to minority groups the process of writing is critical in coming to terms with their status as outsiders in 'mainstream' society.[14]

The other alleged limitations of the Mass-Observation sample can, however, be dealt with adequately. First, the sample is in no way meant to provide crude quantitative material that can be measured in the usual opinion poll manner. Nevertheless, the size of the sample – over 600 people completed the spring 1990 directive – allows for a massive range of responses even if they do not accurately mirror the population at large. Secondly, the writings are subjective and need to be treated as such. The respondents often write at great length and it is the quality of the material produced that is critical. The Mass-Observers have time and space to articulate their views and often do so in extended responses often using a life-history approach. Moreover, there is a great honesty in the responses – it is notable in this particular survey how initial reservation about expressing true feelings wears off as the survey progresses (a trend that mirrors closely the directive responses on race and nation carried out by the early Mass-Observation in the 1930s and 1940s). Such depth, with its concurrent ambiguities, nuances and contradictions, provides a far richer account than the snap reaction to an opinion poll question. The Mass-Observation material is closer to oral testimony with the additional bonus that the respondents feel unconstrained by those carrying out the investigation. The University of Sussex organizers are trusted but do not act as a barrier to communication.[15]

For the purposes of this chapter the timing of the directive was excellent. It was circulated when the domestic debate about the Rushdie affair was still prominent in British society. Furthermore, there had been other recent specific debates such as that involving Muslim schoolgirls and headscarves, the emerging Hong Kong Chinese question, as well as Norman Tebbit's infamous 'cricket' loyalty test comments.[16] The 200 male and 400 female respondents provide a remarkable map with regard to questions of difference in modern Britain. These range from a man from Kendal in the Lake District who reports that he 'rarely s[ees] an Asian or Moslem and ha[s] encountered only one negro in years' through to a middle-aged housewife in Lambeth who perceived herself, as a white person, to be in a minority. In this respect, the survey provides the human element missing in the ethnic spatial variations quantified in the 1991 census which shows that districts vary from having 42.3 per cent of their population as (non-white) ethnic minorities (Newham) to the Western Isles (0.3 per cent ethnic minorities). What, however, do they say about the politicization of difference in contemporary Britain? What is the cause of ethnic conflict and how does this or could this be translated into the political arena?[17]

The problems facing neo-nazis attempting to make an electoral breakthrough in Britain are made clear by the directive replies. On the surface, the quite frequent comments made such as that of a woman in Birmingham that she

> fe[lt] that the racism nowadays is towards the white people, everyone seems to be frightened to not give everything possible to help the coloureds but no-one gives a thought to helping the white youngsters

would seem to suggest that there was mileage in the BNP's slogan of 'rights for whites' (echoing the frightening success of that slogan by right-wing demagogues in the American south such as David Duke and Pat Buchanan). Nevertheless, the final comment of the Birmingham respondent was to warn against such policies because they would actually lead to the undesirable *growth* of National Front type groups.[18] The sample of 600 included a fair smattering of unreconstructed racist bigots:

> Since the Racial Discrimination Act came into being, UK has

131

been overwhelmed and over-run by coloureds, 25 years ago we had the cream of the races. Now we are overrun by the dregs

as a woman from Warley put it, yet not one was in favour of a far-right organization. In contrast to a Mass-Observation survey carried out on 'Race' in June 1939, no one in the 1990 directive stated clearly a belief in an inherent biological inferiority of black people.[19] Moreover, in what might be deemed to be the positive side of the report in terms of the state of racism in contemporary Britain, only one respondent wrote in favour of repatriation, stating that she would

love to be transported back to the fifties . . . – I don't want to be cosmopolitan. I'd like to see the majority of immigrants happily back in their own countries living a good life not in shanty towns and starving.[20]

Even the supporters of Powellism were resigned to the continuing presence of black people in Britain: one from Kington declared that Enoch was right, and followed this by pointing out that there were

enough IRISH, SCOTS, and WELSH in this LAND OF MINE, ENGLAND, without letting others in – not, repeat not, necessarily because of their colour, but BECAUSE OF THEIR CULTURE.

Yet he, however, had to acknowledge that very few immigrants and their children would want to go back 'home'. The respondent was therefore resigned to losing his national identity: for him, the battle had essentially been lost. Others had retreated to their own racially pure white enclaves such as Derby Conservative club, which a member happily admitted was

not the place to choose if one's interests extend to differing cultures – that is why I chose to be a member and would be at odds to any attempt at infiltration by others of disparate racial backgrounds.

A woman from the Isle of Man sums up such concerns but also the near impossibility of politicizing racism in the form of neo-nazism:

I still feel an unease at the number of coloured people when I am in England, but this is because I'm not used to them. I know that many are second or more generation British and they have every right to be there. There is no going back now, so there must be cooperation between the cultures.[21]

The directive establishes the clear outer limits of racist discourse in popular British politics. It also, however, shows the tensions that have emerged in the battle to have ethnic pluralism accepted in society as a whole. Have, then, racist politics become internalized, channelled into control of minorities at home now their effective exclusion from outside has been achieved and accepted by the major political parties?

The majority of the directive responses accept that cultural diversity is to be welcomed. Again, this might be seen as another positive aspect of the survey even if there is a bias in the sample towards left–liberal *Guardian*-type readers. Yet it is often what lies beyond the briefer, surface comments of acceptance that is more revealing of liberal attitudes in Britain and the limitations of pluralism in contemporary society. Sometimes the directive responses move very quickly from stating that 'cultural diversity is basically a good thing' to tirades against minority behaviour. A liberal, retired chartered accountant having praised the 'enlarge[ment of] one's horizons' brought about by diversity, immediately attacked Asians for

> attempting to dictate to our authorities, and screaming 'Racist' if anyone disagrees, and the authorities bending backwards to accommodate them, we who were born here, and have fought two bloody wars to keep our heritage, are fast becoming second class citizens.[22]

Others are less blatant but there is a frequent refrain, as a retired man from Stoke put it, that 'Cultural diversity is quite all right unless it produces culture clashes'. Inevitably, the Rushdie affair was used with immense regularity throughout the responses as an example of minorities getting out of hand. But, rather than being seen as untypical, the Rushdie affair was frequently used as just one illustration of minorities overstepping their place and demanding 'exceptional rights'. A retired director from Sevenoaks provides a succinct shopping list of problems involving ethnic particularism that are perceived as the root cause of racism in Britain:

> The Salman Rushdie death threat. The excesses of the 'loony left' in spending public money on bizarre ethnic objectives. The North Farm riot in Haringay followed by inflammatory remarks by the coloured mayor Bernie Grant. Various examples of an unwillingness to integrate (e.g. teaching Hindi, or teaching in Urdu, at certain schools).

Indeed, for some, it is the very *idea* of ethnic difference that causes

133

them unease – even if, in reality, it is in a form that is totally invisible and does not affect the majority population at all. The ongoing debate about the *eruv* in Britain (in essence, an area marked by symbolic boundary lines which enables strictly observant Jews to carry items outside their homes on the Sabbath) is a telling example of this. As the organizer of one campaign against an *eruv* in a London suburb put it:

> To start demarcating a six-square mile area of London so that a minority can defy their religious beliefs is rather extraordinary. It's a small section of the community exerting their will over the rest.[23]

Race relations legislation was used by many to illustrate the special rights enjoyed by minorities at the expense of the 'British'. The belief that race relations boards still exist as a form of thought police (some fifteen years after their demise) indicates the sense of popular grievance that the state, after having inflicted mass coloured immigration on the population from the 1950s was, equally without consultation, imposing positive discrimination from above. Although the directive revealed some awareness of the existence of racial harassment in Britain, in essence problems to do with ethnic diversity are blamed on the minorities themselves. Often, however liberal the writer, the final responsibility for the evidence of tension is seen to rest with the ethnic group itself and ultimately the solution is felt to lie in the group's willingness to conform. In this respect, the comments of a teacher in Brent are particularly revealing. Having described cultural diversity as 'brilliant, terrific, fabulous', she then added:

> I strongly believe in the teaching of English language and culture first – as this is Britain, and it makes nonsense to try and teach all the different other cultures first. You must give primacy by location.[24]

From this, it is significant that the directive replies often mention the Jews (and, a little less frequently, Italians and east Europeans) as ideal past immigrant groups. As a retired worker from Birmingham put it:

> Now the Jews have integrated into our society [and] all the ethnic groups should aim to do the same.[25]

Yet the perspective from these 'model' immigrants and their children is sharply different. One London Jew asked, 'how many years and generations do Jews have to live here before they can regard themselves as English?' A woman of east European origin living in Bradford adds that 'whatever people may say there [are] a lot of prejudices against Poles'. Nevertheless, she found that 'we are now held up as a shining example of immigrants who fit in (unlike the Asian read Muslim community)'.[26] In fact, the directive gives plenty of examples of the continuation of anti-Semitism in every-day British life which offer a contrasting picture to recent opinion polls on the subject carried out by the American Jewish Committee. A London resident relates:

> Relative racial harmony there may be in this quiet little sub-urban backwater but anti-Semitism is alive and well.[27]

Taken as a whole, the directive shows the power of 'Englishness' and its ability on the one hand to force minorities to conform and, on the other, to exclude those deemed to be different in all aspects of everyday life. With regards to the latter, it is hard to imagine that opinion polls would give such a revealing account as that provided by the Mass-Observation respondents of the racial discrimination practised by people who regard themselves as far from intolerant. A self-confessed *Guardian* reader and company director relates sifting through a large batch of job applications for an engineering position:

> We just *had* to reject about 40 of them immediately. I put my weight behind the rejection of a highly-qualified Indian just because he was a h[ighly]-q[ualified]-I[ndian]. Awful? Not when I had had experience of no less than *six* of such people, up to that time, and had been unimpressed on each occasion.

A retired medical secretary highlights how

> There does seem to be a great amount of racialism at large and I can remember when I worked in an office and became involved in job applications, many people I worked with (in the NHS) would reject any noticeably Asian names. I cannot remember there being such intolerance of German, Greek, Italian, etc. names. So sometimes, even by virtue of marriage, an applicant reduced her chance of getting an interview, no matter whether or not she had the qualifications to do the job.

Indeed, there is a danger that concentrating on structural reasons alone (crucial though they are) for discriminatory practice can lead to the downplaying of personal agency in diminishing the life chances of those of colour. The directive indicates the importance of the day-to-day subtle processes that are at the heart of the informal politics of racial inequality and that represent the reality of education, health, social service, housing and workplace provisions and opportunities in contemporary Britain.[28]

For the majority in the sample, their ideal of ethnic diversity takes the form of theme park difference. A woman from Stockport referring to Manchester's Chinatown illustrates this well:

At the moment the area is not too big and makes a quaint attraction and alternative shopping area but if it were to double in size, as it would if entry from Hong Kong was unlimited, it would threaten the Englishness of Manchester centre.

Ultimately, pluralism has to be subsumed under the hegemony of what is seen as the true English national identity. A college librarian from Swindon reveals how easily this could be turned to a political but non-fascist purpose:

I am against the liberal view that, as we live in a multi-cultural society, our children must willy-nilly learn about all the religions of the world and celebrate Ramadan and the Chinese New Year as well as Christmas and Easter. No doubt it is great fun for primary schools to make Chinese dragons, but I feel that so much of this liberal education has been at the expense of our children learning about Christianity ... the emphasis should be on the history and traditions of the state religion – Christianity. [The nativity story is crucial.] Without this knowledge much of our art and literature is lost to them. I do not wish to see the English culture (and I use the word advisedly, rather than British) swallowed up into a mish-mash of various cultures.[29]

It was, of course, such concepts of Englishness that were utilized by Margaret Thatcher in her rhetoric but also in her policies, most notably in the field of education. What is clear from the spring 1990 Mass-Observation directives is how blatantly racialized Englishness has become.[30] When respondents were asked to define their national identity, many could only do so in negative terms, highlighting the difference of ethnic minorities:

As the indigenous life of this country continues to change in order to accommodate the unforgiving and entirely alien laws of Islam and Afro-Caribbean tribalism – I wonder – how long before we become merely 'the whites'? ... Because I want to preserve what is left of the Englishness of my country, I am a conservative in the true sense and forced into the political arms of Conservatism by the extremes of a black-motivated opposition.

And in similar vein:

We are only a small island and are fast becoming a multi-racial society. I am proud to be English and would not like to think that my culture and heritage would one day be lost in a multi-cultral [sic] society ... I think that we British are frightened to comment on the many aspects of foreigners who live in Britain in case we are thought to be called a racialist ... I believe the British character is one of self-discipline, fair play, and strength. I believe the British way of life could be in danger of being corroded if we are encouraged to be multi-racial. It seems to me that with Mrs Thatcher's government at least we are trying to establish some semblance of the British character.

As a teacher from Carlisle (herself in favour of ethnic diversity) observed, 'Margaret Thatcher has tapped a nerve of the people of Britain by appealing to a sense of Britishness'.[31] It is unfortunate that themes of race and immigration in the existing literature on 'myths of the English' are absent. Yet stereotypical and essentially invented constructions of English culture are used not only to exclude but to preserve fragile, racially dependent means of belonging.[32] Here is the case of a teacher in Watford describing her husband in the directive, who is about to dance

'with his Morris team in Walthamstow, which [she suggests] has the largest Pakistani population in the country. It is St George's Day, and the team member who has organised the event is making little flags for the dancers to wear, AND is having Land of Hope and Glory played, stung ... by the money that is invested in ethnic communities in the Borough'.

She writes after the event that it attracted a large crowd that was almost totally white. The one exception was an Asian man, who quickly disappeared into his own home: a bijou 'English' cottage complete with climbing roses. The schoolteacher, in contrast to her husband, seems to revel in this last image. His blatantly fraudulent vision of the English past is juxtaposed with what she perceives as the reality of everyday life in a London suburb.[33]

It is indeed significant that those in the sample who see the necessity of cultural diversity also reject any attempt to define Britishness or Englishness in a static or narrow way. In the process, some also reject the restraints imposed by patriarchal definitions of nation – more women than men in the survey accept a very pluralistic vision of society. As Jane Mackay and Pat Thane suggest for the period from the 1880s to the 1920s:

> A clearly defined, uncontested, image of the Englishwoman is surprisingly elusive in this period of construction and redefinition of Englishness. The classic English man of the period was held to combine certain qualities, including leadership, courage, justice and honour, which were defined as distinctively 'English'. He has no exact female equivalent.

Their analysis can also be applied to the post-war period: even, ironically, to the Thatcher years. Although female Mass-Observers from the 1990 sample are no less prone to racism and xenophobia as a whole, they are exceptional in being over-represented amongst the minority who are willing to deconstruct the concept of nation (and especially its male representation in the form of 'John Bull' or 'Morris Men'). Instead, these women (and a very small percentage of men) present an alternative reading of Britain's past and present, as well as its potential for the future which is totally dependent on the rejection of homogeneity. British history, rather than being used to buttress the unchanging nature of society is seen in a totally different light:

> We, as a family, really miss the 'ethnic' element in the population, if we spend a couple of weeks away in the 'English' countryside. It seems to me that the diversity of British culture is directly related to her rich and varied history

and similarly:

> The arts and sciences, the extension of all human knowledge have issued from diversity, e.g. the Flemish immigrants to the Jews from the continent to this country.[34]

The idea of a 'chocolate box' heritage-industry-constructed idea of Englishness is also firmly rejected:

> I am a strong believer in the value of diversity . . . I think there

is a romantic notion of the English identity which is cottages in Sussex with roses and tea, but it is all crap. The British have a very diverse culture.

A plural society with cultural difference is an excellent thing. It is a living, evolving society, with potential. Not a museum, which is the great fault of Britain today.[35]

In contrast, the benefits and joys of thinking beyond artificially devised boundaries are stressed by those engaging in a postmodernist idea of identity:

I really enjoy meeting people from different countries. The world is getting smaller in terms of 'community' . . . living in a plural society should and can be an enriching and rewarding experience and one I would hate to be without

the plural society with cultural diversity is a good thing. I don't really understand a lot of so called 'nationalisms' – I don't think there is a national identity to protect

I have never felt that I belong to a minority in British society because Britain is a very mixed country, and [don't] see 'British' [as] mean[ing] anything

different cultures can only broaden our understanding and appreciation of life. I feel that a plural society, with cultural diversity is therefore only to the advantage of the country as a society can only become more enriched by exposure to new ideas, customs and attitudes to life. This should make Great Britain less isolationist and draw it closer to the rest of the world and Europe especially.[36]

To some, the whole future of British society is dependent upon accepting such concepts:

the plural society with cultural diversity is a good thing. Only hope for Britain, really.

The last word in this respect should be left to a woman of Asian/ Irish parentage:

I see it as a great advantage because I have a life and a country of my own, and two extra lives and countries belonging to my parents.[37]

These alternative, positive comments on 'the plurality of British society [as being] one of its assets', as a civil servant from Brighton puts it, are quoted at length even though they represent only a minority of the respondents (roughly 5–10 per cent of the total). They make the point clearly that the basis of conflict is *not* difference itself, but Englishness as a racialized, and in recent years, a politicized exclusive project.[38] From one perspective national identity has been eroded, so that, in the words of a retired railway worker

Every Mohammed and Singh now call themselves British. Nowadays when I sign in at a Hotel or Guest House I put 'English' to represent my identity.[39]

It is such sentiments that Thatcherism and its successors have so ably exploited. From another angle, provided by a librarian in Watford, the key question is 'how long [will it be] before we accept "Patel" as a British name'? As the comments of British minorities themselves – both black and white – suggest, this may be a long time in coming. The statement of a teacher in Sheffield of Chinese origin that 'I feel fairly paranoid when I enter a different environment where the majority is white' is indicative of the potential power (already largely realized in terms of state immigration control and asylum policy) of a racialized nationalist (but essentially non-fascist) discourse in British politics and culture.[40]

NOTES

1 Runnymede Trust, 'The British National Party and the Millwall By-election: History and Reactions', Briefing Paper, 1993; Michael White, 'What took them so long?', *Guardian*, 18 September 1993 for a sense of relief at Millwall; *Guardian*, 6 July 1994. For a general analysis of these issues see Tony Kushner, 'The Fascist as "Other"? Racism and Neo-Nazism in Contemporary Britain', *Patterns of Prejudice* 28(1), 1994, pp. 27–45.

2 For a recent and thorough survey see Institute of Jewish Affairs, *Political Extremism and the Threat to Democracy in Europe* (London: Institute of Jewish Affairs, 1994); Colin Holmes, *A Tolerant Country? Immigrants, Refugees and Minorities in Britain* (London: Faber & Faber, 1991).

3 See *Searchlight*, January 1992, January 1993 and January 1994 for membership figures of the contemporary far right and Richard Thurlow, *Fascism in Britain: A History, 1918–1985* (Oxford: Blackwell, 1987) and Tony Kushner, *The Persistence of Prejudice: Antisemitism in British Society During the Second World War* (Manchester: Manchester University Press, 1989), chapter 1 for a historical perspective.

4 On the local context of 'Docklands' see David Cesarani, 'Between a dock

and a hard place', *Guardian*, 21 September 1993; Dean Nelsen, 'Local democracy goes to the Dogs', *Observer*, 19 September 1993; Tom White, 'Dogs at War', *The Big Issue*, 16–22 November 1993; for corruption in local politics see Geoffrey Alderman, 'M. H. Davis: the Rise and Fall of a Communal Upstart', *Jewish Historical Studies* XXXI, 1988–90, pp. 261–2; on the failure of the British Union of Fascists in this area see Mass-Observation Archive, University of Sussex (M-O A) File Report 39 on the Silvertown by-election in February 1940 and its survey on antisemitism in the East End in 1939: TC Antisemitism Box 1.

5 In 5 May 1994 local elections the BNP and National Front contested 53 seats and won 21,335 votes. Beackon saw the size of his support increase to 2,041 but saw a marked decline in the proportion of his vote with a much larger turn-out. For a detailed analysis see CSO (Board of Deputies of British Jews), 'Local Elections – 5th May 1994', 1994; Sally Weale and John Potter, 'Spectre of BNP has only faded in part', *Guardian*, 17 September 1994 on the Shadwell by-election and *Jewish Chronicle*, 23 December 1994 for Lansbury.

6 On British memory and the Second World War see Patrick Wright, *On Living in an Old Country: The National Past in Contemporary Britain* (London: Verso, 1985); Angus Calder, *The Myth of the Blitz* (London: Jonathan Cape, 1991) and Tony Kushner, *The Holocaust and the Liberal Imagination: A Social and Cultural History* (Oxford: Blackwell, 1994); Vernon Bogdanor, 'The public relations of PR', *Guardian*, 17 April 1992 which 'dismisses claims that proportional representation aids fascism'; *CARF* (Campaign against Racism and Fascism), September/October 1992 on the failure of the BNP outside London.

7 Zig Layton-Henry, *The Politics of Immigration: Immigration, 'Race' and 'Race' Relations in Post-war Britain* (Oxford: Blackwell, 1992), pp. 119–21, 210.

8 For race, culture and politics in the 1980s see Paul Gilroy, *There Ain't No Black in the Union Jack: The Cultural Politics of Race and Nation* (London: Hutchinson, 1987); Floya Anthias and Nira Yuval-Davis, *Racialized Boundaries: Race, Nation, Gender and Class and the Anti-racist struggle* (London: Routledge, 1992); Michael Keith, *Race, Riots and Policing: Lore and Disorder in a Multi-racist Society* (London: University College Press, 1993).

9 For one of the best overviews see John Solomos, *Race and Racism in Britain* (2nd edition, London: Macmillan, 1993). Dilip Hero, *Black British White British: A History of Race Relations in Britain* (3rd edition, London: Paladin, 1991) attempts to examine popular attitudes but does so largely based on opinion polls.

10 *The Times*, 8 October 1981 for figures of 26 per cent supporting compulsory repatriation and 18 per cent in favour of voluntary, financially supported repatriation; Robert Miles and Annie Phizacklea, *White Man's Country: Racism in British Politics* (London: Pluto, 1984), chapter 4; *Independent on Sunday*, 7 July 1991 and Kaushika Amin and Robin Richardson, *Politics for All: Equality, Culture and the General Election 1992* (London: Runnymede Trust, 1992), chapter 3 for more details of this survey carried out by the Runnymede Trust.

11 Michael Banton, 'Optimism and Pessimism about Racial Relations', *Patterns of Prejudice* 22 (1), 1988, p. 8 for the 1964 figures; London Research Centre figures quoted in *Searchlight*, May 1993 and see similar findings (highlighting the differences between Asians and Afro-Caribbeans in this area) in Tariq Modood, Sharon Beishon and Satnam Virdee, *Changing Ethnic Identities* (London: Policy Studies Institute, 1994), pp. 89, 97.

12 For a defence of Gallup, see Robert Worcester, *British Public Opinion: A Guide to the History and Methodology of Political Opinion Polling* (Oxford: Blackwell, 1991); Bryan Cheyette, *Constructions of 'the Jew' in English literature and society: Racial Representations, 1875–1945* (Cambridge: Cambridge University Press, 1993); Homi Bhabha, 'Of Mimicry and Man: The Ambivalence of Colonial Discourse', in idem, *The Location of Culture* (London: Routledge, 1994), pp. 85–92.

13 For the history of Mass-Observation see Nick Stanley, ' "The Extra-Dimension": A Study and Assessment of the Methods Employed by Mass-Observation in its First Period 1937–40' (unpublished Ph.D., Birmingham Polytechnic, 1981); Dorothy Sheridan, ' "Ordinary Hardworking Folk": Volunteer Writers in Mass-Observation, 1937–50 and 1981–91', *Feminist Praxis* 37 and 38, 1992, pp. 1–34; Mass-Observation Archive: Directive Respondent (M-O A: DR) Spring 1990.

14 For a critique, see Angus Calder, 'Mass-Observation 1937–1949' in Martin Bulmer (ed.), *Essays on the History of British Sociological Research* (Cambridge: Cambridge University Press, 1985), pp. 121–36; Modood *et al.*, *Changing Ethnic Identities*, Introduction, and Policy Studies Institute, *The Fourth National Survey of Ethnic Minorities* (forthcoming, PSI). It should be added that a sustained effort has been made by the organizers at the University of Sussex to recruit more minority observers. See *Guardian*, 1 January 1990.

15 For the earlier directives on nation and race see M-O A: DR June 1939, October 1940, March 1943 and July 1946; Dorothy Sheridan, 'Writing to the Archive: Mass-Observation as Autobiography', *Sociology* 27 (1), 1993, pp. 27–40 and David Bloome, Dorothy Sheridan and Brian Street, 'Reading Mass-Observation Writing: Theoretical and Methodological Issues in Researching the Mass-Observation Archive', *Mass-Observation Archive Occasional Paper* 1, 1993, pp. 1–22 (University of Sussex Library).

16 Malise Ruthven, *A Satanic Affair: Salman Rushdie and the Rage of Islam* (London: Chatto & Windus, 1990); Lina Appignanesi and Sara Maitland (eds), *The Rushdie File* (London: Fourth Estate, 1989) and Tariq Modood, *Not Easy Being British: Colour, Culture and Citizenship* (London: Trentham Book, 1992), part 3 for the Rushdie affair; for the headscarf issue see *Guardian*, 19 January 1990 and Melanie Phillips, 'Preserving the freedom not to be free', *Guardian*, 26 January 1990; *Guardian*, 21 April 1990 for Tebbit, cricket tests and the Hong Kong Chinese.

17 M-O A: Spring 1990 DR S2137; DR C108; David Owen, 'Spatial Variations in Ethnic Minority Group Populations in Great Britain', *Population Trends* 78, Winter 1994, pp. 23–33.

18 M-O A: Spring 1990 DR A2168; Douglas Rose (ed.), *The Emergence of*

David Duke and the Politics of Race (Chapel Hill, NC and London: University of North Carolina Press, 1992).

19 M-O A: Spring DR 1990 J1998; M-O A: Directive June 1939: 'Race'. I am currently working on a comparative study of the original and revived Mass-Observation with regard to such issues: *Observing the 'Other'; Mass-Observation, Racism, Ethnicity and Immigration* (London: Routledge, forthcoming).

20 M-O A: Spring 1990 DR C108. In this respect, the Mass-Observation survey offers a contrasting picture to that offered by opinion polls on immigration matters. Nevertheless, the majority of the respondents do feel that further immigration should be curtailed with a minority (less than one-fifth) positively welcoming the prospect of future arrivals.

21 M-O A: Spring 1990 DR P1434; R1418; D2123. The survey as a whole indicates the importance of Powell for those articulating an ideology against cultural pluralism confirming the analysis of Paul Gilroy, *There Ain't No Black*, chapter 2. See also Tom Nairn, *The Break-up of Britain* (London: Verso, 2nd edition 1981), chapter 6.

22 M-O A: Spring 1990 DR F212. In this respect, the survey shows the inherent dangers of surface multi-culturalism, or 'the three Ss' – saris, steel bands and samosas.

23 M-O A: DR G2180; C100; Ian MacKinnon and Simon Midgley, 'Victory for Jewish community in battle over "eruv" ', *Independent*, 22 September 1994. See *Jewish Chronicle*, 1993 and 1994 passim for coverage of the *eruv* debates.

24 For the origins of the Race Relations Boards see E. J. B. Rose *et al.*, *Colour and Citizenship: A Report on British Race Relations* (London: Oxford University Press, 1969), Part VI 'Roy Jenkins and Legislation Against Discrimination: A Case Study'; M-O A: Spring 1990 DR P1434; B1887 and F1634 on their alleged nefarious influence; H1543; W2117; B1882; G1483 and J1998 on the 'imposition' of immigration; H828; H909, B2304 for the awareness of racial harassment; B1887 for the Brent teacher.

25 M-O A: Spring 1990: DR G1531; H276; L1422 and L2063.

26 M-O: Spring 1990: DR H655; K2287. On Bradford's immigrant past see Bradford Heritage Recording Unit, *Destination Bradford: A Century of Immigration* (Bradford: Bradford Libraries and Information Service, 1987); Colin Holmes, *John Bull's Island: Immigration and British Society, 1871–1971* (London: Macmillan, 1988), pp. 246–7 on changing local perceptions of European Volunteer Workers in post-war Britain.

27 For references to (or articulation of) anti-Semitism in contemporary Britain see M-O A: Spring 1990 DR D2206; R450; S1810; S2067; B60 and B2389; Jennifer Golub, *British Attitudes Towards Jews and Other Minorities* [American Jewish Committee Working Papers on Contemporary Anti-Semitism] (New York: American Jewish Committee, 1993).

28 M-O A: Spring 1990 DR D2205; J1586; Trevor Jones, *Britain's Ethnic Minorities: an analysis of the Labour Force Survey* (London: Policy Studies Institute, 1993); C. McCrudden, D. Smith and C. Brown, *Racial Justice at Work: The Enforcement of the Race Relations Act 1976 in Employment* (London: Policy Studies Institute, 1991); P. Braham, A. Rattansi and R. Skellington (eds), *Racism and Antiracism: Inequalities, Opportunities and*

Policies (London: Open University Press, 1992); Susan Smith, *The Politics of 'Race' and Residence: Citizenship, Segregation and White Supremacy in Britain* (Cambridge: Cambridge University Press, 1989) for patterns of life chances with regard to ethnicity and racism; Robert Miles, *Racism After 'Race Relations'* (London: Routledge, 1993) and A. Sivanandan, *A Different Hunger* (London: Pluto, 1982) for differing class analysis of racism in Britain.

29 M-O A: Spring 1990 DR J931; B2304.

30 It is also apparent from the survey, however, that the interplay of race and nation is not a new feature of British history. Past immigrant and minority groups have also played a key role in helping to define the sense of self in terms of an 'alien' other. A housewife from Bosgrove remembers her childhood in the 1930s when, in her family,

> 'THEY' [as well as the servant classes] also included various other groups who were disturbingly different from People Like Us, e.g. the Jews – about whom disparaging jokes were constantly made by my elders.

See Peter Figueroa, *Education and the Social Construction of 'Race'* (London: Routledge, 1991); Alec Fyfe and Peter Figueroa (eds), *Education for Cultural Diversity: The Challenge for a New Era* (London: Routledge, 1993). For specific debates about the history curriculum see Juliet Gardiner (ed.), *The History Debate* (London: Collins & Brown, 1990) and Tony Kushner, 'Heritage and Ethnicity: An Introduction', in idem (ed.), *The Jewish Heritage in British History: Englishness and Jewishness* (London: Frank Cass, 1992), pp. 1–28; M-O A: Spring 1990 DR 1650.

31 M-O A: Spring 1990 DR R1418; F1145 and G1846. See also G2089 and H1774.

32 Themes of race and ethnicity are largely missing from Martin Wiener, *English Culture and the Decline of the Industrial Spirit 1850–1980* (Cambridge: Cambridge University Press, 1981); J. Grainger, *Patriotisms: Britain 1900–1939* (London, 1986); Robert Colls and Philip Dodd (eds), *Englishness: Politics and Culture 1880–1920* (London: Croom Helm, 1986) – with the exception of D. Boyce's article on 'The Marginal Britons: The Irish', pp. 230–53; Roy Porter (ed.), *Myths of the English* (Cambridge: University of Cambridge Press, 1993). In contrast see the (uneven) collection of essays in R. Samuel (ed.), *Patriotism: The Making and Unmaking of British National Identity*, Volume II: *Minorities and Outsiders* (London: Routledge, 1989).

33 M-O A: Spring 1990 DR A1530. See Eric Hobsbawm and Terence Ranger (eds), *The Invention of Tradition* (London: Canto, 1983) for the comparatively recent origins of national 'traditional' culture; Waltham Forest actually has the fifth highest concentration of Pakistanis in Britain according to the 1991 census. See Andy Teague, 'Ethnic Groups: First Results from the 1991 Census', *Population Trends* 72, p 14 and Office of Population Censuses and Survey, *1991 Census: County Report: Outer London Part 1*, Volume 1 (London: HMSO, 1993), p 149 which gives a Pakistani population of 6,256 or 6.3 per cent of the total of Waltham Forest.

34 Anthias and Yuval-Davis, *Racialized Boundaries*; Jane Mackay and Pat

Thane, 'The Englishwoman', in Colls and Dodd, *Englishness*, pp. 191–229 especially p 191; M-O A: Spring 1990 DR B2197; D153.

35 M-O A: Spring 1990 DR W976 (a Jewish respondent); W2186.

36 M-O A: Spring 1990 DR D2239; H2173; H2372 and J2356; Stuart Hall, 'Old and New Identities, Old and New Ethnicities', in A. King (ed.), *Culture, Globalization and the World-System: Contemporary Conditions for the Representation of Identity* (Basingstoke: Macmillan, 1991), pp. 41–68.

37 M-O A: Spring 1990 DR G1041; D161.

38 M-O A: Spring 1990 DR L1991.

39 M-O A: Spring 1990 DR P1372.

40 M-O A: Spring 1990 DR B2260; T2245; Mark Ashford, *Detained Without Trial: A survey of Immigration Act detention* (London: Joint Council for the Welfare of Immigrants, 1993) and Paul Gordon, *Citizenship for Some?* (London: Runnymede Trust, 1989) on recent immigration, nationality and refugee policy and practice.

9

THE REVENGE OF CIVIL SOCIETY

State, nation and society in France

Max Silverman

According to the French sociologist Sami Naïr, the breakdown of the links between state and nation – which can be seen as a general phenomenon today – is perceived in France very specifically as the revenge of civil society on an oppressive state. He says:

> The past has been reconstructed by means of a sort of teleological reading of the present in which the disarticulation of the links between state and nation are seen not so much as the result of a general, world-wide process but more as the revenge of civil society on a state which has always oppressed it.[1]
>
> (Naïr 1992, p. 19)

I would like to consider a number of general features of this 'disarticulation' between state and nation and to discuss how far the French experience can be distinguished from that of other modern industrial nation states.

CIVIL AND CIVIC IN THE MODERN ERA

The end of the modern era of the formation of the properly national state, which I believe is the case today, means the end of the era of the attempted 'uniformization' of a national culture by means of the state. In other words, what became conflated in the high moment of the modern period – a conflation of citizenship, nationality and culture (Leca 1991a, p. 314) – is today in the process of fragmenting. Three points are worthy of note here and highlight the transformation that has taken place.

First, one major aspect of the construction of a uniform national culture and the accompanying abstract construction of the 'citizen' was the conflation of two contradictory principles: the civil and the civic. The first of these, the civil, refers to the private individual and is underscored by the principles of liberalism, the market and inegalitarianism; the second of these, the civic, refers to the individual who is part of a community of rights and is underscored by the principles of intervention, egalitarianism and solidarity (Leca 1991b, pp. 324–5). There were bound to be contradictions between these two conflicting visions of the individual.

The second point worthy of note is that whilst the civil and the civic were subsumed within the apparently homogeneous and unproblematic concept of the citizen, this abstract figure was itself conflated with the yet more abstract figure of 'Man'. However, the universality of 'Man' – humanity seen in terms of 'fraternité', 'the brotherhood of men' (Anthias and Yuval-Davis 1993, p. 28) – is, in reality, in contradiction to the particularity of the 'citizen', who is bounded by a nation and a state. We are 'Men' (sic) and citizens but the two do not always coincide. The conflation of 'Man' and citizen – a conflation of natural and national law, France seen as the incarnation of humanity – merely obscured the contradictions but they were clearly there in 1789. Tzvetan Todorov (1993, p. 186) points out how Sieyès, in his famous *Qu'est-ce que le tiers état?* of 1789, 'identifies readily with natural reason, or natural law, whereas his discourse in fact starts with the idea of the nation. When he distinguishes between the two, it is in order to link them in an apparently unproblematic sequence.'

Hence, the third point is that this citizen – deemed to be the same as 'Man' – was defined primarily in relation to the national state – deemed to be the same as humanity. As Sieyès says, 'The national will ... never needs anything but its own existence to be legal. It is the source of all legality' (*Qu'est-ce que le tiers état?*, p. 126, quoted in Todorov 1993, p. 186). This sentiment was echoed in Article 3 of the first French Declaration of Rights, written in August 1789, which states 'The principle of all sovereignty resides essentially in the Nation' (quoted in Todorov 1993, p. 186). From this point on – but especially in the latter part of the nineteenth century – the will of the people was, in theory, to be expressed by the unitary voice of the state. Similarly, citizen and nation, citizenship and nationality became virtually indistinguishable. As Brubaker (1992, p. 43) points out: 'As a democratic revolution, the French revolution institutionalized

147

political rights as citizenship rights, transposing them from the plane of the city-state to that of the nation-state, and transforming them from a privilege to a general right'.

Within the term 'citizen' there is, then, a whole cluster of different discourses frequently pulling in different directions yet whose problematic nature becomes obscured within an apparent coherence of purpose and design. Whether one would share Hannah Arendt's belief that 'the victory of the bourgeois (the competitive private person) over the citizen' was 'the single major catastrophe that befell Political man and Woman in the nineteenth century' and that 'this catastrophic victory set the scene for the triumph of the "totalitarian syndrome" ' (Heller and Fehér 1988, p. 97) is another question. A more modified view is provided by the political scientist Jean Leca (1991b, p. 203) who sees the conflation of the civil and the civic not only benefiting bourgeois individualism but also favouring the civic concept:

> Citizenship is not only indispensable to bourgeois society to maintain the abstraction of an apparent universalism and to legitimize class domination under the guise of the state, as Marx maintained. Citizenship is even more of use to the welfare state to sustain civil society through increasing social rights of individuals and organizing these within a concept of the needs of the community.

Arendt adopts a thoroughly critical posture with regard to modernity, whilst Leca is far more nuanced.

Whatever one's view is on this, both positions would agree that it was the state – more properly, the national state – which came to act as the main focus condensing and regulating social and political questions and questions concerning the private and the public individual.[2] This came about in the nineteenth century: first, by means of the legitimization of bourgeois and patriarchal values under the guise of neutrality and universality, dependent on the liberal, ideological 'trick' of positing a dichotomy between civil society and the state and a corresponding dichotomy between *droit privé* and *droit public* (cf. Renaut 1993, pp. 7–9); second, by means of the organization of collective rights through the establishment of the welfare state. Of course, this was also the case in other modern democracies, yet in France the state-based nature of rights, the state-focused nature of social questions in general and the fundamental principle of universalism were perhaps more powerful than elsewhere.

POSTMODERN SOCIETY

Today things look rather different. The apparently seamless ties between nation, state and citizen (and culture) have become 'unravelled' through a number of developments which have split apart their problematic unity. Much has already been said about the dual processes of globalization and localization of capital, communications and culture which have undercut the role of the national state in regulating contemporary developments.[3] This has effected a profound change in the role of the state in regulating social questions. One has to look no further than the current condition of the welfare state: Europe's invention, according to Ignacio Ramonet (1994, p. 7), who describes it as 'this arsenal of socio-economic safeguards, captured by the workers' movement and at the heart of modern European civilisation'. Today one of the greatest problems in Europe, as Ramonet points out, is 'quite simply the survival of societies as communities of solidarity in the face of the severe rise in unemployment, exclusion and recession'. Solidarity is losing out to individualism as the state becomes progressively privatized; or one might say the civic question is becoming more and more submerged within the rise of the civil.

A whole politics constructed in direct proportion to the strength of the state is also crumbling: a politics based on the idea that the only way to transform society was the capture of the state. As Laurent Cohen-Tanugi points out in relation to France:

> given that the nation was single and indivisible, and the state was its incarnation, the aim of all political combat was the conquest of the state, which was the sole legitimate instrument capable of transforming society.
>
> (Cohen-Tanugi 1989, p. 75)

Now it is no more a question of *transforming* society through a capture of the state apparatus, using the revolutionary rhetoric of old (Touraine 1993). All talk today is of *managing* change (Cohen-Tanugi 1989, pp. 16, 20) which, for a large part, emanates from sources other than the institutions of the state. It is no more a question of an 'emancipatory' and centralized politics but a shift to what Anthony Giddens (1991, pp. 209–32) has termed 'life-politics' or 'sub-politics'. From the 1960s onwards there has been a politicization of a whole range of issues – questions of gender, sexuality, environment, bio-

149

technology and so on – which are as much related to local and global factors as to specifically national state institutions.

There has also been a profound culturalization of social questions which again has little to do with the national question. Identity has become deinstitutionalized and finds itself today inserted within a localization/globalization network in which the national question becomes increasingly superfluous. Social relations, as Scott Lash points out, 'are increasingly extra-institutional' (Beck, Giddens and Lash 1994, p. 214). Zygmunt Bauman puts this well:

> The much talked about *globalization* of economy and cultural supplies, together with the defensive insufficiency of any political unit taken alone, spells the end of the modern state 'as we know it'. 'National economy' is today little more than a myth kept alive for electoral convenience ... In virtually every field, monopoly of power over their respective population falls from the weakening hands of the state ... (A)s old functions, one after another, slip away from the nation-state, taken over by the institutions which escape its political sovereignty, the state can do without mass mobilization of its citizenry.
>
> (Bauman 1993, p. 139)

In France, as in Britain, this release of civil society from its tutelage under an overbearing and unitary state has led to a mixed response. Many are now willing to heed the sort of sentiment expressed here by Alain Touraine:

> Do not let us give in to the temptation, born in the Eighteenth Century, to equate Man and citizen; this grandiose hope which led to such awful catastrophes, because it destroyed all the barriers which could limit absolute power.
>
> (Touraine 1992, p. 401)

Yet this critique of the worst consequences of universalism are coupled with fears of the consequences of totally abandoning the principle of universalism underlying the conflation of Man and citizen. One could say that what one is seeing in France today is the unravelling of what was always a problematic unity, and the appearance of the latent contradictions of the modern period.

So, on the one hand, new voices are heard, cultural/religious differences have become legitimate tools for political mobilization, pluralism and diversity are more 'up-front'. On the other hand, a breakdown in uniformity and the unitary state leads many to fear a breakdown in the traditional process of integration (especially through the institutions of the state), a fragmentation of society along particularist lines and a loss of social cohesion. Furthermore, the reduction in the power of the state to uphold the civic question and the principle of equality, and to act as a check on the inequalities of the market-place has left the path open to a revenge of civil society founded on unbridled liberalism, a narrow individualism or a resurgent tribalism exploiting mythologized ethnic histories. Sami Naïr describes this transformation well:

> Whilst the major preocccupation of the republican concept (of citizenship) was the concern with universalism, the proposed model of an abstract ideal as the goal of all ordinary citizens, equality as the *sine qua non* of communal life, the construction of a neutral public space – the new concept is centred on the individual subject, rejects the abstract project, prioritizes liberty over equality and opens up the public space to the clash of cultural particularisms.
>
> (Naïr 1992, pp. 44–5)

In the most pessimistic French scenarios, the reduction of the citizen to the atomized individual/consumer has frequently been associated with the transformation from an active 'thinking' subject to a passive, mindless object at the mercy of the market (Naïr 1992, p. 210) and bombarded by a barrage of 'cultural' artefacts in which anything counts as cultural (Finkielkraut 1987; Debray and Fumaroli 1993). Here we have an apocalyptic vision of the total passivization of the citizen. Is this merely alarmist talk designed simply to reinforce the dubious agenda of a return to the universalism, abstract citizenship and high cultural values of old? Or does it accurately describe the situation of individuals bereft of guidelines in a society whose institutions, values, and moral and ethical codes are all in a state of flux?

Perhaps a bit of both. It is true to say, in general terms, that the former conflation of the civil and the civic within a state-based definition of the citizen has today given way to a conflation of a different order – that between civil society and consumerism, within a market-led definition of the citizen. In our current virtually state-privatized societies, citizenship is becoming equated with consumerism – truly the revenge of the market against the state in the form of an aggressive neo-liberalism armed with the new ideological construction of freedom in the form of buying power. (One thinks

151

immediately of John Major's Citizen's Charter in the UK. Is this a charter for citizens or consumers, and where is the distinction between the two?) In this view of the citizen, the civic is either dropped completely (Margaret Thatcher's 'there's no such thing as society, only individuals'), or transformed from a space regulated by the natural entitlement to rights to one that is regulated simply by a variety of contractual arrangements and bargaining power. As Chantal Mouffe (1993, p. 80) has pointed out, in the liberal conception 'it is the citizen which is sacrificed to the individual'. Jean Leca (1991b, p. 209) sees this state of affairs as marking the death knell of citizenship, for 'without some sort of sense of community there is no citizenship, for a "political community" is not simply a collection of individuals'. The inevitable consequence of defining society simply as a collection of individuals is, according to Alain Touraine and his colleagues at the Ecole des Hautes Etudes en Sciences Sociales in Paris, the current *dualization* of society: that is, a division of society into citizens (defined as those who can compete in the market) and all those without the means to compete and therefore excluded from participation in society.

If it is true that the market is the only player left to determine social relations and questions of value, then this is indeed a cause for concern. It is difficult to argue against the Fukuyama 'end of history' thesis (1989) when one sees so many cases of liberalism triumphant and the left – shorn of its old socialist rhetoric – in disarray. France today is a classic example of this scenario. On the other hand, the nostalgia for the Enlightenment values of old – as an alternative to the rampant amoralism (and frequently immoralism) of the unfettered market – is not only inappropriate for today's pluralist societies but also implicitly (and sometimes explicitly) intolerant and ethnocentric. The French headscarf affairs (1989 and 1994) – in which a number of Muslim girls were excluded from school for wearing their Islamic headscarves, hence breaching the code of secularism in state education – highlighted the levels of ethnocentric intolerance to which the secular fundamentalism of the Republican Enlightenment tradition could go (Silverman 1992). Of course, these are troubling issues for all modern industrial nations. The issue here is how far the French experience is any different to that of other countries. For an answer to this question, it is interesting to look again at the state-based tradition in France to which I have already referred, and its effect on recent developments.

STATE AND CIVIL SOCIETY

Let us pursue the effect of the state-based tradition in France on two aspects of the contemporary situation: concepts of difference and pluralism, and concepts of democracy. First, today's fear of an anarchistic revenge of civil society, coupled with the view that difference and pluralism constitute the path towards a fragmentation of social cohesion – a fairly widely-held view in France – can perhaps be best understood only by acknowledging the ideological power of the universalist, egalitarian and state-based republican tradition in that country. The distinction between the public and the private in France was underscored by an extremely powerful myth of a neutral, unitary and enlightened realm (the public) above all particularisms (the private). The public realm and the space of citizenship were successfully depoliticized and aestheticized, thus stripping the citizen of all particularist features and, as we have said, making a direct equation between citizen and 'Man', citizenship and humanity.

This process should be seen within the historical context of the triumph, at the end of the nineteenth century, of the republican consensus concerning the nature of the citizen. Henceforth, blood and soil definitions of the citizen of the type propounded by the writer and politician Maurice Barrès and the extreme right-wing organization Action Française (rooting the citizen deterministically within a community, a place, a culture and a nation) could be convincingly opposed by the message of egalitarianism and universalism so that they appeared to be polar opposites. This binary opposition was underpinned by the notion – expressed by Ernest Renan in his famous talk at the Sorbonne in 1882 entitled 'What is a Nation?' – of a clear dichotomy between the French version of citizenship (political-legal, consisting of a voluntary association of individuals) and the German version (ethnocultural, consisting of a pre-determined and organic concept of the community). Whereas the latter could only ever be parochial (and at worst racist), the former was elevated beyond the limited perspective of local custom and culture to the realm of the truly universal and indivisible. By associating ethnocultural or more overtly racial theories with the German tradition, republican apologists could more easily claim the neutral, progressive, rational, race-free, universalist and egalitarian tradition for the French.

In reality, however, the French version of citizenship, rather than being a political–legal concept *as opposed to* an ethnocultural concept, should more properly be seen as a very effective blending of the

153

political–legal and the ethnocultural, whilst thoroughly effacing its ethnocultural particularism (and other contradictions) through a process of depoliticization and naturalization. Citizenship was merged with cultural conformity, the second seen as the condition of and the means to attain the first.

With such a powerful myth in place it is not too difficult to see how today the 'problem' can be interpreted as an invasion of the cultural into the political sphere, the particularist into the universal sphere, the differentialist into the assimilationist sphere (as if cultural particularism had been absent before). In the discourse of many – not only those on the extreme right – this invasion of the cultural into the political is linked with the idea of the invasion of the cultural difference of the new 'immigrants' (used euphemistically to signify 'North Africans' and their children) and the accompanying invasion of the differentialist discourse of anti-racism into the 'neutral', individualist and universalist sphere of the French republican tradition, leading to the racialization of French society (Yonnet 1993). Here 'cultural difference' – a product of what Agnes Heller and Ferenc Fehér (1988, p. 6) have termed 'the breakdown of the grand narrative of secularization' – becomes a euphemism for 'anti-France'.

Second, the joyful embracing by some of a neo-liberal perspective and the unquestioning conflation of citizenship and consumerism, and of pluralism and liberalism is, according to some French commentators (and commentators on France), due to a relative absence of a liberal-democratic tradition in France compared to some other countries. Laurent Cohen-Tanugi has put it like this:

> The profound inability of French political culture (especially on the Left) to dissociate public utility, sociability and virtue from the state, its inability to articulate law and the market, ethics and society, has put a block on thinking 'the political' in any other way than in relation to the state, to the consequent detriment of civil society and, in the final analysis, to democracy.
>
> (Cohen-Tanugi 1989, p. 77)

Although Cohen-Tanugi himself is precisely one of those who is quick to equate liberalism and democratic pluralism ('democratic liberalism signifies today more than ever before in France democratic *pluralism*', 1989, p. 47), his previous statement contains more than a grain of truth. He argues that, unlike in other countries where a culture of liberalism and democracy went hand in hand, France's construction of a uniform national culture established by means of a strongly interventionist state prevented this partnership and led to 'a weakening of civil society' (1989, p. 78. See also Judt 1992).

Whether one accepts this thesis or not, it does seem as though 'the revenge of civil society' is more dramatic in France than in other western democracies. The national state apparatus and its ideology were certainly more entrenched than in Britain and therefore have further to fall. The new liberalism – just as the new nationalism (or national populism) – seems much more brash, perhaps because there is a greater vacuum to fill. As in the former communist states, the strength of the backlash is perhaps in direct proportion to the power wielded by the state beforehand. A good example of this is the vigorous revisionism of intellectual history which is taking place now that the former Cold War orthodoxies have disintegrated. The vicious attacks on what are depicted as the morally blind, hopelessly prescriptive, authoritarian nature of former gurus (far more ferocious than anything seen in Britain) are frequently the bearers (either explicitly or implicitly) of a neo-liberal, democratic agenda (see for example many of the articles in the influential journal Le Débat).

The crucial questions, of course, are now the following: does the collapse of the left's faith in the struggle for collective rights (largely through the appropriation of the state) and the talk today of *individual* rights mean that questions of citizenship are today inevitably couched in the neo-liberal language of individualism? Is the current 'valorization' by the new left of civil society over the state simply a blind for the hegemony of this language? Is there a consensus now on this language across the political spectrum? According to Sunil Khilnani (1990), the answer to all these questions is, unfortunately, 'yes'. He believes that the current debate in France is not evidence of a renewal of a 'citizenship of participation', but simply the dissolution of the values of citizenship into 'a narcissistic individualism' (pp. 181–2).

However, perhaps this view is overly pessimistic. Although the decline of the state and the re-emergence of questions to do with civil society might favour the forces of individualism within a liberal philosophy of the free market, this does not mean that there is not also another side to this debate. The problem of how to discuss questions of equality, citizenship and solidarity without recourse to the old rhetoric of the radical transformation of society through the appropriation of the state, or, on the other hand, a neo-liberal conflation of citizen and consumer *is* being vigorously debated in France. The text by Sami Naïr, *Le Regard des vainqueurs* (to which I have

155

already referred above), in which he calls for an active citizenship appropriate to today's new economic and cultural paradigms, is one example. Another is the appearance over the last two years of two hefty tomes by Alain Touraine (1992 and 1994) on modernity and democracy. This body of work is built around the rediscovery of the subject – that is, the individual constructed as social and political actor. Touraine argues that in our post-industrial societies we need a new relationship between the universal and the particular, between rational law and the rights of the subject, between social integration and individual freedom. He explicitly warns against the danger of political subjects becoming mere consumers of policies and material goods, a situation compounded by the increasing fragmentation of postmodern life:

> In opposition to both totalitarian principles and the idea of a society reduced to a market-place, we must conceive a democracy built on social movements which defend the human subject against the double impersonality of absolute power and the rule of the market.
>
> (Touraine 1992, pp. 397–8)

Touraine tries to steer a middle path between the general and the particular. His is a guarded acceptance of diversity: aware both of the dangers of the totalitarian nature of rational universalism and of the wholesale acceptance of 'the right to difference' and a politics of identity (the latter seen in terms of ghettoization and tribalism). His colleague Michel Wieviorka (1993b) argues for a similar articulation between common rules and individual freedom which avoids the jungle mentality of the market-place. Touraine and Wieviorka are asking similar questions to those posed by a number of commentators in Britain. Chantal Mouffe has described the problem in the following terms:[4]

> How to conceptualise our identities as individuals and as citizens in a way that does not sacrifice one to the other? The question at stake is how to make our belonging to different communities of values, language and culture compatible with our common belonging to a political community whose rules we have to accept. As against conceptions that stress commonality at the expense of plurality and respect for difference, or that deny any form of commonality in the name of plurality and difference, what we need is to envisage a form of commonality

that respects diversity and makes room for different forms of individuality.

(Mouffe 1993, pp. 80–1)

Although the political expression of concepts of new citizenship might be in its infancy, the debate is already advanced.

In conclusion, we might say that the decline of the state and the revenge of civil society is a mixed blessing in France. The overbearing nature of the national state and its profoundly entrenched narratives of legitimacy mean that it is all the more difficult to step out from under their shadow now that things have changed so much. This leads to the consequent danger of grabbing at dangerous discourses to fill the vacuum. On the other hand, the breakdown of a unitary national state formation and its legitimizing discourses (as, in a different way, with the former communist states) has led to a wide-ranging debate around questions of nation, state, culture, the market and citizenship, and holds out the prospect of a major reformulation of the relationship between individual and society.

NOTES

1 All translations from the French are my own.
2 In the words of Michel Wieviorka (1993a), 'the state itself was the place in which social relations became condensed and focused. As the "welfare state", it played a decisive role in regulating the "social question".'
3 See for example Hall, Held and McGrew (eds) 1992, especially the chapter by Tony McGrew entitled 'A global society?'.
4 See also Weeks 1993, p. 206; Heller and Fehér 1988.

REFERENCES

Anthias, F. and Yuval-Davis, N. (1993) *Racialized Boundaries: Race, Nation, Gender, Colour and Class and the Anti-Racist Struggle*, London: Routledge.

Bauman, Z. (1993) *Postmodern Ethics*, Oxford: Blackwell.

Beck, U., Giddens, A., and Lash, S. (1994) *Reflexive Modernization: Politics, Tradition and Aesthetics in the Modern Social Order*, Cambridge: Polity Press.

Brubaker, R. (1992) *Citizenship and Nationhood in France and Germany*, Cambridge, Mass.: Harvard University Press.

Cohen-Tanugi, L. (1989) *La Métamorphose de la démocratie*, Paris: Editions Odile Jacob.

Debray, R. and Fumaroli, M. (1993) 'Dictature de l'image?', *Le Débat* 74, March–April.
Fukuyama, F. (1989) 'The end of history?', *The National Interest* xvi, Summer.
Finkielkraut, A. (1987) *La Défaite de la pensée*, Paris: Gallimard.
Giddens, A. (1991) *Modernity and Self-identity: Self and Society in the Late Modern Age*, Cambridge: Polity Press.
Hall, S., Held, D., McGrew, A. (eds) (1992) *Modernity and its Futures*, Cambridge: Polity Press/The Open University.
Heller, A. and Fehér, F. (1988) *The Postmodern Political Condition*, Cambridge: Polity Press.
Judt, T. (1992) *Past Imperfect: French Intellectuals, 1944–1956*, Berkeley and Los Angeles, Calif.: University of California Press.
Khilnani, S. (1990) 'Un nouvel espace pour la pensée politique', *Le Débat* 58, January–February, pp. 181–92.
Leca, J. (1991a) 'La citoyenneté en question' in P.-A. Taguieff (ed.) *Face au racisme*, volume 2 'Analyses, hypothèses, perspectives', Paris: La Découverte.
——(1991b) 'Individualisme et citoyenneté' in P. Birnbaum and J. Leca (eds) *Sur l'individualisme*, Paris: Presses de la Fondation nationale des Sciences Politiques.
Mouffe, C. (1993) 'Liberal socialism and pluralism. Which citizenship?', in Judith Squires (ed.) *Principled Positions: Postmodernism and the Rediscovery of Value*, London: Lawrence and Wishart.
Naïr, S. (1992) *Le Regard des vainqueurs: les enjeux français de l'immigration*, Paris: Grasset.
Ramonet, I. (1994) 'Un horizon d'espoirs', *Manière de voir 22, Le Monde Diplomatique*, May.
Renaut, A. (1993) 'Genèse du couple état-société', *Projet* 'Citoyen en quel État?', 233, Spring, pp. 7–16.
Silverman, M. (1992) *Deconstructing the Nation: Immigration, Racism and Citizenship in Modern France*, London: Routledge.
Todorov, T. (1993) *On Human Diversity: Nationalism, Racism, and Exoticism in French Thought*, Cambridge, Mass: Harvard University Press.
Touraine, A. (1992) *Critique de la Modernité*, Paris: Fayard.
——(1993) 'Républicains ou démocrates?, Débat entre Paul Thibaud et Alain Touraine, *Projet* 'Citoyen en quel État?', 233, Spring, pp. 26–34.
—— (1994) *Qu'est-ce que la démocratie?*, Paris: Fayard.
Weeks, J. (1993) 'Rediscovering values', in Judith Squires (ed.) *Principled Positions: Postmodernism and the Rediscovery of Value*, London: Lawrence and Wishart.
Wieviorka, M. (1993a) 'L'État et les sujets', *Projet* 'Citoyen en quel État?', 233, Spring, pp. 17–25.
Wieviorka, M. (1993b) *La Démocratie à l'épreuve: nationalisme, populisme, ethnicité*, Paris: La Découverte.
Yonnet, P. (1993) *Voyage au centre du malaise français*, Paris: Gallimard.

10

MIGRATION, REFUGEES AND ETHNIC PLURALITY AS ISSUES OF PUBLIC AND POLITICAL DEBATES IN (WEST) GERMANY

Karen Schönwälder

In May 1993 Germany's parliament decided to restrict severely the constitutionally granted right to political asylum. This decision was preceded and accompanied by an enormous public debate and an unprecedented upsurge of racist violence. Referring to these conflicts, and the forthcoming parliamentary decision, Jürgen Habermas wrote in *Die Zeit* that, within only three months, and behind the smoke-screen of a dishonest debate, West Germany had been mentally more deeply transformed than in the previous fifteen years. That the arson attacks of Rostock and the killings of Mölln were answered by accelerated steps towards severe restrictions of the right to political asylum, thus branding the foreigners as the source of hatred of foreigners, signalled, in his view, a severe decay of democratic and republican standards: Germany was experiencing an attempt to transform its political self-definition towards a renewed ethnic nationalism.[1]

Unquestionably, asylum and, linked to it, immigration and the presence of those called 'aliens' (*Ausländer*) have been central themes of recent political and public debates in Germany. The politiciz-ation[2] of the issue can hardly be compared with the way immigration or questions of ethnicity are currently dealt with in Britain, although there may be more similarity with France. In the last fifteen years asylum and migration have consciously and without reluctance been made major topics of party political campaigns. In the regional state of Hessen the Christian Democrats (CDU) in 1989 fought elections

159

KAREN SCHÖNWÄLDER

under the slogan that every vote for the CDU would be a vote against voting rights for aliens. In the summer of 1992 their party secretary, Volker Rühe, advised the local branches to focus on asylum and to attack the Social Democrats (SPD) as responsible for every additional refugee.[3] In 1992–3 the CDU/CSU constantly attacked the Social Democrats who, by (initially) refusing to agree to alterations to the Basic Law, were sabotaging a solution to the 'asylum problem'. The Social Democrats themselves countered by advertising that it was the CDU/CSU who blocked measures to limit refugee numbers from being effectively implemented. In Germany there is definitely no inter-party consensus on the suspension of political party competition on race-related issues (as is assumed for some periods of British post-war politics).[4]

What is the background to, and the significance of, the prominence of refugee and migration issues on the public agenda? Is it true that it is mainly the media discourse and the elites with their privileged access to the media who are responsible for racist attitudes and consequently for outbreaks of violence, as claimed for example by Jäger and Link?[5]

There is indeed some evidence supporting this interpretation. The notion that Germany was being flooded, that millions were about to come from the south and the east and that Germany's affluence, for some even its existence as a nation, were under threat, had been hammered into the brains of the population. In June 1991 aliens and asylum rocketed up the scale of themes Germans regarded as important, overtaking unification and the Gulf War, to become priority no. 1 for the West Germans until February 1992. It returned to that position in the following summer and autumn.[6] An increase from 10 per cent naming asylum and aliens as top issues to 70 per cent holding that opinion only a few months later (in October and November 1991) demonstrates the dependence of public opinion on agenda-setting in the media. In 1991 and 1992 asylum was the topic of otherwise politically uneventful seasons. Twice these publicity booms were followed by outbursts of violence: among other incidents the attacks on refugee hostels at Hoyerswerda (1991) and Rostock (1992). In the spring of 1993 the racist murder of Turkish residents at Solingen coincided with the parliamentary decision to restrict the provisions on the right to asylum in the Basic Law. Although it was claimed that restrictions had to be enforced to prevent the continuation of racist violence (thus interpreting the latter as a popular demand that had to be met), it is quite obvious that violence and

160

hatred had been encouraged by the exclusionist rhetoric and that racists would only be further encouraged by their apparent success.

And yet, one might argue that it is too simplistic to assume that racist violence is stirred up by unscrupulous politicians – that conflicts are created by politicians and the media. Indeed, Habermas, in the article mentioned above, attacked the major parties for becoming accomplices of an obtuse, resentment-laden section of their electorate, thus focusing on popular racism and xenophobia. Klaus von Beyme has argued that there is a discrepancy between a patriotism of the enlightened elites that centres around the constitution and the popular nationalism of the underprivileged masses.[7] Obviously, the part which 'elites' and the media on the one hand and, on the other hand, the 'ordinary' population play with respect to the development of racist and hostile attitudes, and the interaction between the two factors are not sufficiently clear, or at least explanations are not consensual. Although the rest of this chapter will concentrate on the political and (wider) public debates, they constitute only one part of the story. To explain the receptivity to racist or xenophobic interpretations of current experiences and problems researchers are debating old and new questions: do conflicts erupt due to competition for scarce resources and when there is high unemployment and economic crisis? Are such problems a recurrent feature of modern society or do the process of modernization and the merger of the two German states account for major changes? How relevant is manipulation or at least the opinion-forming influence of political and media debates compared to spontaneous processes among the population? Do politicians encourage racism or do they only react to conflicts caused by the huge numbers and the unconventional behaviour of the immigrants, as one influential study claimed only recently?[8]

Keeping this wider context in mind, the following text will concentrate on the ways in which the topics of migration and ethnic plurality occurred in public discussions. It will attempt to trace the history of and background to the enormous recent politicization of the issue.

THE ABSENCE OF PUBLIC CONTROVERSY IN THE EARLY YEARS OF LABOUR MIGRATION

There is a famous photograph from September 1964, showing a man on a motorbike holding a bunch of flowers in his hand. He wears work clothes and a hat and looks a bit frightened. Two other men, dressed in suits, are present; both hold microphones. The man on the motorbike is Amando Sá Rodrigues from Portugal. The bike is the present he received as the one-millionth 'guestworker'. The media event around this jolly occasion would hardly be called a dangerous politicization of immigration. Labour migration was, by that time, more or less a labour-market issue in West Germany; it was dealt with by the Federal Ministry of Labour and Social Order, employers, trade unions, the Federal Institute for Employment and – far less influential – the churches and some welfare organizations.[9] The message of this event in 1964 was one of a friendly Germany welcoming desperately needed help.[10] (The reality was often less amicable.)

In 1954, when the idea of recruiting workers from Italy was launched by Ludwig Erhard, the Minister for Economic Affairs, it aroused some controversy. Did not Germany itself have enough unemployed? Had all the German refugees and expellees from eastern European and the East German territories already been integrated? The trade unions had reservations and agreed only on the condition that foreign workers would be granted equal wages and social rights.[11] But for the next ten or fifteen years migrant labour would be an issue of little public interest, removed from political controversy and not associated with any substantial unrest. There are four major reasons for this:

First and most obvious, the West German economy, from the late 1950s, desperately needed additional labour, in particular after the border with East Germany was closed and workers from the east could no longer come of their own accord.

Second, at the time of the Paris Treaties and the preparations for the European Economic Community, West German politicians were eager to suppress any parallels with the past. After Italy's withdrawal from the Axis in 1943, about 600,000 soldiers who refused to fight on the German side had been forced to work for Germany's victory and had received awful treatment.[12] Roughly ten years later their presence in West Germany was presented as a contribution to European Unity, in which Italy was a partner Germany could hardly do without. Emphasis was placed on how important it was that the returning south Europeans would report positively about the Germans (although this was not followed by adequate measures against miserable living conditions).[13] Marked by a strongly patronizing attitude, West Germany presented itself as happy to help poorer European countries and to contribute to their development.[14] *Überfremdung* ('being inundated') – the constant and enormously influential spectre of German nationalism since the 1880s – was not to be heard. It seems that no debate about where to recruit additional labour took place. Italy was a traditional source and its government had offered co-operation. Further research may show whether there was a difference between public pronouncements and internal considerations, as in Britain where, very early on, great concern was expressed in closed government circles about colonial immigration. Questions put by members of parliament regarding the possible importation of infectious deseases, communist infiltration, or the import of criminals through migrant labour might point to deeply rooted mentality structures which were, however, unpopular in the 1960s and so were suppressed.[15]

Third: it has been assumed that a conscious strategy existed to maintain silence on this issue in order to allow a return to the utilization of migrant labour without a public debate about its traditions as well as to allow the unnoticed reconstruction of the pre-1945 legal framework for foreign labour and the control of aliens.[16] This, however, remains a hypothesis.

Fourth, how did the population in West Germany react? It can be safely assumed that the presence of nearly 8 million foreign and forced labourers as recently as 1944 and the experience of the brutal, however relatively easily accepted, Nazi labour system, habituated Germans to the presence and the subordination of non-German colleagues – to put it euphemistically. Forced labour was not an issue of public debate after 1945 and was not perceived as part of the Nazi crimes. Perhaps, therefore, U. Herbert is right in assuming that the experience of foreign and forced labour which had not been subjected to a critical review constituted an influential factor when foreign workers reappeared.[17] When, in 1956, 55 per cent of the West German population rejected the recruitment of foreign labourers fears of competition for jobs were probably crucial.[18] With the boom they quickly vanished.

Rare opinion polls for the 1960s show widespread indifference – indeed, their rarity already reflects how low the level of public interest was. When the millionth guestworker was welcomed, 31 per cent of those questioned had no opinion about the presence of migrant labourers. Obviously the issue was not present in public debates in a way that made the formation of a personal opinion a pressing task.[19] In this phase, the normality of foreign labour, the economic boom and the taboos of the post-Nazi era contributed to an absence (at least in the public sphere) of any violent conflicts.

The first significant clashes and debates occurred around 1967 –

with West Germany's first economic crisis and the end of the so-called economic miracle. A few years earlier there had been signs of a debate about a reduction of the number of migrant workers, possibly by increasing the working hours, as favoured by the then Chancellor Erhard.[20] The reasons given were economic. Besides, it has been assumed that Swiss campaigns against *Überfremdung* had some influence on German perceptions.[21] And indeed, in 1964 the Federal Minister for Labour tried to calm down 'worries that the swelling number of guestworkers means an *"Überfremdung"* '.[22] With unemployment occurring again in 1967, although at a very low rate, migrant labourers were attacked as competitors for jobs. Behind the (still official) friendly image of European unity and German development aid for the south, complaints about foreign life-styles emerged. It might, however, serve as an indicator of the still limited political relevance of the theme that the success of the extreme right in the late 1960s was not crucially based on racism against (im)migrants and that the extreme right tried to use this factor only to a limited extent. Other enemies ranked higher: there was still crude anti-Semitism and anti-Americanism, besides openly racist attacks on migrant labourers as a danger to the health of the German *Volk*. When almost half of the population in 1967 insisted that German cultural life should be kept clean of foreign influence they most probably had America, Coke and pop music in mind.

CHANGING PERCEPTIONS IN THE 1970s: 'GUESTWORKERS' AS A BURDEN

It was not until the early 1970s that those who were now often called *ausländische Arbeitnehmer* ('alien employees') became a major issue of public and political debates. For years, foreign workers had (in the sphere of mainstream politics) been perceived almost exclusively as enormously beneficial to the German economy and state. But, from about 1970, some observers began to note that the favourable costs–benefits. calculation was beginning to fall apart: families and children began to make use of an infrastructure which foreign workers had before only helped to pay for (by taxes and social insurance contributions).[23] With attention focusing on schools and accommodation, migrants began to be perceived as a burden on the social infrastructure, and their presence was consequently (although rarely explicitly) questioned. Additionally, the topos of the 'exhausted capacities' now assumed front rank importance where it remains

164

today. Chancellor Willy Brandt suggested, in January 1973, that careful consideration should be given to the question of at which point the society's capacity to absorb migrants was exhausted and social reason and responsibility demanded a halt.[24] As in Britain, but ten years later, it was claimed that without limitations on the numbers of foreigners integration would not be possible. It was the number of foreign nationals which, in the view of the Social-democratic–Liberal government, endangered integration.

In 1973 the climate was one of change towards peaceful relations with eastern Europe and of internal reforms, of 'dare more democracy'. This climate found an expression in the politicization of the immigration issue from the left, when intolerable living conditions were attacked. Indeed, the previous relative silence on the issue of migrant labour should not be taken as indicating an absence of problems. Now, in the atmosphere of social reform and progress migrant workers and their families could appear as a factor which interfered with the project of a reformed society, and sometimes limitation was favoured because the development of a sub-proletariat living in ghettos was regarded as intolerable.[25]

Furthermore, in 1973, the turn from expansion to a 'consolidation' of the welfare system was already near: it became apparent that costs in the health and pensions sectors had risen enormously and the immigrants and possible integrative measures just added an additional burden for the state. Although it was legally hardly possible to remove the immigrant population, the idea that a return to the home countries should be encouraged increasingly formed one part of government policy. The new key term, however, was 'integration'. It expressed the realization, on the part of politicians and the general public, that large numbers of migrants had at least temporarily become settled in Germany and that social problems had evolved which, as 'integration' suggested, ought to disappear quickly. The question of racial discrimination, which appeared relatively early in British debates, was (and is) largely absent from the public political agenda in Germany. Here, guestworkers were seen as the 'social problem no. 1' (and not as victims of discrimination), and integration was largely perceived as necessary adjustment on their part.

The introduction of provisions which prohibited foreign nationals from moving to towns and cities where they already made up 12 per cent of the population or more reinforced the idea of immigrants as a liability and of a magic threshold above which communities could no longer bear the 'burden' of foreigners.[26] Still, the rationale for the limitation of immigration was, in the first place, defined financially. However, in 1982 the government referred to social peace and the necessary consent of the German population as demanding a limitation on the number of aliens. Although it was often referred to indirectly, ethnic coexistence became a theme.[27] It was the Social Democratic Chancellor Schmidt who (in 1975) emphasized that the Federal Republic would not allow a 'nationality problem' to be forced upon it.[28]

After 1973, attitudes towards migrant labourers or, increasingly, immigrants changed for the worse. While it is quite clear that this was not related to the numbers of immigrants, it is difficult to prove which factor played the major part: the economic crisis of 1973–4 on the one hand or, on the other, the politicization of the immigration issue with the major signal: immigrants are a burden, immigration has to be stopped. The politicization of immigration in the early 1970s was not caused by an instrumental use of the issue, neither did riots provoke a public debate. It was a result of economic considerations and the (reluctant and incomplete) public realization of a neglected reality.

'NATIONAL IDENTITY' VERSUS ETHNIC PLURALITY: THE 1980s

Between 1979 and 1982 attitudes towards migrants underwent a significant change. Two-thirds of the West German population (according to opinion polls) in 1982 thought that the guestworkers should return home – this figure was up from 39 per cent in 1978. Only 11 per cent supported intensified measures for integration. Just three years before, support had been 42 per cent. Almost everybody now felt able to assess the characteristics of immigrants – clearly an indicator of the presence of the issue in the public sphere. Extreme right-wing parties now turned to the theme and set up campaigns to stop the influx of foreigners. The 'Heidelberger Manifest' of 1981 demonstrated academic support for racist concepts. Violent attacks happened. Clearly, the years around 1980 mark a turning point in terms at least of the open expression of xenophobic and racist attitudes.

The political and public debate that obviously formed the background to these developments was marked by three new trends: now *Überfremdung* the old nationalist and racist theme since the late nineteenth century, which had been largely taboo after 1945, was reintroduced into the debate. A number of articles in respectable newspapers and journals now stated that it was impossible to integrate a large number of immigrants and, in particular, the Turks. J. Schilling claimed in several articles that a compulsory repatriation was unavoidable; numbers had to be brought below the 'British danger line'.[29] In the *Bundestag* the Chairman of the CDU faction, Alfred Dregger (and similarly Dietrich Spranger for the CSU), introduced a new tone: it was time to take account of the justified interests of the Germans with their claim to preserve German national identity. Dregger stated that a small country, crippled after two World Wars, was not able to take in too many immigrants. The CDU-politician introduced four categories of alien. In particular two groups could not be assimilated and could hardly be integrated: the Turks with their different culture, mentality and religion, and the Africans and Asians (possibly coming via Britain and with British passports). Return should be the rule, rotation an option to be reconsidered.[30] Despite this radicalization, SPD- and FDP-politicians emphasized common ground and the need to stop further immigration.

The second trend, as signified in Dregger's speech, was a process that might be called 'racialization', meaning the identification of particular immigrant and refugee groups as eternally different. Anti-immigration arguments began to focus on the population of Turkish descent, which numbered about 1.5 million in 1980 and on refugees who, apart from some from eastern Europe, now increasingly came from Asia (in 1980 220,000 Asians, accounting for 5 per cent of the aliens, lived in West Germany).[31] Indeed, many Germans now complained about the 'different behaviour' of immigrants more than about competition for jobs. The (alleged) internal threat of cultural difference and the transformation of the environment was added to the external threat of human 'floods'. It did not replace the latter – as assumed by Paul Rich for Britain in 1971 – but accompanies it to the present day.[32]

While before 1973 asylum had not been a theme of public debates, from about 1979–80 immigration debates started to take the shape of debates about asylum. According to the linguist Werner Link, around that time the media created the *'Asylantenspringflut'* (the notion of spring tides of asylum-seekers).[33]

The more aggressive tendency against immigration and immigrants, and the renewed talk about *Überfremdung*, can be related to the broader renaissance of intellectual and political conservatism since the later 1970s. Here the parallels with Britain are obvious. In the early 1980s there were the first wide-scale discussions about an alleg-edly sick or disturbed 'national identity' of the West Germans and expressions of a desire to reconstitute this identity. Already, between about 1980 and 1984, there was a search for the creation of a higher, non-rational and emotional idea of the community and its ideals. The main obstacles, however, were not seen in the presence of aliens or immigrants, who were hardly mentioned in this debate, but in the peace movement, Germany's division and the prevailing critical atti-tude to modern German history, which was branded a loss of his-tory.[34] Only the occasional backbencher argued that the wish for national unity could hardly be kept alive if the population in the west changed its national character so much,[35] or that an ethnically changing Federal Republic might lose its legitimate claim to represent the German heritage in rivalry to the GDR.[36] As hardly anybody at that time believed in the possibility of unification these interventions did not find much resonance. And yet, it cannot be ruled out that such considerations influenced the political negation of permanent immigration. Indirectly the open thematization of Überfremdung, as in the case of Dregger, was part of and backed by the de-tabooiing of concepts which were linked with the Nazi dictatorship, and it may have found resonance in latent mentality structures. A revival of nationalism or national identity explicitly or implicitly furthers exclusionary mechanisms against those who do not belong to the old cultural and historical nation. However, in the early 1980s the attempt to recreate a 'national identity' was a defensive move against critics, and not entirely successful. The trends towards a delegitimation of nationalism and towards the development of a political confidence or a non-national self-definition in the population were too strong.

A third new trend to emerge at this time was the polarization of the debate. While migrant labour had previously been a consensual issue – the federal government in the 1970s and 1980s usually empha-sized its co-operation with the Länder[37] – a parliamentary debate in February 1982 demonstrated that the CDU and the CSU had left the common ground. It might be said that the extraordinary and aggres-sive use of the immigration and asylum theme in political controversy which has marked recent years started around 1980. In the crisis of the Social-Democratic–Liberal government the Conservatives very obviously used the theme to push the political climate further to the right. This instrumental attitude becomes even more obvious since, after 1982 (when Helmut Kohl became Chancellor of a new centre-right government), the immigration and refugee issues were clearly scaled down. With the exception of a brief campaign in 1986, they were more or less unimportant as public and political theme. It is these cycles that demonstrate the instrumental use of the theme.[38] Although there were policy changes (including a new aliens act) they did not go as far as the rhetoric had promised.[39]

At the same time, under the heading of 'the multicultural society', a nascent debate about the future shape of (west) German society was led by the churches and the trade unions. Thus, people who supported the ideas of tolerant co-existence and of plurality instead of assimilationist integration tried to counter rising hostility and racism. It was not only the political right who promoted a politicization of the issue. In the 1990s it became a key demand of supporters of ethnic plurality to encourage an open and widespread debate about a positive attitude to (regulated) immigration and about the future shape of Germany as a country of immigration. Conservative politicians have argued that it is exactly this politicization, the open and positive talk about immigration, which causes arson attacks on refugee hostels. Obviously such criticism attacks the positive attitude to immigration and ethnic plurality and not solely its public discussion. Public discussion of the issues of immigration and ethnic plurality can have positive effects, as the campaigns for voting rights in local elections and, more recently, against racist violence in Germany demonstrate.

Throughout the 1980s not only was there no overall shift towards hostility, but vocal support was also expressed for friendship and tolerance. During the 1980s opinion polls show positive trends even while unemployment remained high. In the CDU, besides the nationalist trend signified by people like Alfred Dregger, politicians like Heiner Geissler (at that time more influential in the party than today) favoured a more moderate course which would refrain from aggressive language.[40] Many analysts then saw these 'modernizers' as the trendsetters in the Christian Democratic Party. They were understood to signal a move away from old-fashioned nationalist conservatism and towards a more European and world-market-oriented profile which was meant to be attractive to women, youth and to those members of the middle strata who were interested in individual freedom and so-called postmaterialist ideals rather than in a national community. As it turned out, the CDU could relatively successfully hold on to power while relegating the modernizers to the fringe.

CONFLICTING TRENDS IN PRESENT-DAY GERMANY

How deeply has the merger of the two German states changed the framework in which immigration and multi-ethnicity are discussed and xenophobic or racist attitudes develop? Did Germany indeed, during the summer of 1992, change more deeply than in the previous fifteen years, as claimed in J. Habermas' provocative statement quoted above?

The appeal to a national community seems to be confirmed by recent history, and it may gain more popularity than in the 1970s and 1980s. It is one concept within a struggle about the redefinition of the identity of the greater Federal Republic of Germany that Germany should now, at last, return to being a 'normal' nation which feels proud of itself and its history. Supporters of a non-national and non-ethnic self-definition of the German state have been harshly attacked for their alleged neglect of the national factor and the future of the German nation, and they have lost ground.[41]

The 'self-confident nation' tries to free itself from the taboos of the 1950s and 1970s which then restricted open racism and xenophobia. Now a direct line is drawn between 'national identity' and the relationship towards immigrants. Don't the Germans, it is claimed, have the right to protect their identity? Increasingly, and as one product of a liberation from the 'moral corsets' of the post-Nazi era, it is maintained that hostility to immigration is a perfectly understandable and legitimate self-defence of a people or culture that sees its survival threatened. It seems that *Überfremdungsängste* (fears of being inundated) has become a perfectly normal term which reflects this notion. 'The state has to take action if *its citizens* feel threatened', a former head of a government commission against violence stated: it has to fight the threat and to bar further immigration to accommodate the subjective feelings of one part of its population.[42] It is a remarkable recent trend that, instead of the former stereotypical refusal to accept that Germany is a country of immigration, multiculturalism, once a key-term of a pro-immigration faction, is now aggressively and in a more elaborate way addressed by its opponents. Far right arguments are further introduced into mainstream publications and debates. J. Schmid for example, a renowned professor of population studies in Bamberg, has attacked the multicultural society as impossible in principle because cultures have or strive for territory and property. His views, and similar arguments put forward by the retired Trier professor E. Faul, largely overlap with extreme right-wing stances.[43] Cultures, or, in Faul's words, 'firmly contoured peoples' identities' (*fest konturierte Volksidentitäten*) appear as fixed and competing units and are – explicitly – related to living spaces. The retired Trier professor of political science explained to the participants of a seminar of the Konrad-Adenauer-Stiftung that immigration from the east should be considered a process which could potentially amount to a partial conquest, thus tying up with the expulsions of Germans from eastern Europe in the late 1940s. A German economy (*deutsche Wirtschaft*), meaning high productivity, efficiency and social security, Schmid's almost openly racist argument further runs, cannot be operated by the increasing number of foreign immigrants. It has become common to associate large-scale immigration of non-Europeans with a scenario of 'Lebanization', US-style slums and a 'babylonic' society with enormous social splits and conflicts, dangerous streets, political disintegration, etc. An arbitrary disintegrative blend, as Faul describes ethnic plurality, inhibits self-development. Frequently immigration has been described as an existential threat to Germany and western Europe.

Given the social tensions and problems of political integration in Germany today, there is an enormous temptation to use an issue which has in the past consistently rewarded the conservatives and might now provide an integrative mechanism for the new German state. The population in the west, which was not enthusiastic about unification anyway, faces rising taxes and declining living standards. With the redundancy of anti-communism and a nationalism focused on the recovery of territories, old integrative mechanisms are gone. In the east, only one-third of the population still believe 'we are one people' – as the slogan of 1989 proclaimed.[44] Here, in the territory of the former GDR, the social and political ruptures, the loss of value systems and of clearly defined, if not brilliant, perspectives together with disappointed (unrealistic) expectations add up to an unstable situation.

In the face of economic problems and political disillusionment, a sense of community (others might say solidarity) is desperately longed for. Wolfgang Schäuble, the chairman of the CDU/CSU faction and a possible successor to Chancellor Kohl, for example, argued that this community ought to be based on the idea of the 'nation', a concept that provides the non-rational acceptance of responsibilities and an understanding for the common whole. Such a community, conscious of itself, he further pointed out, is not in danger of fearing an *Überfremdung* if confronted with many foreign faces.[45] But, it should be added, it remains a nationally constructed community distinct from those with the 'foreign faces'. It lies within the logic of a national community which is based on blood bonds or culture and history that immigrants (at least of recent decades) are excluded, and they can hardly be expected to find such an appeal attractive. However, protests by immigrants against the financial burdens of unification, which as tax-payers they have to share, or against the privileged recent immigrants and competitors from the east, has (astonishingly enough?) not yet been heard or seen.

There is certainly pressure from below and not only unscrupulous politicization from above. Habermas, in his article cited above, criticized the leading parties and politicians for giving way to the obtuse and resentful parts of their electorate. Political debates and media campaigns about the alleged abuse of the right to asylum and about alleged floods threatening the Germans have contributed to releasing potential hostility and racism. There is a spontaneous search for scapegoats and an activation of traditional structures of prejudice, in particular if they are enforced by political debates and a political process that seems to confirm the belief that Germany has to protect itself against pressures and demands from outside. Conflicts between long-term residents and newcomers should not be neglected either. For the four years from 1988 to 1991 immigration (including East Germans and 'ethnic Germans') has been estimated at 3.6 million.[46] Local authorities have come under considerable pressure. At the same time, the enormous material help for those regarded as ethnic Germans shows how arbitrary concepts of fixed absorbative capacities are. The widespread refusal to see the 'ethnic Germans' as 'true Germans' demonstrates the limits to the fiction of a German *Volk* and how resistant popular interpretations are to government and media campaigns.[47]

Nevertheless, the importance and influence of media frenzies is growing. The spectacular electoral successes of the extreme right which preceded the demolition of the Berlin Wall have frequently been related to a crisis of the integrative force of the political system and the big parties. With traditional loyalties and a milieu-related political socialization losing force, voters, in particular young people, have become more vulnerable to fashions and more likely to act outside the preformed paths of voting and supporting the established parties. As the shift from electoral support for extreme right-wing parties to less strictly organized arson attacks shows, this tendency also affects the extreme right.

Any attempt to assess the potential for nationalist tendencies in German politics should take into account that an appeal to a national community in Germany has to be balanced with Germany's economic dependence on exports and the world market and the strong pro-European orientation. The damage to Germany's image abroad was one decisive factor in the rejection of violence against refugees or immigrants on the part of all leading German politicians.[48] Signs of realism are noticeable when leading CDU politicians nowadays admit that immigration has taken place and occasionally accept that integration does involve an adjustment on the part of Germans as well.[49] Chancellor Kohl has stressed that the more than 6 million foreign nationals in Germany belong there and ought to be integrated. The CDU/CSU has, however, disappointed hopes for positive developments by obstructing the already widely agreed introduction of a vague constitutional clause on the state's respect for the identity of national minorities. Its programme for government again confirmed the ridiculous claim that Germany is not a country of immigration. When, on the other hand, Richard von Weizsäcker, a strong supporter of the national idea, handed over the job of Federal President he spoke clearly and powerfully about 'natives' and 'newcomers' (*Einheimische und Zugewanderte*), not of Germans and aliens, and emphasized the need to face immigration and to reform the law on nationality. His successor, Roman Herzog, remained vague, however.[50]

In torchlight demonstrations all over Germany, hundreds of thousands of people in 1992–3 demanded 'no violence' and peaceful coexistence. These activities influenced the political climate towards a rejection of violent attacks and reduced the support for extreme right-wing groups. At the same time, it should be noted that these protests, although impressive, came relatively late. They have not yet led to the formation of a civil rights movement. Initially, the attacks on refugee hostels were greeted by a high level of understanding for the attackers in the population.[51] The motives and problems of the youthful attackers were debated more than the situation of the victims. Do not exclude them, the author Martin Walser pleaded, for they are our protesting children.[52] The notion that, if their methods were wrong, the concern of the arsonists was legitimate, was clearly present.

In the debates following the 1992 Mölln attack on Turkish residents in particular (and to a lesser extent the siege of refugee hostels) one characteristic feature was that the problem addressed was violence not racism: 'violence' from right and left, from criminals (not right wingers) as well as Turkish or Kurdish extremists.[53] Racist violence was thus depoliticized and separated from the context of discrimination against immigrants. In an absurd re-interpretation of the issue, a Vice-President of the *Bundestag* and former member of government suggested that violence was caused by an over-liberal education, a weakening of the state and a decline of traditional values which was, among other things, caused by the allied re-education after 1945 – a line of argument leading us back to the nation, authority and traditional values as counter measures.[54] Erwin K. Scheuch, a well-known sociologist who was called as an expert to the European Parliament's inquiry into racism in 1985, has recently argued that hostility towards aliens, even organized violence, does not have very much to do with foreigners or a growth of racism. Instead, it should be subsumed under politically legitimated violence – as started by the left in 1968 and as occurring in many countries – violence that is in Germany enacted to attract attention, not to harrass or kill foreigners. The Germans in general were not hostile to foreigners but rightly defending their identity, the right not to be made a minority.[55]

Germany is a foreigner-friendly country – this has been the stereotypical claim of the early 1990s. Altogether, hostility and racism are more often neglected than tackled. This attitude marks a clear difference to Britain. It remains to be seen how the trend towards renewed nationalism and the European and world market orientation will be balanced in the future. After restrictive measures have succeeded in reducing the number of applications for asylum, immigration could possibly be moved further down the public agenda for some time. But Germany has changed in the early 1990s. The upsurge of violence and the public debate on immigration and ethnic coexistence signal deeper shifts in inter-ethnic relations.

NOTES

1 J. Habermas, 'Die zweite Lebenslüge der Bundesrepublik', *Die Zeit*, 11 December 1992. In August 1992 refugee hostels in Rostock were besieged and set on fire by a mob. In November 1992 three Turkish residents were killed by a racist attack on their home in the north German town of Mölln.
2 I use politicization in a narrow sense to describe phases in which an issue becomes the subject of open political conflicts and public debates.
3 See the advertisement by the CDU in the *Frankfurter Rundschau*, 8 March 1989; Rühe's letter is documented in *Die Deutschen und die Frem-*

den. taz journal (1991/92). I shall use the acronyms CDU for *Christlich Demokratische Union* and CSU for *Christlich Soziale Union*, the Bavarian Partner of the Christian Democrats.

4 On Britain see A. M. Messina, *Race and Party Competition in Britain* (Oxford: Clarendon, 1989), p. 2; Z. Layton-Henry and P. Rich (eds), *Race, Government and Politics in Britain* (London: Macmillan, 1986), p. 5. Both books point at a temporary repoliticization in the early 1980s.

5 S. Jäger and J. Link (eds), *Die vierte Gewalt. Rassismus und die Medien* (Duisburg: DISS, 1993), p. 12. The authors refer to L. van Dijk.

6 There are regular opinion polls in which the participants are asked to name in their view, the most important political themes: see M. Jung and D. Roth, 'Politische Einstellungen in Ost- und Westdeutschland seit der Bundestagswahl', *Aus Politik und Zeitgeschichte* (B19), 1992, pp. 3–16; 'Asylstreit entscheidet Wahl', *Der Spiegel* 44, 1992.

7 'Forum: Deutschland nach Solingen', *Gewerkschaftliche Monatshefte* 44, 1993.

8 H. Willems in co-operation with R. Eckert, S. Würtz and L. Steinmetz, *Fremdenfeindliche Gewalt. Einstellungen, Täter, Konflikteskalation,* (Opladen: Leske & Budrich, 1993); for some recent research results see my review article in *West European Politics* 18(2), 1995.

9 On the influence of different institutions and on aliens policy more generally see B. Huber and K. Unger, 'Politische und rechtliche Determinanten der Ausländerbeschäftigung in der Bundesrepublik Deutschland', in H.-J. Hoffmann-Nowotny and K.-O. Hondrich (eds), *Ausländer in der Bundesrepublik Deutschland und in der Schweiz. Segregation und Integration: eine vergleichende Untersuchung* (Frankfurt/M. and New York: Campus, 1981), pp. 124–94 (hereafter Huber and Unger, *Determinanten*). See also H. Esser and H. Korte, 'Federal Republic of Germany', in T. Hammar (ed.), *European Immigration Policy* (Cambridge: Cambridge University Press, 1985), pp. 165–205.

10 T. Blank, 'Eine Million Gastarbeiter', *Bulletin des Presse- und Informationsamtes der Bundesregierung* 160, 30 October 1964, p. 1480: "Ich möchte deshalb die Gelegenheit nutzen, den Helfern aus dem Ausland für ihre bisherigen Leistungen herzlich zu danken."

11 See the *Bundestag* debate on 17 February 1955 (*Verhandlungen des Deutschen Bundestages*) and, in particular, the speech by deputy Odenthal, SPD, who summarized the debate (ibid., pp. 3387–90). See also S. Bethlehem, *Heimatvertreibung, DDR-Flucht, Gastarbeiterzuwanderung. Wanderungsströme und Wanderungspolitik in der Bundesrepublik Deutschland* (Stuttgart: Klett, 1982), p. 145 (hereafter Bethlehem, *Heimatvertreibung*).

12 U. Herbert, *Geschichte der Ausländerbeschäftigung in Deutschland 1880 bis 1980. Saisonarbeiter, Zwangsarbeiter, Gastarbeiter* (Bonn: Dietz Verlag, 1986), pp. 142–3 (hereafter Herbert, *Geschichte der Ausländerbeschäftigung*) [English translation: U. Herbert, *A History of Foreign Labour in Germany, 1880–1980: Seasonal Workers, Forced Labourers, Guest Workers* (Ann Arbor: University of Michigan Press, 1990)].

13 MP Gerlach, SPD, in the debate in the Bundestag on 27 June 1962, quoted in *Das Parlament*, 4 July 1962, p. 8.

14 See for example *Das Parlament*, 3 August 1960; A. Simon, 'Die Lage der Gastarbeiter in der Bundesrepublik', *Die Neue Ordnung* 15, 1961, pp. 344–9.

15 See the examples of parliamentary questions quoted in *Das Parlament*, 15 May 1963, 18 December 1963 and the 'Bericht der Bundesregierung über die Beschäftigung ausländischer Arbeitnehmer', *Bundestags-Drucksache* 4/859 (1962) which answered questions put by the SPD.

16 K. Dohse, *Ausländische Arbeiter und bürgerlicher Staat. Genese und Funktion von staatlicher Ausländerpolitik und Ausländerrecht. Vom Kaiserreich zur Bundesrepublik Deutschland* (Berlin, 1985), pp. 144, 177. U. Herbert questioned Dohse's theses: *Geschichte der Ausländerbeschäftigung*, p. 193.

17 Ibid., pp. 9–10.

18 Unless indicated otherwise, all references to opinion polls are taken from K. Schönwälder, 'Zu viele Ausländer in Deutschland? Zur Entwicklung ausländerfeindlicher Einstellungen in der Bundesrepublik', *Vorgänge*, 30, 1991, pp. 1–11.

19 Equal numbers saw them as a problem, or thought that they got along quite well.

20 See his policy statement (*Regierungserklärung*) of 1965 in which he argued that there were limits to a recruitment of even more alien workers because it would lead to higher costs. Instead, weekly working hours should be increased by one hour, *Bulletin des Presse- und Informationsamtes der Bundesregierung* 179, 11 November 1965, p. 1439 (hereafter *Bulletin*).

21 S. Bethlehem, *Heimatvertreibung*, p. 148.

22 *Bulletin* 160, 30 October 1964, p. 1480.

23 See for example W. Steinjahn, 'Wirtschaftliche Aspekte der Ausländerbeschäftigung', *Die neue Ordnung*, 29, 1975, p. 307, who pointed at a declining net use (*abnehmender Nettonutzen*) of the migrant workers who began to make use of infrastructure provisions.

24 Policy statement (*Regierungserklärung*), *Bulletin* 6, 19 January 1973, p. 54.

25 Sommer, *Die Zeit*, 6 April 1973.

26 These measures were implemented in 1975 but given up already in 1977 because, due to international treaties, their application would have been possible only with respect to Portuguese and Yugoslavs. See Huber and Unger, *Determinanten*, pp. 155–8.

27 See, for example, J. Eick, 'Die Schallmauer ist erreicht. Zum Gastarbeiter-Problem', *Frankfurter Allgemeine Zeitung*, 23 May 1973. The article mainly referred to limits of the social infrastructure but expressed particular concern about immigration from Turkey and non-European regions.

28 Quoted in Bethlehem, *Heimatvertreibung*, p. 156, based on *Die Welt*, 13 February 1975.

29 J. Schilling, 'Multikulturelle Gesellschaft oder Repatriierung? – Ausländerpolitik im Widerstreit von christlicher Toleranz und Staatsräson', in H. Geißler (ed.), *Ausländer in Deutschland – Für eine gemeinsame Zukunft*, vol. 2 (München, 1982), pp. 123–130, 130. Similar statements by Schilling were published in *Die Zeit*, 21 January 1980; *Christ und Welt*, 9 January 1981.

30 *Verhandlungen des Deutschen Bundestages*, 4 February 1982, pp. 4891–5.

31 In 1980 visa requirements were imposed for people coming from Sri Lanka, Iran, Ethiopia and Afghanistan.
32 P. B. Rich, 'Conservative Ideology and Race in Modern British Politics', in Z. Layton-Henry and P. B. Rich (eds), *Race, Government and Politics in Britain* (London: Macmillan, 1986), pp. 45–72 (60).
33 J. Link, 'Medien und Asylanten: Zur Geschichte eines Unworts', in D. Thränhardt and S. Wolken (eds), *Flucht und Asyl. Informationen, Analysen, Erfahrungen aus der Schweiz und der Bundesrepublik Deutschland* (Freiburg i. B., 1988), pp. 50–61 (52–3); S. Wolken, 'Asylpolitik in der Bundesrepublik Deutschland. Politik gegen politische Flüchtlinge?' in ibid., pp. 62–97.
34 See K. Schönwälder, 'Auf der Suche nach der "deutschen Identität". Ein Literaturbericht', *Blätter für deutsche und internationale Politik*, 30, 1985, pp. 1450–65. B. Willms, who argued that an integration of aliens was incompatible with national identity, constituted an exception, see ibid. p. 1455.
35 Dr Olderog (CDU/CSU) in the *Bundestag*, 24 June 1988, *Verhandlungen des Deutschen Bundestages*, p. 6048.
36 J. Schilling, 'Multikulturelle Gesellschaft oder Repatriierung?' (n. 29 above), pp. 126–7.
37 'Antwort der Bundesregierung auf die Große Anfrage der Fraktionen der SPD und FDP "Ausländerpolitik"', *Bundestags-Drucksache* 9 (1629), 5 May 1982.
38 D. Thränhardt, 'Die Bundesrepublik Deutschland – ein unerklärtes Einwanderungsland', *Aus Politik und Zeitgeschichte*, (B24), 1988, pp. 3–13; S. Wolken, 'Asylpolitik in der Bundesrepublik Deutschland' (n. 33 above).
39 See, with a different emphasis, D. Thränhardt, 'Die Ursprünge von Rassismus und Fremdenfeindlichkeit in der Konkurrenzdemokratie. Ein Vergleich der Entwicklung in England, Frankreich und Deutschland', *Leviathan* 21, 1993, pp. 336–57. See also K. Sieveking, 'Neue Ausländergesetzgebung – deutsche Überfremdungsängste. Zur Ausländerrechtspolitik seit 1982', *Demokratie und Recht* 16, 1988, pp. 412–19.
40 See the general attitude of the CDU conference on aliens in Germany in 1982 (H. Geißler (ed.), *Ausländer in Deutschland – Für eine gemeinsame Zukunft*, 2 vols, München, 1982).
41 See for example articles by E. Fuhr, *Frankfurter Allgemeine Zeitung*, 29 September 1990; K. H. Bohrer, *Frankfurter Allgemeine Zeitung*, 13 January 1990.
42 H.-D. Schwind, 'Sind wir ein Volk von Ausländerfeinden?' *Frankfurter Allgemeine Zeitung*, 24 June 1993, my emphasis.
43 E. Faul, 'Das vereinigte Deutschland – europäisch integrierte Nation oder diffuse "multikulturelle Gesellschaft"?' *Zeitschrift für Politik*, 39, 1992, pp. 394–420; J. Schmid, 'Das deutsche Asylrecht angesichts des Umbruchs im Osten und des Weltbevölkerungsproblems', *Politische Studien* 43, 1992, pp. 39–55. See also E. Schiffer, 'Ausländerintegration und/oder multikulturelle Gesellschaft', *Politische Studien* 43, 1992, pp. 56–66, Schiffer was a higher civil servant in the Ministry of the Interior.
44 Lecture by W. Fach, Conference of the German Political Science Association, Potsdam, 1994.

45 W. Schäuble, 'Der Platz in der Mitte', *Frankfurter Allgemeine Zeitung*, 6 July 1994.

46 *Frankfurter Allgemeine Zeitung*, 8 April 1993.

47 In an Allensbach survey only 31 per cent of those questioned said that they regarded '*Aussiedler*' as true Germans, 40 per cent were not sure, 29 per cent said they were not true Germans: *Allensbacher Jahrbuch der Demoskopie 1984–1992*, eds E. Noelle-Neumann and R. Köcher, Munich: Saur, 1993, p. 520.

48 See, as one example, the *Wirtschaftswoche* of 16 October 1992, with the heading 'Violence against aliens: Germany pays the price'.

49 See for example J. Gerster, 'Illusion oder realistisches Ziel? Ausländerintegration eine wichtige Zukunftsaufgabe', *Die neue Ordnung* 42, 1988, pp. 269–79. At the same time he emphasized that Germany is a state for the Germans and should continue to be shaped by German culture and history.

50 See the texts of the speeches in *Das Parlament*, 15 July 1994.

51 In opinion polls 34 per cent expressed understanding for violent actions 'because of the aliens problem' (*Der Spiegel* 44, 26 October 1992, reporting results of October 1992). According to an Allensbach survey 20/21 per cent (east/west) in October 1991 and 26/27 per cent in September 1992 thought that most Germans showed understanding for those who perpetrated violent attacks, *Allensbacher Jahrbuch der Demoskopie 1984–1992* (n. 47 above), p. 541.

52 M. Walser, 'Deutsche Sorgen', *Der Spiegel* 26, 28 June 1993, pp. 40–7.

53 See, as pointed examples, the declarations of the CSU's party conference as reported in *Bayernkurier*, 14 November 1992, and an article 'Wider Gewalt' in the *Frankfurter Allgemeine Zeitung*, 1 June 1993.

54 H. Klein, 'Die Deutschen und ihre Identität', *Deutschland Magazin* 23(4), 1994, pp. 30–3.

55 Niemand will gern zur Minderheit gehören. Rechtsradikalismus und Fremdenhaß, zwei deutsche Chimären', *Frankfurter Allgemeine Zeitung*, 10 February 1993.

11

THE NORTHERN LEAGUE

Changing friends and foes, and its political opportunity structure

Carlo Ruzza and Oliver Schmidtke

The revival of regionalist movements in an increasingly integrated European Union presents some important yet little-explored issues with implications extending far beyond the often noted fact that small regions are more viable in a larger economic space. When people reassess their economic interest in relation to a specific territory, they are not simply reacting to changing economic realities. They engage in a cognitive and affective process of construction of spatial boundaries and of the redefinition of social and civic identity. Here we will consider the ascendancy of the northern Italian movement *Lega Lombarda* or *Lega Nord*[1] by examining the transformations of the social identity of activists in connection to the leadership's adaptation to changing political opportunity structures. Over the decade during which it has held national relevance in Italian politics, the Lega has changed its criteria of classification of members, allies and enemies. We will review these changes, the ambiguities that accompanied them, and connect both to changes in the social and cultural background of activists and to changes of the global institutional context.

At first glance, the Lega Lombarda/Lega Nord in Italy might appear to exemplify many of the characteristics of the European ethnic or territorial movements. While it may be a newcomer on the Italian stage, the Lega has become the strongest political force in northern Italy and has played a key role in shaping the changes that the Italian political system has recently undergone. One cannot account for the astonishing electoral success of the Lega, however, simply by drawing parallels with the general rise of regional movements across Europe. The established theories about ethnicity are insufficient in seeking to come to terms with the phenomenon of the

Northern Leagues in Italy. Unlike many other European regionalist movements, where an *internal colonialism* model applies (Hechter 1975), the Lega had not engaged in a long-lasting fight for self-determination centred on appeals to historically rooted symbols and forms of collective identity. Lombardy lacked a specific regional identification until the mid-1980s, and only recently cultivated its present identity through broad political mobilization. In essence, the Lega manufactured what Anderson has termed as 'imagined community' (Anderson 1983), but it has done this in the remarkably short period of a decade, without the support of a truly different language or of a distinctive political history. In addition, the Lega has aided the bolstering of other regional leagues that were previously declining, such as the Venetian League. The Lega has also prompted the formation of new leagues, which all subsequently converged into a large *Northern League* (effectively dominated by the Lega Lombarda and hence used synonymously). We believe that political and cultural dynamics that facilitated the rapidity of the development of this movement, supported by the extensive utilization of media-conscious political spectacles and rapidly manufactured symbolism, differentiate the Lega from traditional territorial movements, and instead illustrate paradigmatic developments in 'identity politics' and movements' adaptation to changing political opportunity structures.

HISTORY

The Lega Lombarda was founded in 1982 by a charismatic leader, Umberto Bossi, who was inspired by a small, already established northern Italian independence movement, the *Union Valdotaine*. The Lega acquired some visibility in 1985, when it first competed in the electoral arena. Initially, it participated in a few local elections and obtained 2.5 per cent of the valid votes in the province of Varese. In 1987 it took part in the Lombardy regional election and was chosen by 2.7 per cent of registered voters. This figure grew to 6.5 per cent in the European election of 1989, to 16.4 per cent in the regional election of 1990, and to 20.5 per cent in the national election for the Senate of 1992. Since then, the rapid growth of the Lega has continued, but in the context of a rapidly changing national situation. In the March 1994 General Election the Lega gained a decisive position in the ruling coalition led by Silvio Berlusconi, leader of the *Forza Italia* party, and joined by the right-wing formation *Alleanza Nazionale*. After serious quarrels with Berlusconi, in December 1994 the

Lega left the national administration and helped to inaugurate Dini's government. In its successful ascent the Lega was not directly helped by the media, whose attitude remained largely negative, and certainly not by alliances with established parties, who consistently attempted to marginalize the Lega.[2] They regarded it as too unreliable, 'out of the system' and locally focused to be considered as a potential ally. Yet, the Lega's success brought this new formation to a position of responsibility and power in the Second Italian Republic.

The recent massive changes in Italian politics have resulted from a crisis that delegitimized the ruling class. The alienation between civil society and ruling class that was a permanent feature in Italian politics was only intensified by a set of corruption scandals involving politicians and industrialists. In this respect, the rise of the Lega was crucial for redefining the terms of political action. The Lega's much-publicized indignation at the extent of the political corruption unearthed by a Milanese judge was instrumental in sensitizing public opinion and stopping the old elite from successfully taking their 'business as usual' attitude as in previous crises. The Lega's attack on political parties and central government in Rome, and its more generalized questioning of state services and institutions associated with the political establishment made a political alternative feasible. The protest in the name of regional self-determination has opened an agenda beyond old lines of conflict. In so doing, the Lega has contributed to citizens' cynicism towards politics, while also mobilizing formerly depoliticized groups in Italian society, such as shopkeepers and artisans.[3]

The Lega shares some common traits with other regionalist movements, such as mythologies concerning the uniqueness of language, culture and territory. But the Lega also expresses distinctive features that go beyond traditional regionalist grievances. Its strong anti-southern and anti-immigrant identification reminds one of the type of 'enemy politics' more frequently associated with right-wing movements. Equally distinctive is its proud assertion of the work ethic and Lombard affluence as main identifying cultural features. We will examine these traits in the context of the rapid process of reconstruction of aspects of Lombard identity.

The Lega and changing features in constructing the 'enemy'

The easiest and emotionally most efficient way to invigorate the feeling of a (regional) collective identity and to persuade people to act in accordance with that feeling is to convince people that a definitive 'enemy' threatens their way of life.[4] The Lega's symbolic strategy for bolstering its legitimacy bears the hallmarks of a series of effective and politically profitable publicity campaigns. Its strategy was to offer easy answers to complicated political problems. At any point in time, the Lega identified an easily detestable enemy against whom its members could channel their activity. A narrowly focused regionalist movement necessitates a clearly defined enemy. A movement that has become institutionalized in a complex national political system needs to convince members to project their identity in a more abstract manner. The greater the degree of complexity of a political system, the more useful a shared definition of a concrete enemy proves to be to the rhetorical strategy of a movement. The identification of an explicit and easily recognizable enemy promises an indisputable frame of reference and hence an effective basis for political mobilization in a complex environment. One should view the emphasis on the 'other' in Lega rhetoric against this background. In the Lega construction of the enemy, we will identify three phases of progressive institutionalization in a changing political system.

First phase

Anti-southerner and anti-immigrant feelings were especially integral parts of the Lega's effort to furnish a territorially conceived identity in its formative stage. These feelings were grounded in the traditional hostility between northern and southern Italians, and their expression was unhindered in a narrowly focused and territorially circumscribed social movement as was the Lega in the early 1980s. Being rooted in popular culture, this hostility was taken for granted, and its free expression was positively encouraged. The cultural and socio-economic divide between the northern and southern regions of Italy provided an easy starting point for defining a regional identity which already held broad acknowledgement in Italian society. During this phase, the culprits in the traditional view of the Lega Lombarda are the southerners, whose particularistic culture and absence of a work ethic is said to have colonized the Italian state and its political parties. Many Lombards believe they hold radically different values; they feel part of a '*mittel* European' culture. They are proud of their economic success and feel exploited by the south of Italy. The Lega argued that the 'natural' or indigenous values of the Lombard and northern Italian culture in general are conducive to morally healthy, productive,

182

prosperous and efficient communities. They asserted that a destruction of these values had occurred through the negative influence of other cultures, particularly southern Italian influences. As a result of this, a problem of unsatisfactory public services and political corruption had emerged in Lombardy and all over Italy.

As a solution, the Lega advocated a new awareness of Lombard's cultural identity, and through the Lega their acquisition of a directive role in Italian politics. This would bring about a regeneration of Italian politics through a renewal of the political class, and the indictment of all corrupt politicians. The Lega portrays the values of the northern community as the blueprint for change that the entire country is supposed to follow. Expressing an openly missionary attitude, Bossi's movement presents the citizenry of the small producers and shopkeepers with their particular work ethics as the renovating principle by which the malaise of Italian society is to be cured. While large sections of Italian society viewed Lega members as crude racists, Lega members themselves vigorously rejected accusations of racism. Representatives have repeatedly claimed in public that the Lega does not have anything against southerners as such.

Second phase

Particularly after its first electoral successes, the Lega has sought to shift the emphasis of its political campaign from southerners to other types of enemies. Increasing immigration from the Maghreb region and from central Africa constituted the new target. These people were a visible and marginalized group that as non-voters presented little threat to the movement.

After gaining the strongest political voice in northern Italy, and then developing a national frame for its political mobilization, the leadership of the Lega reduced the emphasis on internal differences within the Italian state, and shifted the concentration of its rhetoric from the unequal distribution of resources between the north and south to a concentration on the 'evil' malaise that foreigners and centralized national bureaucracies had inflicted on Lombardy.[5] In the mid-1980s, when the Lega shed its explicitly ethnic allegiance and partially adopted a territorially defined identity, southerners ceased to be the main enemy. A southerner who had lived in the north for a sufficiently long period (five years was the estimate of many activists) could become a Lombard provided he or she accepted the values of the new culture. While the Lega continued to refer to the value of the culture of Lombardy, it no longer attached any concrete political meaning to these references. Only foreigners were clearly excluded. Lega leaders would explain that their integration was just too difficult to succeed because their original culture was too different.

The Lega accuses the national government of promulgating an immigration policy that threatens the rights of Lombards. The promotion of an opposition between 'us' and 'them', the members of the Lombard community and the undesirable recent immigrants, lies at the core of the Lega's mobilization efforts. The 'Lombardy first' campaign has inspired northern proposals for restricting the influx of immigrants and foreign workers. For this reason, Giorgio Bocca, a well-known editorialist, characterized the vote for the Lega in 1990 as a symptom of the widespread racism of Italian society.[6]

The Lega's effort to link a territorially defined collective identity based on the rejection of immigrants with a strong notion of individual virtue has nevertheless raised certain ambiguities. The position of the Lega on this question can be exemplified by its opposition to the attempt of former Minister of the Interior Martelli to change the law on immigration in 1990 (the so called *'legge Martelli'*).[7] In its official discourse, the Lega mainly portrays immigrants as potential competitors for scarce jobs and public resources, rather than exhibiting direct hostility towards the outsiders because of their 'otherness'.[8] The Lega has argued that all members of the Lombard community have a right to jobs and accommodation that must be fulfilled before new members can enter the community. The Lega thus justifies its demand to restrict the 'settlement of foreigners', though, theoretically at least, the boundaries of the Lombard community retain a potential porousness. The Lega thus does not conduct an overtly racist campaign of intolerance towards everything that is (phenotypically) different. Rather, it projected a racist message in the language of rights, arguing that present Lombards had a right to a reasonable standard of living. The Lega's position, in harmony with its highly individualistic market-type ideology, is thus not an arbitrary complement but a significant element in the newly emerged collective identity framed around socio-economic lines. The potential integration into the 'community of producers' marks the criterion upon which 'belongingness' to the community is judged.

The ethnocentric dimension of the Lega rhetoric was not always so discreetly packaged. During its formative years, the Lega benefited from its description of immigrants generally, and immigrants from the Third World in particular, as the main threat to the cultural integrity and stability of northern communities. As Bossi stated, 'the cultural difference is just too great. The difference in skin color is detrimental to social peace. Imagine if your street, your public square, was full of people of colour, you would no longer feel part of your own world.'[9] This early rhetoric clearly excluded the possibility that immigrants might possess individual merit from which the northern communities could benefit. Although the Lega more recently has sought to downplay its racist attacks against immigrants and southern Italians, the creation of an outside enemy in order to strengthen its own collective identity has been an integral part of its political success.

More than superficial tactical considerations are at stake, however. The critical point is how one can define the features of belonging to a community in which a territorially defined collective identity has not been sanctioned by articulated attributes confirmed by established habits and rules. To be convincing, the boundaries constructed on such features have to be confirmed by concrete experiences in daily life. They have to resonate with the continuously changing perceptions of reality held by the assigned constituency. Simultaneously, however, they have to be stable enough to furnish those indisputable legitimating resources needed to formulate the rights of the designated community. The latter point partly explains why the Lega still periodically refers to an ethnic identity, in spite of the declining political relevance of the ethnic designation. The very authority of territorial politics is based on the notion of a stable and uncontested collective identity. Regarding the case of the Lega, it is instructive to have a closer look at the related reflections of the leader of the Liga Veneta and former president of the Lega, Franco Rocchetta. Together with Gianfranco Miglio,[10] he represented the faction within the Lega Nord that was most strongly committed to an ethnically defined notion of identity. He contended:

> Localities like Tuscany, Lombardy, Veneto or Sicily, they are really European nations. Each of our regions is a homogenous society. Usually there is a great coincidence between the administrative boundaries, and the historical, economical and social boundaries.

When asked whether the homogeneity is ethnic or linguistic in character, he maintained:

185

An extremely thick and an extremely rich homogeneity. Each region, and every region is breathing in its own rhythm and mechanisms. They have existed for millennia . . . It is not simply a linguistic problem, or a cultural problem. It is a spontaneous organization of society in a particular way. Economic structures and ways of life of Venetians are exactly the same in South America and in Veneto. Simply because culture is more than music and language. It is the way to organize your society spontaneously.[11]

The random character of the properties that define 'the community' is obvious. The Liga Veneta leader, Franco Rocchetta, asserts that a viable national community arises from the 'spontaneous' organization of societal life which, while historically rooted, reflects the ahistoric values of the nation. The authority of history, the claimed indubitable fact of at least four ethnically grounded peoples in the north of Italy,[12] faces a contemporary situation in which the associated collective identity is far from clear. Essentially, features of belonging are inarticulate. Implicit in Rocchetta's statement is the notion of 'naturalness' of each national community which, while apparent to members, lacks a form that can be expressed in objective terms. The effectiveness of such a framing of communal belonging for political mobilization is evident. While this criterion implies that the community has solid boundaries constructed over a long historical period, the ambiguity allows the actual definition of the boundaries to remain flexible. Changing values and features of social life may be referenced to give meaning to the abstract notion of a 'national' identity.

It is against this background of a flexible collective identity that the Lega has been able to reformulate the features of the antagonism between the 'Lombard,' or northern community, and its supposed adversaries. The combination of increasing electoral success in the early 1990s and the accelerating legitimation crisis of the established parties generated an opportunity for the Lega to assume the role of the major opposition force against the nation state's political establishment. In addition to claiming to represent the northern region, the Lega now also explicitly claims to represent the deserted political centre. The Lega has had to achieve two tasks to make its new claim credible. First, it has had to counter its image as a racist, narrow-minded and self-interested force from Lombardy and Veneto, promoting illegitimate parochial interests. The demarcation from the *extracommunitari*[13] and southern Italians – by now targeted as a new potential constituency for the Lega's federalist ideas – was hence replaced by the reinforced fight against the Roman parties.

In addition, the Lega had to co-ordinate the only loosely connected northern leagues to facilitate the efficient pooling and use of the material and ideological resources each respectively had at its disposal. To achieve this task, a further redefinition of its collective identity and amplification of its communicated interpretive frames of reference became necessary.

Third phase

Gradually in the 1990s the Lega evolved from stigmatizing foreigners and Italians from the *Mezzogiorno* (Southern Italy) to concentrating on an agenda of federalism and regional self-determination. As Bossi pointed out in an interview, what the Lega is really against is 'the state, authoritarianism, and the dominance of the centres of power. Therefore we cannot be racist.'[14] In this last phase the enemy had been redefined, from a concrete social group to a more abstract threat that included both the state as a distant and inefficient structure and specifically, corrupt politicians and lazy bureaucrats.

In the 1990s, the demarcating boundaries of the community had to be further enlarged in such a way that the Lega could attract a broader constituency. Correspondingly, the political discourse needed to be reframed to extend the scope of the political goals and to present the Lega as a political agent on a par with other, nationally operating parties. In effect, the political discourse of the Lega was redirected towards genuine, non-territorial political goals.

This transformation enabled the Lega to widen the scope of its political goals and to broaden its base of support. More importantly, the new identity enabled the Lega to employ a flexible strategy to respond to opportunities created by the implosion of the old, established political order in Italy based on the *tangentopoli* system of bribes and patronage. In so doing, the Lega became primarily an agent of political change on a national scale.

DILEMMAS INVOLVED IN THE LEGA'S POLITICAL MOBILIZATION

Considering globally the changing conceptions of the enemy, some general conclusions can be drawn. The variations of racism that appear in the Lega's discourse are not 'essentialist' conceptions of biological differences, but ones that focus on the social process by which social collectivities are categorized and attributed with stereotypes in order to justify inequalities. However, there emerges at some junctions a cultural essentialism that, although distinct from theories of biological determinism, can be equally as intolerant of differences and of the possibility of change.[15] At other times a more inclusive discourse develops, which could potentially lead to an expansion of the movement.

As the case of the Lega indicates, there are certain limits to integrating new members into the political project. Any broadening of the constituency unavoidably threatens to weaken the sense of boundaries that is indispensable for a territorially shaped collective identity. The less distinct the symbolic and ritual confirmation of the boundaries of the assigned community becomes, the less strong are the features of integration. To sustain its political mobilization the Lega has to constantly reproduce the notion of superiority, which demarcates the community *vis-à-vis* the 'profane' and corrupt nation state centre. Its moral crusade, epitomizing the core idea of a cultural form of collective identity, depends on a convincing picture of the 'Other' as the object of missionary aspirations. Still, notwithstanding these endemic risks of blurring the demarcating boundaries of the 'Other', structurally the collective identity on which the Lega's political mobilization is based does not impede the development of widely applicable standards of inclusion.

To expand its influence beyond the north, the Lega had to devise strategies for attracting votes in the south. The quest for expansion none the less entailed some serious risks for the Lega. Foremost among these was the need to reconstruct the image the party portrayed of southern Italians without losing credibility among voters in the north. In the early years, the Lega had characterized the south as the breeding ground of political corruption and clientelism. The Lega needed to construct a strategy that could open membership to Southern voters without compromising the party's past. At the same times, the Lega had to convince voters in the south that it had shed its racist roots, while not alienating its supporters in the north who had been receptive to the racist message. The Lega decided to tone down its rhetoric and desist from engaging in openly racist practices against people from the *Mezzogiorno* and the *extracommunitari*. Now, the Lega has to cope with the radicalized fruits of its own original attempt to build up a strong collective identity based upon the antagonism between the 'Us' and the 'Them'. Outspoken racist factions within the Lega accused the leadership of collaborating with, or at least of adopting an excessively tolerant attitude towards, those labelled as aliens in the northern communities. In effect, the openly racist anti-southern stand, initially an integral part of its collective identity, has lastingly disqualified the Lega in the south of Italy and, to a lesser extent, in the political centre.

Through its present strategies, the Lega has jeopardized the very essence of its success. The main difficulty in the Lega's effort to sustain its mobilization can be traced back to a critical redefinition of its integrating collective identity. The northern leagues have gradually weakened their formerly constitutive territorial reference, softening the demarcation of the boundaries of its constituency. In the process, the Lega has also weakened the appeal it once held for northern voters – who could feel when they joined the Lega that they had joined a special community in tune with their needs – and thereby diluted its ability to mobilize committed support for political change. Moreover, the Lega has moved from a position of assailing the government through popular protest to membership of the formal government opposition. This change of status, likewise, has alienated the would-be anti-institutional populist actors who formerly supported this party. Both developments of the Lega's collective identity have allowed a broader and more far-reaching political mobilization, as – in a more advanced stage of its mobilization – they have simultaneously become the source of the Lega's first electoral setback in the 1994 general elections.

Reflecting the problems in spurring further mobilization the results in the 1990 Regional Elections and the 1992 and 1994 General Elections show that the Lega is strong only in its traditional strongholds (see Table 11.1). In Lombardy, Piedmont and, particularly, in Veneto the Lega could even increase its share of the votes. In the centre of Italy, and here first of all in the left-dominated Emilia-Romagna and in Toscana, the Lega had to accept a notable setback. It is worth recalling that it was the centre that was declared a main political target (especially by Bossi) in order to go beyond the territorial restrictiveness the Lega has to face. As in its early days, the Lega has in fact been far more successful in those areas with a distinct Catholic culture, in the 'white zones', than in those traditionally shaped by a communist–leftist political subculture, like Emilia-Romagna or Toscana. The further ambition to gain a foothold in the south of the country is obviously a total failure. The result of the European election in May 1994 even more radically confirmed this electoral

189

trend. Evidently the Lega's explicit aim to tap new social groups, particularly in the centre, has failed.[16]

Table 11.1 Regional distribution of electoral support for the Lega Nord: elections for Regional Council in 1990 and General Elections in 1992 and 1994 (Chamber of Deputies)

Region	1990 %	1992 %	1994 %
Piedmont	8.6	14.9	15.0
Lombardy	68.9	44.1	45.1
Liguria	4.1	5.2	4.3
Trentino-Alto Adige	–	1.7	1.5
Veneto	10.5	16.9	21.7
Friuli-Veneto	–	4.0	4.6
Emilia-Romagna	5.0	8.6	6.0
Toscana	1.2	2.4	1.7
Other regions	1.4	2.4	1.7

Media influence

So far we have considered the Lega in its direct relation to the political system. But there is a public sphere where cultural images resonate with emerging discourse from civil society and the media that also needs to be considered.

All regionalist and nationalist movements dwell on the theme of belonging to communities, and thus often articulate issues of citizenship and nationalism in their communications. They are often opposed by national political parties, and at times by counter-movements, that oppose or reinterpret their claims of the sacredness of the boundaries of a territorial community. The cultural exchanges between the two types of movement reflect debates taking place in public discourse and, in turn, influence these debates. Not only issues of resource allocation, but also 'packages' of idealized personality traits are contested and redefined in the course of these exchanges. What is at stake is how a culture perceives itself. In this process of re-elaboration of mythologies, the media plays an important part. With Gamson,[17] we differentiate public discourse from media discourse. The media form just one arena among others where discussion of societal themes occurs. Thus an important area of discourse such as the debate on ethnic relations has a media dimension and is also the subject of discussions in families, political parties, work organizations and other discussion arenas. So far we have illustrated changes that were oriented by the changing political opportunity structure of the Lega. However, to be effective the leadership of a movement is not free to change the definition and boundaries of membership irrespective of the broader cultural discussion taking place in society and echoed in the media.

If the importance of the media arena is universally recognized, it is also important to investigate the arena of discussion that takes place in every-day life. Social movement demonstrations and other protest events are often the impetus for media coverage; and in ascending order, such Cadres' framing of issues is likely to be reported and thus constitute the initial presentation of topics.

The frames produced by movements could have been accepted by the media only in their agenda-setting dimension. However, the solutions proposed are likely to be re-evaluated by journalists according to dynamics emerging in the area of media discussion (Ruzza and Schmidtke 1993). It is to those dynamics that public discourse is sensitive, although it does not mirror them faithfully. It does, however, limit the extent to which a social movement discourse can adapt to a changing set of political opportunities.

Specific networks re-elaborate media positions and produce autonomous frames that are related both to aspects of their experience and to current media discussion. The Lega, like other recent nationalist social movements, has defined multiculturalism as a threat to indigenous populations and to community integration. In doing so, it has responded to situations of ethnic competition, but has also responded to an emerging media discourse and to a typical organizational need of social movements: the constitution of an enemy that, by mere virtue of its existence, creates the 'us' versus 'them' feeling that supports activism and sustains the identity of the challenger. The definition of 'the enemy' has varied significantly in different countries over time, but it is often the latest immigrant group to have arrived. Rival groups of longer-standing residents tend to ascribe negative traits to the most recent migrants, but the image of 'the enemy' changes over time as new groups arrive and new framings emerge in public discourse. In this situation, the nationalist movements' ideas have emerged, on the one hand, on the basis of ethnic competition for the resources of the welfare state, and, on the other, on a need for community that has been undermined by the changing structure of several labour markets and patterns of urban life in Lombardy, just as in other western countries.

The important criteria for the definition of insider and outsider status vary, but often some difference acquires a symbolic relevance and are considered to represent in a condensed way the essence of the difference. The symbol can be a dialect, or even merely an accent. An auxiliary set of myths and symbols is often adopted more or less intentionally to create and maintain cultural boundaries. The classical nation state repertoire that includes anthems and flags is self-consciously stressed by right-wing nationalists and redefined by regionalists. 'Stories' deemed to typify aspects of the 'other' are not the only symbol utilized in the process of defining the enemy. The other forms of symbols may or may not have a factual basis.

Typical in this respect has been the reaction to the earthquakes which rocked the southern Italian province of Irpinia in the early 1980s. Volunteers from the north streamed to the south to provide assistance. Rumours spread in the north that the volunteers encountered a lack of co-operation from members of the local population who were unwilling to engage in manual work and were more inclined to wait for state assistance. The Irpinia earthquake was later contrasted with an earthquake in the Friuli region in the north, where victims, according to northern folklore, worked industriously to repair their damaged villages. These and other similar 'stories' have functioned as stereotype-constituting mythologies, and have supported the conception of the enemy discussed in phase one of the changing Lega ideology.

These episodes, and the process of public reinterpretation and mythologization surrounding them, form an important source for an ongoing construction of social boundaries. News stories then act upon a pre-existing conception of different ethnic groups often based on prejudice such as the perceived lack of work ethic of different immigrant groups. Social movements like the Lega have been instrumental in publicizing these negative stereotypes at a time when their open status was not legitimized.

In phase two and three new emerging stories in the media concerned political corruption and the collapse of the political system that had ruled Italy for 45 years. Hence, as it was politically expedient, definitions of the enemy could also be easily reoriented in these terms.

THEORETICAL FRAMEWORK

We need now to consider the trajectory of the Lega in the broader context of other similar movements. The increasing attacks on foreigners and minorities in several European countries suggests the re-emergence of a culture of 'enemy thinking' in European politics. Several observers have pointed out that this culture is connected to generalized experiences of economic deprivation and of ethnic competition for jobs and welfare-state resources. However, these factors need to be analysed in the composite cultural context of modern life as the identification of social boundaries is a multifarious cultural process involving several spheres of life. This includes the impact of media discourse and the discourse of other relevant organizations that engage in a constant contest for the interpretation of public events. The exchanges between different sources of identity-building results in multiple influences on the development of a sense of community and citizenship. This context favours a particular, though not new, political worldview. A composite 'enemy' scapegoat replaces the more complex and universalistic social evils disparaged in modern political discourses. For instance, the seeming immediacy of interests held by competing ethnic groups provides the venue for ethnic scapegoating as the class-based Marxist explanations of social misery appear unconvincing in the face of the increasing fragmentation of lifestyles in the West, and the loss of appeal of those ideals associated with the collapsed Eastern bloc. Both organized, heterophobic social movements and isolated attacks on immigrants reflect the salience of this interpretation of political reality.

Regionalist movements are among the recent beneficiaries of these trends. In recent years, geopolitical factors such as European integration – which makes regions viable economic units in a larger supranational community – have made economic considerations newly relevant in the EU. In this context, regionalist movements call into question the traditional allegiance to nation states. Some movements have arisen which primarily seek to better the fiscal and economic conditions of their region. Such movements have reevaluated the boundaries of the polity in terms of the psycho–social aspects of belonging to the heterogeneous communities that nation states have once been, and, thus, these movements may constitute a new type of social movement. Members of these movements have also re-emphasized a sense of regionalist belonging in terms of issues of political representation which have accompanied a broader sense of disenchantment with politicians and political structures of several European countries. The basis of regionalist identities is varied, but it is often rooted in perceptions of ethnic community. However, a distinction needs to be made between 'historical' small nations, such as Scotland, Wales or the Basque region, and areas that are relatively new and artificial constructions with only a rather modest cultural identity based mainly on affluence, such as Baden-Württemberg, the Rhone Alps, and Lombardy (see Harvie 1994: 66). Precisely because economic affluence is at the heart of cultural self-definition, economic migrants to these areas, who are generally from disadvantaged groups, are more likely to be perceived by established residents as the invading enemies from the outside world who bring with them the threat of deprivation. Migrants thus help to symbolize the boundaries that define an otherwise fragmented community from the outer citizenry; they make internally visible the presence of external boundaries. As economic issues are the main criteria to legitimize group-belonging, economic measures tend to be sacralized, associating good work performance with morally valued personality traits such as hard-work and ingenuity. These traits are celebrated in the propaganda material of proactive social movements such as the Lombard League that contribute to 'package' dissent in cohesive new mythologies of ethnic identity (see Ruzza and Schmidtke 1993). But 'good economic behaviour' is different from historically more frequent definitions of otherness that have to do with essentially unchangeable traits. It is less clearly defined, historically more changeable and thus more adaptable to changing political opportunities structures. We plan to show that within the boundaries of issues of economic performance, the Lega's enemy has at various times strategically changed, modifying in the process the utopian vision of community that the movement espouses. These changes have, in turn, altered the scope and nature of political action in ways unanticipated by cadres.

ROOTS OF THE DIFFERENCE THAT DEFINES THE 'THEM'

At a general level the concept of citizenship has been anchored in different principles, with a main distinction made between ethno-territorial principles of citizenship and civil–political ones. The definition of an enemy is crucial, as it supports social identities. The enemy is the 'them' to be opposed. The existence of 'the enemy' provides internal cohesion for the movement, and makes an articulation of grievances and goals possible at the political level. Perception of differences is often qualified in terms of asserted culturally incompatible traits rather than on the basis of a realization of mere conflicting interests. But as 'notions of cultural difference and processes of boundary maintenance arise from aspects of social organization, not from "objective" cultural difference' (Hyllard Eriksen 1993: 58), it is important to understand what are the relevant social patterns that sustain perceptions of difference.

Despite indicating a crucial phenomenon, the concept of ethnic nationalism is rather imprecise, as in different regions it encompasses widely divergent elements, which raises doubt about the utility of the value, and underscores the necessity of delimiting its scope. Regionalist groups promote the autonomy of specific ethnic nations within larger nation states.[18] Nationalist–regionalist movements have been extensively studied in specific 'historic' regions but little work is available on their impact outside these specific regions in 'newly' affluent areas. This is especially relevant as some of these areas possess very heterogeneous populations.

Although different in many respects, regionalist and nationalist formations share many traits, such as the belief that cultural boundaries should be coterminous with political boundaries, and a concern for 'protecting' communities. As a consequence, such movements often identify an 'enemy' that they claim to fight. In some cases, regionalists and nationalists may identify the same enemy. In other cases, regionalists and right-wing nationalist groups target different 'enemies'. Regionalist parties are concerned with a specific dominant group of their nation-state, such as the Welsh's concern with the English, whilst the right-wing nationalists define the enemy in 'racial' terms as the 'non-whites'. The two sets of concerns may of course both be present at the same time, but more frequently there is a difference of political emphasis which corresponds to a different characterization of the enemy. The two types of movement propose different methods to enhance the communities of concern. The idealized solution proposed by right-wing nationalist movements is the expulsion of immigrants or moves in that direction.

Regionalist parties, which range in political orientation from right to a fairly radical left, generally focus on ensuring the institutional primacy of their nationals in their regions. However, in some cases, they might also advocate the expulsion of non-nationals. A dimension of contemporary regionalism rarely examined is the relationship of regionalists to the welfare state. An important issue is whether the 'them' is considered a non-resident of the region, or whether there are more inclusive criteria such as traditional roots in the community or the mastery of a language. That is, a central factor in a movement for self-understanding concerns the issue of boundary definition.

CARLO RUZZA AND OLIVER SCHMIDTKE

STRATEGIES IN THE CONSTRUCTION OF SOCIAL BOUNDARIES

The issue of boundary construction is a general one that is common to all social movements and thus to regionalist movements. Boundaries can be drawn along essentialist or constructionist lines. In the essentialist case, differences are seen as innate, even if they are merely cultural, and in the constructionist case, as socially produced. As Calhoun (1994) notes, this difference characterizes not only theoretical frameworks that movements' analysts employ, but the theories that activists employ to frame the nature of their movement and the purpose of their activism.

In tying their political identity to a territorial demarcation, regionalist movements potentially unlock access to the resources of their region and simplify their efforts for mobilization. To achieve legitimacy and saliency, however, the would-be regionalist movement must convince a sizeable proportion of the people living in a particular region that they have political interests which differ from those of the people in surrounding regions. In most cases, regionalist movements have striven to achieve this goal by emphasizing shared cultural experiences and feelings of deprivation inflicted by outside forces that have been passed from one generation to the next. Usually language and other unique cultural customs used in daily life give a stable sense of a collective identity. The definition of 'Us' is not so much a matter of a reflexive process, but rather one based on inherited tradition.

Two conflicting dynamics have impacted the sense of belonging in most regionalist movements. On the one hand, the increasing mobility of people around the globe combined with economic incentives to move, as well as the spread of individualist values by the Western media, have helped to break down traditional communities by removing members of the younger generations and introducing residents from other cultural backgrounds. The sense of belonging to a regional community is increasingly becoming a reflexive process, that is, a matter of choice, rather than result of birth into a specific community. At the same time, the choice of a culturally-based belonging has grown increasingly attractive to people feeling alienated by the atomistic lifestyle predominant in Western Europe. Many regionalist movements have thus increased their mobilization by providing the disaffected with the choice to join an organization that will provide them with a collective identity.

A concept of community is built on the simultaneous operation of processes of inclusion and exclusion. A movement seeking to offer a political identity to its members must construct clear boundaries between its members, 'Us', and non-members, 'Them'. The longer-term success of regionalist movements often rests on the degree to which a movement can convince its members of the naturalness or inevitability of the Us/Them distinction.

The degree of rigidity or flexibility in the definition of membership to a territorially-based movement in turn impacts upon the political strategies the movement can employ. The particular codes upon which the collective identity is based provide the political movement with critical resources in mobilizing their assigned constituency. These codes determine the range in which political goals can be conceived and issues politicized without contesting the overall integrating collective identity. Here it is necessary to underline that the formation of a politicized collective identity is an explicit challenge to the dominant cultural order. It determines how people locate their claims in a cultural system, as well as designating the range of targets and tactical actions that members will perceive as legitimate.

Analytically, one can identify two distinct routes for a grounding of belonging in Western societies. Regionalist movements tend to cluster into two ideal types, with each type using different strategies for defining membership. With reference to the Lega, we have shown that changing structures of political opportunities can re-define movements' identity. The first of these types is the essentialist, or *primordial* type. It uses codes and rituals to emphasize the supposedly 'natural givenness' of a community. Many regionalist movements frequently frame their appeal in essentialist terms. Primordial movements seek to strictly regulate contact with the outside world to protect the intrinsic value of their culture from pollution or dilution. Thus, these communities employ a rigid demarkation between 'Us' and 'Them'. Such collectivities seek to retain or recall members rather than to recruit new members.

The alternative ideal type of collective identity is integrated by ideologies of *cultural distinctiveness*. This type of coding of a collective identity tends to employ criteria for membership which require acceptance of certain philosophical ideas rather than criteria based on genetic or other non-choice-based features. The orientations of this way of demarcating the boundaries between the 'us' and the 'them' is potentially universalistic. The virtues that are said to be the defining criteria for belonging to the community are not bound to a strictly defined ethnic criteria or cultural endowments which are categorically given by descent. Although normally built on a notion of superiority of the territorially defined community, the often undefined boundaries for foreigners are, in principle, open, as long as they are willing to adapt to the mostly implicit rules of the game. This type of collective identity explicitly invites people to 'convert' by the help of education and cultural assimilation. It is in fact integral to this type of collective identity that it develops a 'missionary attitude', presenting its own societal order as a superior social model. Still, this form of collective identity is characterized by a noteworthy ambivalence regarding its integrating features. While such communities assert cultural openness of their boundaries for legitimating reasons, they still work with an underlying idea of communal homogeneity. On this basis, severe practices for cultural assimilation can be formulated and enforced. The belonging to a territorially conceived community, the mode of cultural inclusion, is not entirely made subject to discursively generated and explicitly stipulated civic rights. Rather, it often works with a culturally framed notion of an integrated identity whose standards are formulated on implicit rules. The newcomer is accordingly asked to undergo rites of initiations in which he or she will have difficulty adapting and over which she or he can exert little influence. The more this cultural type of collective identity is naturalized and rationalized by non-discursive modes of integration, the stronger can the 'rules of obeyance' be enforced *vis-à-vis* the outsider.

A movement asserting a cultural collective identity, as opposed to a primordial one, can attract support from a wider range of people whose interests in other matters may conflict. Traditional European regionalist movements, which have worked to fortify existing roots in historical nationalism, aim to preserve the features that divide their community from the national culture. Culturally integrated territorial movements, on the other hand, are not restricted to the legitimizing symbols of their indigenous community, nor are they dependent on the traditional regional elites. As a result, the second ideal type of movement generally enjoys an advantage in its ability to mobilize. Focusing on the difference between ethno-regionalist forces and those populist movements which employ a strong notion of communal belonging, Diani elaborates:

> Ethno-nationalism differs from populism in the greater emphasis it places on cultural symbols; while ethno-nationalism is usually committed to preserve, and in cases re-vitalize, specific signs of

difference such as language or cultural traditions, populism is more inclined to build up a rhetoric discourse upon them.[19]

Table 11.2 further clarifies the difference between each of the types.

Table 11.2 Crucial elements in defining boundaries in primordially and culturally integrated forms of collective identity

	Primordial collective identity	*Cultural collective identity*
Character of Boundaries	Unsurmountable for outsiders; non-negotiable endowment of indigenous population	Crossable through adaptation and compliance to fluid cultural standards of inclusion
Criteria for membership	Strict, ultimately ethnically defined standards of belonging; accordingly framed 'objective' criteria of integration	Discursively fabricated consensus based on explicit cultural values; membership subject to flexible cultural attributes
Integrating Features	Belonging constituted by primary socialization; strong sense of distinctive history and 'uniqueness'	Commonly shared worldviews and cultural values as a reflexive self-interpretation; polemic demarcation from 'Them'
Attitude towards the outer world	Rigid demarcation; uniqueness of community; outer relations perceived as threat; no scheme for integrating outsiders	Missionary attitude; 'exportable' model for societal organization; explicit invites for 'conversion'
Stability of assigned constituency and its integrating features	By definition stable (historically 'invariant') ethnic standards; constituency designated by descent	Changing according to specific model stipulated by cultural value orientation and ideational reference points
Form of political aspirations	Rigid political agenda determined by aim to preserve and enlarge the rights of the ethnically assigned population	Flexible adaptation to changing challenges; normative primacy of territoriality in defining political goals (however, open to different agendas)

The theoretical hypothesis regarding the ideal-type distinction is that the basic codes, by which forms of collective identity are constituted, pre-structure the pattern of political mobilization. By the very nature of the criteria and procedures by which the boundaries of the assigned community are reproduced, the range and quality of the feasible collective actions are set. The underlying assumption is here that the features of collective identity, especially the flexibility of the definition of boundaries and criteria for belonging to the community, are critical incentives and structuring conditions for political mobilization. The intellectual framing provides an ideological resource for mobilizing efforts. The important analytical question in this context is, however, how broad cultural changes influence concrete political behaviour and shape political conflicts. Complex intellectual issues dealt with in mass media need to enter the interpretative order by which people frame social reality in daily life. For a movement to successfully entice people to work towards its objectives, it must project its conceptual frames into the intellectual discourses related to political issues in particular social environments. These frames in turn need to find resonance in the elements of popular culture rooted in daily experience. In this respect, general feelings of deprivation which may result from the perceived belonging to a certain collective identity have to be linked to more elaborated framing processes designed to give these feelings a mobilizing political meaning. We will answer that question with reference to the Lega. Before, however, a broader discussion of identity formation is necessary.

COLLECTIVE IDENTITY IN THE LEGA

In the case of the Lega, the fabrication of an image of collective identity was anything but a uniform and stable process. While still less than two decades old, it has changed its political identity substantially. To a large degree, the Lega's success is due to its capacity to effectively react upon the changing political opportunities and to change its political discourse and tactics accordingly.

The northern leagues expanded beyond their initial localist character, and eventually assumed influence on the national scale. In the 1990s, the Lega became a permanent agent in a political system increasingly in crisis, explicitly striving for national power and basing its aspirations on a platform for institutional change on a national level. Most important in the development of the Lega is the gradual weakening of a regionalist agenda with its related political goals. In shedding its association with an ethnic history in favour of representing the honest, simple, and hardworking person from Northern Italy, the Lega has shifted from the first to the second ideal type, and capitalized on economic divisions between the north and south of this country. The shift to a broadly-based regional identity likewise has prompted the Lega to construct a sense of shared political identity which differs from the majority of regionalist movements.

This political option has been feasible for the Lega given the nature of its collective identity. Bossi's movement was significantly more successful than regionalist movements based on primordial features in re-adapting its political discourse, and hence in convincingly propagating its project during the course of its political fight. Its collective identity was structurally far more flexible and open to frame realignment, which enabled the movement to adapt its values during the course of its mobilization. The flexible adaptation of the cultural collective identity to the challenges of the different stages of the Lega's mobilization proved to be a critical means of constantly re-affirming the correspondence between the movement's political aspirations and the constituency's value orientation. As the history of the Lega shows, the less the collective identity is dependent on stable social structures for its reproduction, the more it is symbolically generated in public discourse as a notion of cultural belonging, and the more flexibly it can be used as a strategic resource in political conflict. Substantial changes in its features are not likely to be perceived as an illegitimate incoherence. Rather, its fluid and inconsistent character is an effective cognitive means to integrate the changing expectations and orientations of the assigned constituency and to adopt to the altering challenges this collective actor meets in the course of its political engagement.

In the case of the Lega, the political agenda is not bound solely to the defence of group entitlement on the basis of a territorially conceived community. The principle of territoriality becomes a symbolic *chiffre* for justifying wider political goals than suggested in the fight for regional self-determination. The image of communal belonging is strategically used in a form of political mobilization that exceeds what is traditionally known as regionalism. National politics and, more particularly, the governing establishment, become the primary target of the politicizing effort. At the core of the Lega's discourse stands the critique of organizing modern political reality. The Lega cleverly combines a populist critique of 'official politics' with a *voto di appartenenza* – a form of political allegiance – constituted by strong features of communal belonging. The main political goals are meant to provide a blueprint of change for the entire society, not for the territorial entity, which on its part primarily serves as a reference point in formulating the collective identity. In its latest phase of mobilization, the territorially framed collective identity served to give the populist protest against the nation-state elite a strong ideational communitarian basis. To understand the Lega's success, one must therefore point to the socio-psychological processes by which the Lega has nurtured feelings of communal belonging.

The traditional European political structures, which have defined citizenship in terms of allegiance to a particular nation state, have come under attack from forces seeking to relocate the source of political authority and identity in entities larger than the traditional states, as well as from movements seeking to shrink the boundaries of the political community. One common element appearing in the rhetoric of challengers to the state from both sides is an emphasis on the importance of the location of an individual's residence. Territorially based conceptions of the state historically constituted one basis for citizenship and ethnic definitions an alternative. Both separated nationhood from other spheres of life and sacralized it in a process that transcended the immediacy of territorial belonging and naked self-interest. As we have seen, with the Lega a new political culture emerged where residence is celebrated in itself as the condensing symbol of other emerging identities and as a substitution for declining ones. The thematization of residence is part of a general redefinition of relationships between individuals, civil society and the state.

For the Lega, residence – which also stands for community – is ideally located in the small village or the city quarter, areas idealized as the *locus* of a sense of community. The Lega members argue that people develop closer feelings of association to such local communities than they do to a more abstract nation state. This belief challenges the supposed 'immediacy' of the people to a distant state. The Lega, like other ethnic, linguistic, and regional community movements, has successfully attributed new political meaning to territorially based collective identities, and subsequently to sub-national agencies and institutions. But it also has created a rich market of nested territorial identities: village; province; region; the whole of northern Italy – all of which bypass the nation-state and identification with Europe. In the richness of these articulations, the formative process of the

Lega was qualitatively different from the cultural processes that accompanied state-building.

Territorial identities are no longer unique, or clearly differentiated from other types of social identities. They compete with traditional Italian ideological identities, notably the Catholic and Communist identities, but also express new political myths such as the idealized Thatcherite state model. Residence is then taken as proxy for an idealized vision of appropriate state–individual relations – a vision of northern self-reliance and entrepreneurship – and contrasted with a southern assisting state, which is captive to outmoded ideologies.

The increasingly prevalent discussion of the crises of nation states in political analysis highlights several factors which have contributed to the processes of globalization. These include a cultural modernization rooted in the transnationalization of the media and patterns of consumption, the fragmentation of lifestyles, and the consequent emergence of a 'market of identities'. The structural counterpart of these trends lies in the transnationalization of the economy and the political success of supra-national entities such as the EU that can claim rival political allegiance and exert independent influence on national politics. But as concepts of 'global citizenship' emerge, Western Europe has experienced an augmentation in the number and strength of movements reasserting the primacy of political identities defined by narrow ethnic, regional, or linguistic boundaries. These movements often seek to attribute new meaning to communal life by redefining the basis on which the individual is politically integrated into the collectivity. In West European societies, ascriptive categories of belonging to an assigned community have again become a reference point of political mobilization. In this sense, nationalist and regionalist movements express issues of identity politics similar to those of the new social movements of the eighties.

CONCLUSIONS

The flexibility in adopting changing political orientations and co-operating with different allies became possible because of the very nature of the Lega's collective identity: its transition from a culturally essentialist to a relativist position. The structural restrictions on political mobilization normally to be found in the case of regionalism did not impede the rise of the Lega. Its demarcating boundaries, its main integrating codes, are delineated in such a flexible way that a broad range of political goals can be legitimated and a very widely defined constituency can potentially be included into its political project. It is this on principle openness in terms of its delineating boundaries and constitutive elements of its collective identity that has allowed the Lega's development from a narrow folklorist movement in Lombardy to an ex-junior partner in national government. Correspondingly, the Lega understood to substantially redefine their 'enemies' in the populist staging of their protest against the Italian nation state and its representatives. Reacting efficiently to newly emerging political opportunities, Bossi and his associates cleverly redefined the attacked opponent. The increasingly discredited Roman politicians gradually replaced immigrants and southerners in antagonism to which the Lega originally formulated its own political identity. By this, the grounds were laid for the Lega's political aspiration to become a national party replacing, in a region, the declining Christian Democrats and Socialists.

In its mature stage, the Lega can be understood as an agent of the ideal type of collective identity that is integrated mainly by cultural features. As such, it represents a highly modern and politically explosive challenge to the established national political parties. At the core of the Lega's outstanding electoral success lies the productive combination of two features both determinant for its political identity. On the one hand, particularly in its formative period, the Lega based its attraction on a strong and symbolically dispersed territorial identity. Initially, this identity was predominantly framed around the claimed incompatibility between the advanced north and the *mezzogiorno* basically reproducing features of traditional regionalism. With the adoption of broader political goals, however, this reference to a marked territory with distinct cultural features was formulated more as a conflict between the honest and hard-working citizens versus the 'corrupt' politicians in Rome. This belonging to a foremost culturally designated community was critical in the process of mobilization. It provided the legitimating resources for the wider political claims as it was the polarizing vehicle by which the political establishment was challenged by a new political agenda.

With its growing electoral success and against the background of the accelerating crisis in the Italian political system, the Lega impersonate the populist protest against the discredited political establishment of the country. Before entering the governing coalition under Berlusconi, the Lega presented itself as the radical opposition against all established political institutions and parties in Rome. Its claims were intensively portrayed as the political voice of civil society revolting against the bankrupt 'political class'. In this communal feeling, the rootedness in a particular 'value community' was a decisive reference point in spurring the protest and in offering a viable prospect of political change with such related political goals as decentralization and federalism.

To adequately understand the challenge that is involved in institutionalization, it is instructive to recall the nature of the cultural collective identity. Its integrating codes are essentially based on the explicit demarcation from the 'Them'. Legitimating resources are hence critically dependent on the plausibility of an image which contrasts the group's own superiority with the deficiencies of those excluded from the culturally assigned community. In the case of the Lega, these forms of aggressive demarcation have gradually lost their mobilizing effects. At an earlier stage, Bossi's organization largely replaced the negative notion of southerners and immigrants by the national parties and politicians as their 'enemy' in political terms. Each direction of enemy construction was conducive to a particular stage of the Lega's mobilization with its particular opportunities. Initially, the polemic demarcation from the south served to fabricate and politicize the collective identity of the northern regions. With the broadening of its political aspirations, the Lega widely abandoned its stress on the dividing line of Italian society. Instead, Third World immigrants were used to belligerently confront what was portrayed as 'alien' to the wider northern community. Subsequently, the image of the 'enemy' changed towards the representatives of the Roman nomenclature, underpinning the Lega's role as a populist protest against the nation state centre, with the rapprochement to Roman institutions and with the rise of other new political forces. This latest reference, however, has become increasingly ineffectual. Not being based on procedural rules for the community's internal organization as the Lega's appeals are too abstract to sustain a high level of mobilization.

NOTES

1 After the first electoral successes of the Lega Lombarda the Lega Nord was founded in 1987. This organization comprises the Liga Veneta, Piemont Autonomista, l'Union Ligure, Lega Emiliano-Romagnola, the Alleanza Toscana and the Lega Lombarda itself. In the following we uniformly refer to this organization as 'Lega'.
2 See Ruzza and Schmidtke 1993.
3 See Ruzza and Schmidtke 1992.

4 In his systematic study of the Lega's electoral campaigns in 1992, Todesco notes that the political framing of the Lega revolves around vigorous attacks on an enemy which span several political domains. Out of a total of forty-three posters used for political campaigns thirty-five, show a distinct reference to an 'enemy' (see Todesco 1992: 287ff.). Almost always these adversaries are named; the following list gives an impression which are the agents from which the Lega demarcates itself and how often they are identified in the Lega's manifestations: 'parties (16), mafia (15), thieves (12), Rome (9), state (centralized) (9), south (6), taxes (2), politics (2), Parliament, bureaucracy, political regime, fascism, clandestine immigration, government, *tricolore* (all 1)' (Todesco, Fabio (1992), *Marketing elettorale e communicazione politica. Il caso Lega Nord*, Tesi di Laurea, Università Commerciale Luigi Bocconi, Milan, p 128).

5 It is in this respect that the Lega's political engagement can be described as highly symbolic in character. The same mechanism is at work that Edelman described as follows: 'In place of a complicated empirical world, men hold to a relatively few, simple, archetypical myths, of which the conspiratorial enemy and the omnipotent hero-saviour are the central ones. In consequence, people feel assured by guidance, certainty, and trust rather than paralysed by threat, bewilderment, and unwanted personal responsibility for making judgements' (Edelman 1971: 83).

6 Bocca 1991: 28.

7 This law was designed to be a response to the problematic social situation of immigrants and the question of how to effectively control the illegal entry of a labour force from outside. The Lega accused Martelli, who was the socialist Minister of the Interior at this time, of not facing up to the urgent problems created by continual immigration with his propositions. The Lega suggested instead a far more radical regulation of immigration, namely, to allow entry to Italy only to those who already have accommodation and a job in the region to which they intend to go. See on the issue of immigration the following articles in *Lega Lombardia Autonomista* or *Lega Nord*: 'Colpo di stato. L'immigrazione del terzo mondo minaccia la democrazia' (no. 6, April 1990) and 'La legge Martelli garantisce solo la partitocrazia di Roma' (no. 26, 18.7.1990).

8 This does not exclude in any way that openly racist attacks by Lega activists are possible.

9 Bossi in an interview in *Epoca*, 20 May, 1990, pp. 12–13. In this context Guido Bolla, the former spokesman of the Lega in Lombardy, stated: 'Our campaign is, in effect, a bit racist, but not against a 'race': rather it is against those that take advantage of us. First come the Milanesi, second come the Lombardi, third come the Italians, and then come all the others' (cited in Leonardi, Robert and Kovacs, Monique 1993: 50–65, esp. p 59).

10 Miglio and Rocchetta left in summer 1994.

11 Interview with Rocchetta published in Tambini 1993/4.

12 Even more articulate is the reference to the 'glorious' past of the Venetian people in an interview given for *Politique Internationale*. Here the homogeneity is explicity portrayed as something systematically obstructed by Roman colonial power. It is still presented as the only legitimate basis

for political reform and change in the Italian nation state (see Rocchetta 1992–3.)

13 With this term Italians commonly refer to immigrants from outside the European community, describing mostly people from Africa.

14 Bossi, 'Ora si. Vogliamo il Governo', interview with Fiamma Nirenstein, in *L'Independente*, 6 Dec. 1991, p 3.

15 For a discussion of cultural essentialism see Calhoun 1994.

16 Taking a more detailed look at the electoral results another figure is worth pointing out: regarding the support for the Lega there are significant differences within the regions, namely Piedmont and Lombardy. There is a striking gap between a rural and an urban setting regarding the electoral affirmation of the Lega. Whereas the Lega lost in Turin and Milan 1.9 per cent and 2.8 per cent respectively, in the non-metropolitan provinces in Piedmont and Lombardy it won 0.8 per cent and 1.5 per cent respectively comparing 1992 with 1994's result (Source: DOXA). One can speak here of a similar development: the Lega somewhat declined in those areas where it expanded its consensus in the early 1990s.

17 See Gamson 1988. See also Gamson 1992.

18 Typically, they claim that specific regions need to be protected from the economic or cultural predatory behaviour of nation states. They advocate an increase of various types of political and economic resource ranging from subsidies for depressed areas to the institutional protection of linguistic differences. Their independence claims range from limited autonomy in specific sectors to seeking secession and promoting ethnic nationalism and statehood. In these claims they are similar to nationalistic groups and it is often difficult to differentiate them. A successful regionalist secessionist movement might become a nationalist party after secession.

19 See Diani 1992.

REFERENCES

Anderson, Benedict (1983), *Imagined Communities*, London: Verso.

Balbo, Laura and Manconi, Luigi (1990), *I razzismi possibili*, Milan: Feltrinelli.

Bocca, Giorgio (1991), *La disUNITA d'Italia*, Milan: Garzanti.

Cappelli, Sergio and Maranzano, Davide (1991), *La Gente e la Lega*, Milan: Greco & Greco.

Calhoun, C. R. J. (1989), 'The problem of identity in collective action', in J. O. Huber (ed.), *The Macro-Micro Divide*, Beverly Hills: Sage.

—— (1994) (ed.), *Social Theory and the Politics of Identity*, Oxford and Cambridge: Blackwell.

Cohen, J. E. L. (1985), 'Strategy of identity: new theoretical paradigms and contemporary social movements', *52–4*, pp. 663–716.

Cross, James P. (1990–1), 'The Lega Lombarda: A Spring Protest or the Seeds of Federalism?', *Italian Politics and Society*, 32, Winter, pp. 20–31.

Diani, Mario (1992), *Ethnonationalism vs. Populism: Competing Master Frames in the Lombard League*, (paper for the 'Culture and Social

Movements' Workshop, San Diego, June 18–20, 1992), Milan: Università Bocconi.

Edelman, M. (1971), *Politics as Symbolic Action*, Chicago, IL: Markham.

Eder, Klaus (1985), 'The New Social Movements: Moral Crusades, Political Pressure Groups, or Social Movements', *Social Research*, 52, pp. 869–90.

Gamson, William A. (1988), 'Political Discourse and Collective Action', in Klandermans, H. Kriesi and S. Tarrow (eds) (1988), *From Structure to Action: Comparing Social Movement Research Across Cultures*, vol. 1, International Social Movement Research, Greenwich, CT: JAI Press, pp. 219–44.

—— (1992), *Talking Politics*, Cambridge: Cambridge University Press.

Giesen, Bernhard (1993), *Die Intellektuellen und die Nation. Eine deutsche Achsenzeit*, Frankfurt am Main: Suhrkamp.

Harvie, C. (1994), *The Rise of Regional Europe*, London: Routledge.

Hechter, M. (1975), *Internal Colonialism: The Celtic Fringe in British National Development*, Oxford: Oxford University Press.

Hyllard Eriksen, T. (1993), *Ethnicity and Nationalism*, London: Pluto Press.

Leonardi, Robert and Kovacs, Monique (1993), 'The Lega Nord: the rise of a new Italian catch-all party', *Italian Politics*, London: Pinter Publishers, pp. 50–65.

Mannheimer R. and Biorcio R. (eds) (1991), *La Lega Lombarda*, Milan: Feltrinelli.

Rocchetta, Franco (1992–3), 'L'Italie Existe-t-Elle?', *Politique Internationale*, Winter, pp. 129–47.

Ruzza, Carlo and Schmidtke, Oliver (1992), 'The Making of the Lombard League', *Telos*, 90, Spring.

Ruzza, C. and Schmidtke, O., (1993), 'Roots of Success in the Lega Lombarda: Mobilization Dynamics and the Media', *West European Politics*, April, pp. 1–23.

Shils, E. (1975), 'Personal, Primordial, Sacred and Civil Ties', in Shils, *Center and Periphery. Essays on Macrosociology*, Chicago: Chicago University Press, p. 111–26.

Tambini, Damian (1993/4), 'Strategy or Identity? The Northern Leagues at a Crossroad', *Telos*, 98/99, pp. 219–48.

Todesco, Fabio (1992), *Marketing elettorale e comunicazione politica. Il caso Lega Nord*, Tesi di Laurea, Università Commerciale Luigi Bocconi, Milan.

12

CONCLUSION

Mary Fulbrook and David Cesarani

The issues with which this book has dealt are both immensely complex and immensely important. Entitlement to citizenship carries with it a host of specific rights and responsibilities: rights to residence, assorted benefits, political representation and participation and, often, associated obligations to the wider community (as for example in military service). Citizenship has wider, affective connotations too: the sense of belonging to a broader community, expressed in symbols and values, and the often quite vehement emotional identification which may be associated with that wider community of belonging. Conversely, exclusion from citizenship may be associated with experiences ranging from the relatively passive lack of entitlement to vote (which cynics might dismiss as the figleaf of representative democracy in any event) through infinitely more problematic and unpleasant aspects of life as 'aliens' in a not always hospitable host country.

In the closing decade of the twentieth century, there is a widespread sense of flux, which is hard to capture in received categories. On the one hand, many commentators have identified transnational trends over recent years which have seemed to signal or signify the end of the era of the European nation state. Participation in a global economic system circumscribes the powers of national governments to control their own domestic economies. The explosion of rapid communications and the internationalization of popular culture – from surfing the Internet, through mass cable and satellite TV, to a McDonalds in every mediaeval town centre in Europe – contribute to the decline of national cultural distinctiveness. The creation and development of supra-national bodies, such as the EU, with increasing powers of regulation, present serious problems for concepts of national sovereignty. And the mass movement of peoples, partially facilitated by these trends, similarly challenges received notions of (largely imputed) 'traditional' national identity.

On the other hand, alongside these trends towards a degree of supra-, trans- or internationalization, there appear to be currents running in the reverse direction. For some commentators, 1989 heralded, not the end of history, but rather history put into reverse gear. The break-up of the multinational empire of the Soviet Union, and the revival of ethnic nationalisms not only in the Soviet successor states but also elsewhere in eastern and particularly south-eastern Europe, appeared to give the lie to those who had been announcing the end of the nation state. The proliferation of right-wing movements within 'fortress Europe', parading racist doctrines in new and sometimes camouflaged culturalist forms, aroused uneasy memories of the late 1920s and 1930s. Closer to the political centre, many mainstream politicians have been arguing for the need to construct a cohesive national identity, to revive notions of community and to revitalize national pride. In Britain and Germany, in particular, this rhetoric has taken on exclusivist and ethnic tones, the opposite to the supposed decline of the nation. At the same time, the alleged arrival of postnationalism was given a massive shock by the ethnic atrocities occurring among Bosnians and Serbs. Just as the perennial 'German problem' appeared to have been solved by unification, and Germans, newly united in a nation state, announced their enduring allegiance to European ideals, the disruptions on the south-eastern fringes of Europe harked back to the Balkan crises with which the twentieth century began.

So how should we seek to understand the complex, cross-cutting developments occurring today in a broader, historical and comparative perspective? In analysing the four cases of Britain, France, Germany and Italy, some lines of inquiry and patterns of development begin to emerge. While no definitive generalizations can as yet be made, some of the issues involved can be disentangled.

THE INTERPLAY BETWEEN LAW, POLITICS, SOCIETY AND ECONOMY

As the chapters above have made clear, it is essential to consider questions relating to citizenship, nationality and migration from an interdisciplinary perspective.

Citizenship is essentially a legal category: yet legal entitlement to citizenship is both a product of political and social phenomena, and in turn has an impact on political and social developments. As Elspeth Guild has shown, the concept of European citizenship is currently – despite the best efforts of lawyers – in a state of some disarray. Ambiguities and anomalies abound, as Patrick Weil pointed up in the example of two Turkish cousins, whose fathers emigrated to France and Germany respectively. The one cousin, born and bred in Paris, was, on moving as an adult to Frankfurt, entitled to vote in municipal and European elections without necessarily speaking a word of German, while the other, born and bred in Frankfurt, educated in German schools and with an intimate knowledge of local affairs, was denied similar rights to representation in what, in every aspect of his upbringing and socialization, was his home. The EU principle of allowing each state to determine its own rules of citizenship entitlement, with no attempt at harmonization in this centrally contentious matter, has saddled the construction of a 'European identity' with a number of inherent difficulties.

These difficulties relate to national differences. A comparative and historical approach points up both the intrinsic mutability of national traditions – for example, the changing connotations and definitions of British citizenship outlined above by Cesarani, or the different phases of development of French 'active' and 'passive' citizenship traced by Patrick Weil – and also the striking differences across different nation states. The 'palette' of four criteria in the French case, among which place of birth and socialization or education take precedence, contrasts markedly with the primacy of ethnic heritage, diluted only modestly by the rather restricted chances of cultural assimilation, in the German case. What is taken for granted as entirely 'natural', an assumption which requires no further explicit examination, by the inhabitants of one state, may differ fundamentally from the way the world is categorized, and insiders demarcated from outsiders, by the inhabitants of a neighbouring state. There is, in other words, no 'essential' definition of citizenship, however essentialist the participants' own views of it may be. Historians, anthropologists and sociologists can usefully collaborate with lawyers and politicians in unpacking the conceptions which come to form the crucial barrier or gateway to the passage of peoples from one area to another and which determine how far they have a say over the conditions which shape their lives and futures.

There are, too, different aspects of the bundle of rights which are associated with citizenship, as pointed out by T.H. Marshall in his classic analysis of the subject. Citizenship in the political sense may or may not be combined with economic and social aspects of citizenship. And discrimination against those defined as 'other' may continue to persist irrespective of formal legal status. There is a widespread assumption that citizenship is in some way closely bound in with a sense of identity, of similarity, yet this may in fact be by no means the case.

CITIZENSHIP, NATIONALITY AND NATIONAL IDENTITY

Conceptions of citizenship have, over the last century or so, been tied in very closely with conceptions of nationality and national identity. Indeed, they are very often entirely conflated: this is in part where the emotive power of citizenship lies. Patriotism may be limited to flag-waving, singing of the national anthem and other symbolic songs, participating in national occasions for celebration or commemoration – or it may mean nothing more than a day off work, an excuse for a street party. National moments of crisis may for some entail military service, not only serving, but even dying for 'one's country'; for others, it may mean disaffection with the policies of the government in power, acute disagreement with the current framing of the nation's destiny (as was, for example, very clear in popular reactions in Britain to the Falklands conflict). Such national identifications are inherently ambiguous, ambivalent in the messages they project and the ways in which citizens identify with, participate in, the national 'moments': as the 1995 VE day commemorations reminded us, there have been not only heroes but also victims, not only perpetrators and collaborators but also resistance fighters, in every state; every nation has its own internal political and cultural rifts. The attempt to construct a notion of homogenous identity is always an active (if not always a conscious) political project on the part of one group or another, realized through a variety of cultural and institutional forms and strategies.

But the construction of national identity has to a large degree been premised on the myth of some form of national homogeneity – however defined. Here again, there is a degree of ambiguity. It is, for example, ironic that the Germans, who have perhaps spilt the most ink over a sustained public quest for the holy grail of a national identity, actually at the same time appear to have the least problematic conception of 'who is a German'. Admittedly, there are shades of German-ness. As Karen Schönwälder points out, by the 1980s the reception given to resettling ethnic Germans from eastern Europe was becoming somewhat less than enthusiastic. Nevertheless, until the fall of the Wall and the discovery that East Germans were almost unrecognizable cousins, there was a very clear assumption about 'being German' simply because one's parents had been. The problem was not so much 'who is a German', but rather, what being German meant. Such clarity of basic identity was by no means echoed in the case of Britain, for example, where – despite lack of serious public debate over the definition of national identity – the predominance of a mythologized 'Englishness' has never gone unchallenged by the Welsh, Scottish, Irish (or even Cornish) inhabitants of this multi-national realm, and where the label 'British' is often only used by those who wish to stress an inclusive concept of identity.

Nevertheless, for all the ambiguities and variations, there has been an almost universal tendency for whichever group is deemed to be legitimate residents in and defenders of the inherited territory to erect barriers to the influx of others – or to define the permitted newcomers as second-class citizens, present merely as 'guests' so long as they behaved properly and were economically useful. Again, Germany – on its own account, 'not a country of immigration', and yet a country which has relied on migrant labour for generations – is a prime example.

Most participants – however 'liberal' in self-definition – in any national community agree that boundary definitions are important, while disagreeing on how to calibrate and 'filter' the in-flows: but there is then often wide disagreement over whether, and how easily, immigrants should be allowed to become full citizens rather than merely permanent residents, and on what basis they may apply. Generally, European states have adopted a somewhat cautious attitude towards initial immigration, with a relatively open attitude (although in many cases increasingly restricted) towards applications for citizenship after certain criteria have been met. The legacy of the Third Reich set Germany in the opposite direction, with relatively open doors for asylum-seekers while retaining an exceedingly restricted concept of citizenship.

There have also been cultural shifts in the terms and character of debates. As a number of authors in the chapters above have pointed out, there has in the last couple of decades been a shift from 'biological' notions, tainted by racist implications and overtones, to more 'culturalist' notions of identity which nevertheless may serve the same purposes of classification with a view to exclusion. Protection of the national heritage appears to be a more acceptable value than protection of the purity of the race, although the practical implications may amount to much the same as far as would-be immigrants are concerned.

The criteria for citizenship entitlement have then in some way been associated with the notion of a national identity, to which those possessing or seeking citizenship must conform. Whether this identity is (unintentionally!) assigned by descent or by location of birth, or whether it is attained more actively by acquisition of certain educational standards and positive adherence to specific values and ideals, varies from case to case. The question now may be whether the often only implicit association between citizenship and national identity should not be broken, or at least weakened.

If citizenship could be decoupled from the assumed need for cultural or ethnic homogeneity, then the current debates about migration and citizenship might be less heated. In the changing international context sketched above, with a fluidity of boundaries both 'upwards', towards the supra-national level, and 'downwards', to regional and local identifications, the role and location of the 'nation state' is clearly changing. Along with structural changes in the economic and political arenas there are already changes in patterns of social and cultural identification. It is time, perhaps, to recognize these more explicitly and to seek to sever the close links between citizenship and national identity. Giving all permanent residents of a particular state the right to vote ('no taxation without representation' has, after all, a respectable political ancestry) without necessarily demanding a high degree of cultural assimilation would hardly represent a fatal threat to the preservation of distinctive cultural traditions in that area.

IMMIGRANTS AND THE POLITICIZATION OF DIFFERENCE

This leads very directly to the issue of inter-group relations. Few people would worry about these issues if they were purely conceptual questions, a theoretical play on words or an exercise in historical comparisons. But as millions of people know only too intimately, they are very real issues on the ground. Arson attacks, racist violence on the streets ranging from insults and muggings to murder, the formation and spread of extremist political movements, are exceedingly frightening and threatening phenomena which cannot be disposed of by a few strokes of an academic pen. In a less easily visible and definable manner, but no less central to the constitution and development of human lives, is the way in which categorization and perception intrinsically shapes the whole of people's existences in unequal societies. The children of immigrant communities may have more difficulties at school, be disadvantaged in the job market, live in poorer housing conditions on less adequate incomes – and these subtle, inter-related, persistent disadvantages may cumulatively add up to a lifetime of poverty, ill-health, decreased life expectancy, lack of self-fulfilment.

Citizenship clearly does not always correlate with a sense of membership of a broader community, and groups and individuals are very often designated as 'other' and discriminated against whether or not they are citizens of a particular state. Racist attacks are hardly prefaced with a polite query as to the victim's legal status. Nevertheless, assumptions about the constitution of a community, what it seeks to uphold and what it is legitimate to defend against perceived threats from the 'other', are subtly built in to a whole range of social processes, from the obvious political extremes to infinitely more refined and complex positions.

As Tony Kushner has shown in his analysis of the Mass-Observation material, above, many seemingly 'liberal', Guardian-reading respondents express the most reasonable sounding sentiments about their rights to sustain a Christian and English tradition against the multiculturalism that celebrates Ramadan on the same level as Christmas. It is but a short step from the arguments about defending the educational content and value systems transmitted in 'our' schools to an implicit downgrading of the traditions of the many children from other backgrounds and cultural heritages. It is a similarly short step to arguing the 'right' to preserve the 'peace and quiet' or the 'character' of a residential neighbourhood against the perceived intrusions of 'alien' music, or the pervading smells of different culinary traditions, or the sight of 'swarms' of children in visibly different clothes playing and talking in unintelligible languages.

Tensions rooted in multifarious issues of everyday life may remain at the level of grumbles and grotesque exaggerations (conflating all Asians as 'Pakis', for example) or requests to the local council for a housing transfer (often accompanied by assertions of 'foreigners' jumping the queue); they may be expressed at the level of overt, constant sniping and bullying and low-level aggression in the street and the playground. Public disquiet, or the raising to public consciousness of such issues, may feed into the rhetoric of established, mainstream political parties, as Karen Schönwälder pointed out took place in Germany in the early 1980s. The apparently legitimate, 'respectable' assertion of the right to defend a 'national heritage' can very easily cast a penumbra of acceptability around more extremist organized political movements. Under specific configurations of circumstances (as in Millwall, or in certain regional elections in West Germany in the late 1980s), local tensions can readily be mobilized and translated into votes for overtly extremist parties. In the case of the Northern League in Italy, as described by Ruzza and Schmidtke, an energetic political leadership can construct and exploit new exclusionist identities against shifting definitions of the foe under particularly fragile national political conditions. Whatever the changing structural and international location of the nation state, nationalism appears to enjoy a remarkable capacity to remain alive and well in a whole variety of forms and expressions.

In all manifestations, intergroup tension is exceedingly problematic, and poses problems to which there are no easy or obvious solutions. Much of the politicization of difference – like all social phenomena – is easier to explain than to control. Intervention is in any event a political matter, and views on particular issues differ enormously across even the 'respectable' political spectrum. Debates have to take place at all manner of levels, with respect to particular issues and the practical implementation of policies. In exploring historical and contemporary aspects of citizenship, nationality and migration in four European states, the chapters above have sought both to make specific contributions to these debates and to situate the arguments in a wider context. Ideally, debates on these issues would be conducted in a spirit of tolerance and harmony, the policies designed in a world with no constraints. But ideal conditions do not always obtain.

If there is any lesson from the range of national experiences and historical traditions analysed in this book, it is perhaps that, whatever the differences of culture, dialect, religion or economy, if immigrants are accepted by host communities as having a legitimate claim to belonging, their integration is infinitely less problematic than if the differences are construed as insurmountable barriers to a sense of common humanity. As the immediate post-war experience of the Germans shows, given the appropriate political will and cultural assumptions, there are no absolute barriers to the total numbers of individuals who can in principle be accommodated on a given territorial area.

Citizenship could be explicitly divorced from the myth of national homogeneity, and toleration of a diversity of cultural, regional or other identities – indeed celebration of this diversity – could become the accepted norm of the twenty-first century. But this of course is to make a political statement which some would see as denying them their proclaimed right to remain in, effectively, a ghetto of perceived homogeneity – which is precisely the issue at the heart of a controversy which will not die so easily. At least, perhaps, the reflections on and contrasts between the four cases presented in this book will help to underline the fact that the construction and politicization of boundaries between people, of inclusion or exclusion, are socially constructed, historically changing phenomena, rather than enduring, immutable entities; and that an informed engagement with these issues in a broader framework will be of some assistance in grappling with the infinitely intractable problems of the real world.

INDEX

218